UNSHACKLED SPIRIT

PRISONERS OF WAR AND THE SECRET SPITFIRE

COLIN PATEMAN

FONTHILL

This book is dedicated to Leading Aircraftsman Peter Pateman 1458281
Royal Air Force Volunteer Reserve
1921-2002

FONTHILL MEDIA
www.fonthillmedia.com

First published 2013

A CIP catalogue record for this book is available from the British Library

Typeset in 10 pt on 13pt Sabon LT Std
Typesetting by Fonthill Media
Printed in the UK

ISBN 978-1-78155-191-2

We are the men who no longer fly,
Mid the threat of fire and flak.
We are the ones who are forced to stand by;
To the fight we can never go back.

Our small domain is encircled by wire,
Not even the ground can we roam.
To wait quietly by the war does require,
Please God why can't we go home?

On days when the weather is very clear,
And we gaze into the sky,
Sometimes we can see what our captors fear!
Our own planes flying by!

Then we on the ground see the scorching flak,
So send up a silent prayer,
To ask him to guide them safely back,
Our classmates in the air.

They are the brave boys we flew with,
Some of whom have yet to die.
Others will come here to join us,
While the rest continue to fly.

Some day when the war is over,
And we hear the battle is won.
Let's hope that he'll have a record,
Of the various deeds we've done

2nd Lt Meredith D. Fink, shot down 2 November 1943.
Stalag Luft I (north compound)

The King in RAF uniform meeting pilots from Fighter Command.

CONTENTS

Preface

During the Second World War, the Royal Air Force and her Commonwealth air forces mobilised a vast array of squadrons and commands. In the footsteps of the regular volunteer reserve, auxiliary air force personnel, and aircrews from the early years, there followed an entire generation of young men who unreservedly served their crown and country.

These willing volunteers were to be denied the opportunities of academic study or a chosen civilian career; something that is possibly taken for granted now. Many of those young men went on to experience terrible events involving bravery and misfortune. Individual pilots in fighter aircraft lost their lives in aerial combat defending Great Britain. Iconic images of vapour trails in the sky over Southern England represent the Battle of Britain, and entire bomber crews of up to eight men died together in the skies over occupied Europe. Thousands of men from Bomber Command failed to return to their airfields; in many instances, nothing was known of their fate. Week after week during the entire period of the Second World War, casualties from all commands were simply registered as 'missing in action'.

On 11 March 1943 in the House of Commons, the right honourable Member of Parliament Mr Boothby replied to a question on the bombing of Germany. He said:

> It is an arresting thought that when we carry out one of our big raids over a German town there may be anything from 3,500 to 4,500 young men in the air, about three miles above the target. When we staged our big raid on Cologne, no fewer than 7,000 young men were in the air over that town together at a given moment. These bomber crews display a quality of cold courage that has never been matched, and which is quite unparalleled in the annals of war.

Tragic circumstances frequently saw pilots and members of aircrews falling from the skies and becoming prisoners to the enemy forces waging war against Great Britain and her Allies. The author has attempted to secure and preserve personal stories from a number of these men – this has been possible by capturing real life experiences created from the author's collection of unique YMCA wartime logs. These were very special books, gifted to only a small proportion of the many thousands of Allied prisoners of war during the Second World War.

Wartime logs inevitably contain artwork, sketches, and detailed writing, as well as small keepsakes retained in cellophane envelopes affixed to the back pages. Wartime logs are always individual, and prisoners of war who were fortunate enough to have one gifted to them regarded them as extremely valuable items. Many of the most important logs were carried by unfortunate prisoners during the long marches enforced by the highest command of Germany during the closing stages of the war. The prisoners of war would have faced difficult choices; as each man's survival may well have depended on how much food he could carry, little room existed for anything else. Thus, the majority of YMCA wartime logs were understandably lost or abandoned between January and May 1945, cast aside in favour of the most basic instinct of mankind – survival.

From original material, the author has been able to create a book that exposes the lives and thoughts of those enduring day-to-day existence behind barbed wire. From a wartime log, these words were written by an anonymous prisoner in 1944: 'Where men were ringed about with wire, which coiled and twisted through the brains, till each barbed strand became a shaft that seared like sharp, relentless flame.' The research and compilation of these incredible wartime logs has created, without question, a unique book that illustrates many examples of personal thoughts and artwork, but also goes further to explain the intense support structure provided by the numerous welfare groups, the role of the British intelligence services, and the efforts and risks taken to smuggle escape aids into the camps.

In addition, and equally as important, this book tells the incredible, and as yet unpublished, account of how a group of Allied prisoners of war were led by one man in the task of purchasing their own Spitfire aircraft while imprisoned inside Germany. The assistance of MI9 was required to understand the wishes of those prisoners, with coded instructions within letters being passed to the War Office. This led on towards a truly inspiring and amazing set of events that eventually progressed to the purchase of a most special Spitfire aircraft, named *Unshackled Spirit*. The Spitfire became operational with the Royal Air Force in 1944, and was flown by a young fighter pilot in the skies over occupied Europe. In that particular camp, and to the brave men who raised the money to purchase the aircraft, any Spitfire seen overhead was, in their minds, their Spitfire.

The collection of personal prisoner of war logbooks has allowed the author to create a book that has never, as far as it is known, been published in this format. Where appropriate, the author has recorded facts, dates, and times according to how they were written by the prisoners of war. Some errors may exist when examined against other written or published postwar material. The author makes no apology for this, as the personal reflections written are from the hands that held the pencil, recording events as they were being experienced. Those same hands created magnificent sketches and artwork, which has to be regarded as historically important to the individuals and to the role that the Allied air forces played during the Second World War.

Unshackled Spirit flew in the skies above those vast barbed wire compounds, and the skies remained the only place to view freedom for the men who had lost their wings.

Colin Pateman
November 2012

Acknowledgements

The author acknowledges the content of the respective prisoner of war wartime logs that form the basis of this work. Personal writings and photographs associated with each prisoner of war remain credited to those individuals. In several instances, additional photographs have been included from the author's collection, and where possible, other items are duly credited. In particular: Chris Moscrop for the material on Stalag 383, Geoffrey Saunders (Australia) for the image of Unshackled Spirit, Churchill College Archives Centre in Cambridge (Duncan Sandys Archives), and the National Archives under the terms of the Open Government License. Other material, particularly photographic work, sits within the public domain created by the Government prior to 1957. The author would finally like to acknowledge the assistance of his wife Sarah-Jane and son Lewis, who both accepted his solitude at the desk.

Introduction

The King's message to the Royal Air Force on the outbreak of the Second World War, 4 September 1939:

> The Royal Air Force has behind it a tradition no less inspiring than those of the older services, and in the campaign that we have now been compelled to undertake, you will have to assume responsibilities far greater than those which your service had to shoulder in the last war. One of the greatest of them will be the safeguarding of these islands from the menace of the air. I can assure all ranks of the Air Force of my supreme confidence in their skill and courage, and in their ability to meet whatever calls may be made upon them.
>
> King George VI

That same day, the Royal Air Force committed fifteen Bristol Blenheim aircraft from numbers 107 and 110 Squadron, together with fourteen Wellington Bombers from numbers 9 and 149 Squadron, to attack enemy warships off Brunsbuttel in the Schillig Roads[1] and Wilhelmshaven. Five Blenheims were shot down, and two of the Wellingtons failed to return. Flight Lieutenant Kenneth Doran was awarded the first Distinguished Flying Cross medal for the Second World War following his actions in the Blenheim operations. It was not long before the newspapers began to publish the first lists of RAF casualties, noting airmen who were 'missing' and 'missing believed killed'. Within the first seventeen names announced by the Air Ministry were 561012 Sergeant G. F. Booth and 548555 Aircraftsman Second Class L. J. Slattery, both of 107 Squadron. These two men were to become the first RAF Bomber Command prisoners of war captured during the Second World War. 10,997 men of Bomber Command were to follow in their footsteps, and become known as Kriegies.[2]

Those events heralded the onset of material losses in aircraft, which mounted with some ferocity. The training of aircrews and the production of aircraft became one of the great many priorities that arose from those early years of conflict with Germany.

I

Unshackled Spirits

Unshackled Spirits in Prisoner of War Camps

In 1940, Winston Churchill appointed the Canadian newspaper magnate Lord Beaverbrook as a new Minister of Aviation Production. Lord Beaverbrook took up the post on 15 May 1940, and was charged with increasing the production of aircraft within the United Kingdom. With production costs high, the Government urged the public to donate funds that would facilitate the purchase of a specifically named or dedicated aircraft. This concept had been successfully used in the First World War and was therefore resurrected by Beaverbrook. The target valuations of £5,000 for a single-engine fighter, £20,000 for a twin-engine aircraft, and £40,000 for a four-engine aircraft were published. The National Archives' currency converter from 1940 to 2005 equates these figures to £143,600, £574,400, and £1,148,800 respectively.

A Spitfire was a snip at £5,000, and 'buy a Spitfire' money collections sprang up overnight. Hurricanes would also be needed, but it was the Spitfire that inspired the public imagination; a fact that continues to exist today. The true contracted cost of a Spitfire to the Air Ministry was almost double that figure at £8,897, with the fuselage alone costing £2,500, and the Rolls Royce Merlin III engine £2,000. Other items of cost included the wings at £1,800, and the tail section at £500. One of the most important parts of the Spitfire were the eight Browning .303 machine guns that cost £100 each, not forgetting the thousands of rivets that cost 6d each. The Ministry of Aircraft Production simply indicated that if the sum raised was over £5,000, the donor would be allowed to name their own Spitfire. Several district-based collections created their own Spitfire fund badges. These were awarded to individual donors so that they could wear the badge to show they had participated towards the collection of funds. This was in itself an excellent concept as it promoted further donations, and of course, to be seen without a badge was not desirable.

Collecting boxes rattled everywhere, and even small, isolated hamlets managed to scrape together £5,000 for a fighter aircraft; a significant sum for locations with such limited headcounts. It very much became a matter of pride

Spitfire fund badge. Each one was numbered to record individual donations.

to have a location or dedication painted adjacent to the pilot's cockpit. Money also arrived from all over the world for a variety of aircraft types. Donations from New Zealand, Iceland, America, Brazil, South Africa and India were received, as well as funds sufficient for the purchase of an entire aircraft that arrived from many countries. Most presentations were for one or two aircraft, but extraordinarily, some were intended for an entire squadron. 152 (Hyderabad) Squadron was funded by the Nizam of Hyderabad. The early donations from the Nizam in 1940 were built upon significant contributions for aircraft during the First World War, thereby cementing the commitment previously undertaken by Hyderabad. The motor industry also donated over £100,000 to purchase Spitfires for No. 154 Squadron. Those aircraft carried various names; amongst them *Lord Austin*, *Go To It*, and *Nuffield*.

Many local boroughs within the United Kingdom organised collections from the average working family who were already struggling with rationing and wartime conditions. In Bermondsey, Central London, door-to-door collections requesting just pennies achieved an impressive collection of 402,000*d*. (There were 12 pennies in a shilling, and 20 shillings in the pound, hence 240 pennies in a pound.) This enterprising pennies collection achieved £1,675 for the Spitfire fund.

Within the production flow of aircraft leaving the factory, designated presentation aircraft had the donor's chosen name stenciled or painted on the fuselage, just in front of the cockpit. While it was thought imprudent to allow aircraft to be named after companies, it appears a few slipped through. Others were given names that were associated with the donor. For instance, Spitfire serial W3215 was named *The Marksman* by Marks & Spencer.

The Air Ministry initially laid down strict rules regarding the representation of the name. The early names were in dull yellow script, but this soon gave way to many variants. Large coats of arms began to appear, with transfers having been provided by the donor. Some names were chalked on simply for the benefit of photographers, but by 1942 a light grey, 2 inch lettering had become standard. Aircraft built at the Castle Bromwich factory were originally distinguished by their presentation names being in italics, but by 1941 the use of italics had been dropped. Photographs and a certificate were sent to the donor, and in some instances a formal ceremony was undertaken, capitalising on the media and news publication.

Most of the names selected for the aircraft had a direct connection to a town or village where the funds had been raised. Others, such as *The Dog's Fighter*, funded by the British Kennel Club, were self-explanatory. The Associated British Cinemas also collected funds on a regular basis and provided sufficient monies for four aircraft, which were named *Miss A.B.C.* Cinemas were one of the only regular entertainment facilities accessible to members of the public during the war, and the combined contributions to purchase four individual Spitfires was a truly inspiring feat. The sum raised totaled £20,712, 4s, 2d.

Several individual Spitfires were purchased anonymously, but with instructions to have the individual aircraft named after a family member; an example being *Heather*. This particular Spitfire carried the donor's daughter's name in the air from 1941 to 1947; a rare example of such a long operational life during the Second World War and beyond.

Interestingly, the Spitfire itself had another, most important connection to a daughter. Annie Penrose was the daughter of Sir Robert McLean, who played a crucial role in the development of the Spitfire through his position as chairman of Vickers Aviation in the 1930s. He worked closely with the gifted design engineer R. J. Mitchell. When it came to giving the new, single-seated fighter a name, McLean suggested his daughter's childhood nickname 'Little Spitfire', the affectionate term he used for his spirited elder daughter. Initially, the Air Ministry had reservations about the name *Spitfire*, as did Mitchell, who rather favoured calling the new aircraft *The Shrew*. Annie Pemrose, 'Little Spitfire', died in 2011 at the age of 100 – she could have given this country no greater legacy.[3]

Newspapers were keen to promote fundraising, and appealed to their readers to 'get a Spitfire'. The newspapers published a running total, with a full listing of donors and donations each week. When a target was reached, the local newspaper would publish a photograph of the Spitfire. The town's Spitfire was something to be proud of, and without doubt, served to raise the morale of the public. By the end of the war, well over 1,500 Spitfires had carried presentation names. Unfortunately, the serial numbers or individual identities of nearly 200 of these very special aircraft are unknown, largely because most of the relevant official documentation was scrapped in the early postwar years.

One of those particular Spitfires was a unique aircraft, named *Unshackled Spirit*. The funding to purchase this particular Spitfire came from the wages of prisoners of war; men who, although imprisoned behind barbed wire in Germany, never lost sight of freedom. It is these men to whom this book is dedicated. Although these prisoners were captured in traumatic conditions, they innovatively created a system to send cryptic letters back to England in order to purchase a Spitfire. This selfless act epitomised the unshackled spirit of Allied prisoners of war, which could not be broken during the Second World War.

D. T. Miles-Osborne, a Sergeant held in Stalag 383, personally knew Duncan Sandys,[4] the parliamentary secretary to the Ministry of Supply. Prior to his ministerial position, Sandys had served in Norway with Miles-Osborne in 151 Battery, Royal Artillery. In 1941, having returned to England, Duncan Sandys was involved in a serious motor car accident. He was being driven by his army driver, who unfortunately fell asleep at the wheel, resulting in the staff car crashing into a stone wall at a fairly high speed. The injuries that Sandys sustained resulted in his medical discharge, and he walked with a significant limp for the rest of his life. As an elected Member of Parliament for Norwood, London, Sandys sought to return to politics alongside the Prime Minister Winston Churchill, who was his father-in-law since he had married Diana Churchill in 1935.

Sergeant Miles-Osborne commenced cryptic communication with Sandys in mid-1943. The communication was based upon the formation of The Duncan Sandys Welfare Fund; a guise created by Miles-Osborne to allow money to be donated from the prisoners of war in Stalag 383 into that supposed welfare fund. The initial communication to Sandys gave no suggestion whatsoever that the funds were to be used to purchase a Spitfire. In fact, the first communication received at the House of Commons required Sandys to respond to Miles-Osborne as follows:

> Many thanks for your letter of 25 May, which I have just received, together with an imposing list of contributions for a welfare fund. Your letter refers to a previous letter of March 14, which I have never received. I am therefore in the dark as to the purpose and nature of the fund.
>
> If it is a fund to help prisoners of war, or for some other good purpose of that kind, I shall of course be only too delighted to do anything I can to help. I should be glad, therefore, if you would send me by return full particulars of the circumstances in which the fund is being formed, and the purpose to which you wish the money to be devoted.

Sandys was clearly unsure of what was taking place, having unexpectedly received a letter that had been written by his old friend Miles-Osborne, which in addition, carried the counter signature of the camp's Man of Confidence

Squadron Quartermaster David Mackenzie. The letter passed through the Stalag 383 censorship procedure without any concerns being expressed. It should be born in mind that Duncan Sandys had been charged with the heavy responsibility of uncovering the German plans for rocket attacks upon the United Kingdom. In mid-August 1943, he actually attended the secret RAF briefing for the Pathfinder bomber crews who attacked Adolf Hitler's V2 research establishment at Peenemunde on the Baltic peninsula.

The Germans used a team of female censors to check prisoners' mail. This had become part of the Luftwaffe's intelligence operation, which was directly

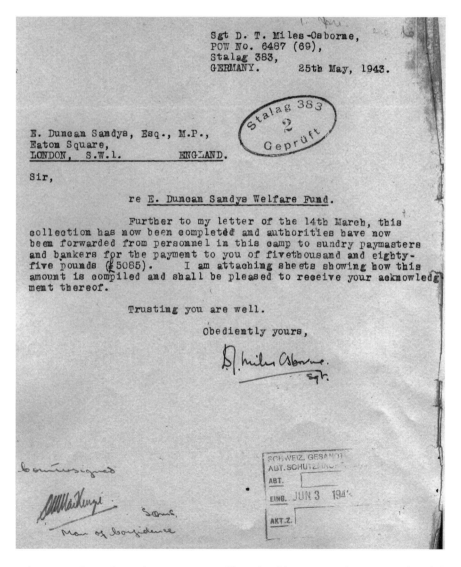

A letter sent by Miles-Osborne. (*OPSI Office of Public Sector Information Churchill Archives*)

linked to the central Dulag Luft intelligence-gathering base. Prisoners' letters could contain useful information, for instance, regarding the state of morale and possible indications of bomb damage inflicted on targets in Britain. Letters passing through the German censorship were stamped 'gepruft', German for 'approved'. Each stamp held the identification number of the censor checking the document. The letter sent by Sergeant Miles-Osborne carried the rubber 'gepruft' stamp '2', as well as the camp identity numbering. The German women grew to know both the individual prisoners and their families through their work. In some instances, the prisoners of war also censored their own outgoing mail; a role created to ensure that there was no sensitive information being unintentionally exposed. When imposed, these measures were instigated by the British senior officers' own initiative; they were by no means prescriptive.

Miles-Osborne had conceived an incredibly audacious act. He sought consent for his plan from a considerable number of men within the camp contingent, including men from across all of the military services. The document sent to Sandys indicated 108 military units, with each regiment or squadron indicating the combined total of monies agreed to be paid by their respective paymasters. For example: the Royal Navy, £4; the Royal Marines, £27; the Royal Tank Regiment, £107 4s; the Gordon Highlanders, £82; the Royal Air Force, £164 4s; the Royal Canadian Air Force £25; the Royal New Zealand Air Force, £15; RASC/EFI, £86 12s; the Royal Australian Air Force, £25; the

Stalag 383. *(Chris Moscrop)*

Royal Horse Guards, £3. Two of the last entries were for £2, relating to GHQ London and the Royal Ulster Rifles. The listing appeared to record a contribution from almost every component of the British and Commonwealth fighting forces. The German censor stamp was applied to the bottom of the dispatched document, indicating that such information could be sent without any censorship whatsoever.

The prisoner of war salaries paid to officers and men differed greatly. While in captivity, German authorities endeavored to employ the men to work in a multitude of ways, for which they were paid an agreed minimum wage. It was not unknown for German employers to visit the camps and bid for such workforces. Officers were excluded from the requirement to work. Both groups of men were still receiving a salary by the normal payment infrastructures dictated by the Government and the Geneva Convention statements. Some deductions were later applied, resulting in reduced payments in to the prisoners' accounts. In Stalag 383, the men corresponded directly to their respective paymasters, who facilitated the diversion of their monies to the Duncan Sandys Welfare Fund.

Extracts from the House of Commons' written answers on 19 November 1941 explain further upon the subject of prisoner of war pay. Viscountess Nancy Astor[5] asked the Secretary of State for war whether imprisoned British service men received a cash allowance equivalent to their pay while interned in Germany. Mr Sandys replied:

The Prisoners of War Convention, 1929, lies down that the detaining power shall pay to officer prisoners of war either their own rate of pay or the rate of corresponding ranks of the detaining power's own forces, whichever is less. On this basis, British officers in Germany receive the German rates of pay for the corresponding ranks, and the balance is credited to the officer's account in this country. No pay is issued by the detaining power to other rank prisoners unless they are employed on work, and so far as British prisoners are concerned, the full pay of their rank in issue at the time of capture continues to be credited to them. An exception to the general rule is made in the case of medical and other protected personnel who receive from the German Government the pay of the equivalent German ranks.

The British Government circulated in early 1942:

Any balance of pay and working pay accumulated by our prisoners and protected personnel from the issues made to them by the German Government will be exchanged on repatriation at the rate of 15RM = £1. Accumulated lager money in an individual's possession can be placed to their personal credit. Such transactions should be carried out through Kommando Fuhrers. Receipts will be given for amounts deposited. Arrangements can be made

through Kommando Fuhrers for the withdrawal of amounts of money that
may be required for special purposes.

In the absence of any further knowledge concerning the events from Stalag 383,
Sandys additionally received direct payments from numerous other sources.
A number of cheques arrived payable to The Duncan Sandys Welfare Fund
from Canada, and personal 'kriegsgefangenenlager' postcards from individual
prisoners of war within Stalag 383. The postcards were thanking him for his
help. Sergeant Miles-Osborne had inadvertently created a situation of great
enthusiasm, which had additionally spread through prisoners' mail to some of
their families in the United Kingdom and the Commonwealth. Unfortunately
and frustratingly for Sandys, the crucial information regarding the intentions
of Miles-Osborne's endeavours still eluded him. His personal assistant Nora
Sabel was tasked with administering what had become a logistical problem
involving an ever-increasing sum of money. On 4 August 1943, she received a
letter from the Navy, Army and Air Force Institute:

> We have received a letter from NX9416 Sgt H. J. Buck AIF PoW 4465 (1450)
> Stalag 383 (formerly Oflag 111C) requesting us to forward you the sum of
> £86 12s in respect of contributions to your welfare fund from twenty-four of
> our prisoners of war at the same camp.

This related to the pledged sum by the RASC/EFI[6] £86 12s on the list of con-
tributors. It has been deducted as instructed by their respective paymasters,
and send as directed to Duncan Sandys.

In September 1943, Regimental Sergeant Major Cooper from the Royal
Army Medical Corp was selected for repatriation from Stalag 383 for medical
reasons. He departed the camp with the intention of contacting Sandys at the
earliest opportunity, as Miles-Osborne required him to clarify their intentions
for the money collected. He was to deliver the following message: 'The so
called Duncan Sandys Welfare Fund provides over £5,000. It is the wishes of
the warrant officers and non-commissioned officers of our empire at Stalag
383 to present a Spitfire to the Wings for Victory Fund.' RSM Cooper was
repatriated to a hospital in Knaphill, Surrey, but was unable to deliver the
message to Sandys until February 1944.

During late 1943, further correspondence had also been received from
Stalag 383. One prisoner, Aubrey Snell, provided something that promoted
Sandys to contact the War Office. His request was for an interpretation of the
'stilted language' contained in the correspondence. The involvement of the
War Office, and ultimately MI9, provided the key to success. Within one of
the 'kriegsgefangenenlager' postcards sent by Miles-Osborne to Sandys was
reference to 'w for v'. This related to Wings for Victory, so the War Office
made arrangements for a welfare fund to be formed to pool the money sent by

the prisoners of war. The Duncan Sandys Welfare Fund was set up to provide funds for the Ministry of Aircraft Production Spitfire Fund. Clearly, the prisoners of war target of £5,000 had relevance to their objective. It was agreed in principle that Sandys would be provided with a letter from the Ministry of Aircraft Production, ensuring that after the war, should any prisoners of war query the allocation of money to the Spitfire Fund, facilities would exist to have their money refunded to them.

With some satisfaction, the financial matters were handed over to the treasury solicitors in November 1943. Instructions were issued for all the respective paymasters to submit funds to the command paymaster at Eastern Division, Ashford Middlesex, via the normal military transfer of payments. Separate arrangements were required for the remaining services and dominion forces. This was by no means a simple process, as it had never been negotiated previously. However, Miles-Osborne had achieved his purpose in representing the prisoners of war in order to purchase a Spitfire from within a German prisoner of war camp; an incredible and brave feat.

On 4 December 1943, Duncan Sandys wrote to Stalag 383, addressing his letter to Sergeant D. T. Miles-Osborne:

> Many thanks for your letter of 7 October, which I have just received. Now that I know the precise purpose to which you wish the welfare fund devoted, I am going ahead with the necessary arrangements. I shall be glad to know whether you wish an inscription of any kind painted on the vehicle. If so, please let me know exactly what you would like.

During late 1943, and continuing into 1944, conditions in the camp were deteriorating. Red Cross food parcels had failed to come through, resulting in every man remaining constantly hungry. The news of the plan having progressed spread with great speed throughout the camp. No doubt pride and a sense of achievement abounded. An accurate scale model was made of the Spitfire by Company Sergeant Major 'Mac' Frederick William MaClaren.

The Ministry of Aircraft Production were kept well advised upon the unusual circumstances concerning the requests of the prisoners of war in Stalag 383. The collection of monies from the Commonwealth countries was proving to be troublesome, purely and simply because of the conditions of war. On 18 February 1944, Duncan Sandys was finally able to place his signature upon the authorisation provided by the Chief Treasury Office from Canadian Military Headquarters.

Considerable time and thought had been given to the Ministry of Aircraft Production's request for a name to be allocated to the purchased Spitfire. On 22 May 1944, Duncan Sandys' personal assistant received a letter requesting the selected name, and advising that the total sum of money received at that

Telephone :
Franklin 2211 Extn. 1147

Telegrams : "Airprod London."

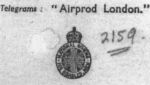

2159.

MINISTRY OF AIRCRAFT
PRODUCTION,

PS6
MILLBANK, S.W.I.

22nd May 1944.

Our Reference ....

Your Reference ....

THE GAOLBIRD.

Dear Miss Sabel,

    You will probably recall that in January
last I spoke to you regarding the "Duncan
Sandys Welfare Fund" and you undertook to let
me know what name should be given to a
Spitfire aircraft to be purchased from the
proceeds of this fund.

    I should be very grateful to learn whether
a decision in this matter has been reached.
We have received to date nearly £4,600 and
we are ready to go ahead to name an aircraft
and to take photographs of it. Will you please
let me know the latest position?

        Yours sincerely,

Miss N. Sabel,
    PS to Joint Parly.Secretary,
      Ministry of Supply,
        Shell Mex House,
          Strand, W.C.2.

Letter received by Nora Sabel on 22 May 1944.

Scale model of *Unshackled Spirit* built by Sergeant Major MaClaren. (*Chris Moscrop*)

time was £4,600. Sandys had considered names of *Triumphant, The Homing Pigeon, Escape to Happiness,* and *The Gaolbird.*

On 14 June 1944, Nora Sabel wrote to the Ministry of Aircraft Production, PS6, advising Mr Camp that:

> Mr Sandys has now decided on the name *Unshackled Spirit.* He thinks that, while the significance of this name will be obvious to all concerned with the fund, it would not be in any way connected with prisoners of war if the aircraft should fall into enemy hands.

Between 14 June and 15 July 1944, one of the Mk IX Spitfires that passed through the production line was selected and identified with the name *Unshackled Spirit,* which was painted upon her fuselage. Two photographs were sent to Sandys' office at the Ministry of Supply in London. One copy was immediately sent to RSM Cooper, the repatriated RAMC officer from Stalag 383, with an accompanying letter advising that he should decide whether or not the picture could be sent to the camp without anyone getting into trouble.

Following Sandys' cautious approach to the War Office, and as a result of the subsequent information that continued to pass between the departments, Nora Sabel wrote to the office, requesting that MI9 send the following message to Corporal McCallen in Stalag 383:[7]

YOUR SPITFIRE WHICH WAS CHRISTENED – QUOTE UNSHACKLED SPIRIT UNQUOTE – HAS BEEN IN BATTLE OVER GERMANY TELL MILES OSBORNE.

Unshackled Spirit. (Geoffrey Saunders)

The War Office confirmed by letter on 4 October 1944 that the requested message to Corporal McCallen had been transmitted. This vital message confirmed to the prisoners of war that their selfless aim to support the war effort and the fight for freedom had been achieved. Sergeant Miles-Osborne and the prisoners of war from Stalag 383 had created a unique and incredible story within the history of the Second World War.

News of the prison camp fund spread at the end of the war. A small article in the *Shenstonian Newsletter* from Solihull School, where Miles-Osborne had been a pupil, was printed in September 1945. It advised that *Unshackled Spirit* had been operationally flying over Germany, having been purchased by funds from the prisoners of war in Stalag 383.

The Mk IX Spitfire *Unshackled Spirit* had been built in the factories conceived under the Shadow Scheme, devised by Lord Swinton in 1936.[8] Those factories were subjected to bombing by the various Luftwaffe campaigns in an effort to disrupt the production of aero engines, airframes and other vital components required to produce the country's fighting machines. It is a measure of the immense productivity of that industry that the labour force employed by British aircraft companies had grown to a peak of an estimated 1,821,000 men and women in early 1944.[9]

2

Wings for Victory

Wings for Victory Saving Campaigns

Almost immediately after the declaration of war with Germany, the British Government urged the counties and districts across the country to contribute money towards the funding for the war effort. Local savings committees were established to invest the cash. Contributions ranging from small, individual amounts to large, corporate investments were accepted into the National War Savings Scheme. This particular savings scheme was created to focus public attention, and instil a feeling of direct participation for local communities. These investments were completely separate from the local Spitfire fund collections and the gift purchasing of specific aircraft. In many instances, the two schemes ran alongside each other, with combined promotions across the country.

The Government sponsored war saving events, which identified specific areas of activity, and required local authorities to designate one particular week in each year as a War Savings week. Throughout the duration of the war, nationally led, regionally coordinated, and locally organised campaigns for War Weapons week, Wings for Victory week, Salute the Soldier week, and Warship week enabled the public to respond to the challenge to meet financial targets set by local committees.

Wings for Victory was the title deployed during the nominated 1943 savings week. The options and returns for investing money were savings bonds, defence bonds, saving certificates, saving stamps, national war bonds and post office savings banks. The Wings for Victory savings were specifically for the purchasing of an aircraft, and in general terms at the time, the investment return was around 3 per cent. The Government understood the value of promoting the savings schemes, therefore saving stamps featured prominently on several areas of promotional images. Stamps could be purchased by individuals and stuck onto bombs that were later pictured being loaded onto Bomber Command's aircraft.

Incredibly, almost every town and village held their own Wings for Victory savings week, with targets being set by the respective local authority, and supported by advertising posters supplied by the National Savings Department. The RAF endorsed the campaigns through personal appearances made by pilots and

Wings for Victory Certificate.

THIS

LOG BOOK

which will record the operational activities

of an Aircraft

is a tribute to the success achieved by

West Renfrewshire
(GREENOCK)
SAVINGS COMMITTEE

in the

WINGS FOR VICTORY

NATIONAL SAVINGS CAMPAIGN · 1943

Target :- £ 1,000,000.
Achievement :- £ 1,341,917. 14/.10.

REPRESENTING 12 LANCASTERS. 12 CATALINAS.
THE COST OF 12 HURRICANES, EQUIPMENT
AND PARTS.

Wings for Victory logbook.

aircrew at numerous events during the designated weeks. In London, Trafalgar Square supported a Lancaster displayed on a plinth. The aircraft drew large crowds, who were then duly encouraged to invest money in the various savings schemes that were being promoted. The Prime Minister Winston Churchill was quoted as saying, 'If we fail, all fails, if we fall, all fall together;' a message that strongly intimated that everyone needed to engage in the war savings.

The local authorities that achieved or surpassed their target funds were presented with a commemorative plaque. The plaque measured 58 cm high and 35 cm wide, and was made of a urea formaldehyde plastic, a form of bakelite manufactured by De La Rue Plastics of Walthamstow; a renowned plastics manufacturer of the time that was under contract to produce different plaques for each of the primary campaigns. All of the plaques were of the same dimensions, and all appeared in the same ivory-coloured finish. Many of these can be still be seen today, hanging in public buildings across the country.

The Wings for Victory plaque 'Per Ardu Astra' depicted a naked warrior with a sword about to slay a three-headed monster. At its base was the inscription:

War Savings Campaign 1943.
Presented by the Air Ministry in recognition of successful achievements in Wings for Victory week.

In addition to the plaques, certificates of honour were issued, with a depiction of the plaque and the signature of the Secretary of State for the air identifiable in the bottom corner of the certificate. It would appear that the certificates were issued to recognise the many cases where the level of investment was significant, but fell just short of the target figures.

All districts were kept aware of what the funds were purchasing, and in many instances, individual logbooks were created for each aircraft. The original crew names were identified, and the operations undertaken were listed for that aircraft. These obviously became outdated very quickly, but the books provided a tangible representation of what had been achieved by the counties and districts. The illustrated example from West Renfrewshire provides that the district of Greenock was set a target of £1,000,000, and achieved the incredible sum of £1,341,917 14s 10d. That sum of money represented the purchase of thirty-six aircraft: twelve Lancasters, twelve Catalina Flying Boats, and twelve Hurricanes.

The aircraft logbook sent to West Renfrewshire was for one of the Lancaster Bombers, with the aircraft serial ND 395. The Lancaster went on to participate in fifteen bombing operations over Germany between 5 January 1944 and 11 April 1944. Tragically, on that fateful day in April, the aircraft failed to return, having been shot down over Aached, Germany. From her crew of seven men, five were killed, one escaped and successfully evaded, while the remaining crew member, Flying Officer McDougall from Canada, was captured to become a prisoner of war in Stalag Luft III.

3

Kriegies

Allied prisoner of war numbers grew progressively as Germany's Third Reich consumed enormous swathes of land across Europe. The Royal Air Force engaged in the Battle for France, where inspiring operations were conducted in outdated aircraft. At that time, the probability of returning from France to England after being shot down still existed, but after the fall of France, the Allied airmen brought the war from their airfields to the occupying forces of Germany on the other side of the English Channel. Fighter pilots, bomber pilots, navigators, flight engineers, radio operators, bomb aimers, and air gunners from across all flying commands volunteered to defend the United Kingdom and attack Germany's great might in the skies over occupied Europe. These brave men, and the supporting Polish, Czechoslovakian, Belgian, Dutch, and free French aircrews were constantly exposed to crash landings, or the threat of being shot down from the sky and parachuted into the hands of the enemy. Those men were precious to the RAF. It is estimated that the training costs were approximately £10,000 to produce a qualified bomber pilot and £15,000 for a fighter pilot.

The earliest prisoners from within the Royal Air Force were pre-war regulars and short service commissioned officers who served alongside the auxiliary and volunteer officers. It would be fair to summarise that many of the men were ex-public school and gentlemen flyers, many of whom had trained at weekends in the various auxiliary squadrons.

The German occupying forces were initially ill-prepared for the numbers of prisoners captured during their onslaught in Europe. In fact, that situation continued to be present for the entire duration of the war. Initially, the German authorities requisitioned appropriate buildings; primarily disused barracks, castles, and fortresses. Many of these had been used for the same purpose during the First World War. Very few new prisoner of war camps were constructed. The German Army was initially responsible for all captured and imprisoned men, and distributed the Allied soldiers, airmen, and sailors across the prison camp structure.

Towards the end of 1940, the Luftwaffe started to assume greater control over aircrew prisoners, and constructed a purpose-built camp for these men,

An early German PoW camp holding Allied prisoners in Poland.

namely Stalag Luft I. The Allied air forces consistently suffered the loss of pilots and aircrews, and the numbers of aviator prisoners of war steadily grew, reaching its peak in 1944. Aircrew prisoners of war were regarded as important by the German authorities, and their expensive training and value to the Allied forces was fully acknowledged by those charged to keep them incarcerated.

By this time, the British Foreign Office had created the Prisoner of War Department, which was headed up by Sir Harold Satow. The War Office created a Prisoner of War Directorate that represented all three services, and was designed to facilitate in all matters that involved the captured forces. The demand for welfare support, and in particular the specific requests for books for prisoner of war camps in Germany during the Second World War, became insatiable;[10] libraries were established in almost all the camps. It is through the myriad of voluntary and humanitarian agencies established during the war that the primary subject of this book, namely the wartime log, is examined.

The wartime log was a book specifically designed, printed, and produced for Allied prisoners of war. Originally, the book was to be issued personally to prisoners so that they could keep a record of their thoughts, memoirs, and artwork. The logs were printed and distributed from Geneva, Switzerland, between 1944 and 1945, as a gift by the Young Man's Christian Association (YMCA) War Prisoners Aid. During the Second World War, the YMCA was

involved in war work with displaced persons and refugees. They set up the
War Prisoners Aid to support prisoners of war by providing books, sports
equipment, musical instruments, art materials, radios, gramophones, eating utensils, and many other essential items that would aid survival in the
wretched prison camps.

The Geneva Convention of 1929 upholds the most important basic rights
for all prisoners of war. The lives of Allied prisoners of war would be influenced
and controlled by the Geneva Convention agreement, and held no boundaries
regardless of what army, navy or air force they were engaged in. Countries
that failed to sign and agree to the convention's terms were not bound by
its articles. Two of the world's main fighting forces, Russia and Japan, were
not signatories to the Geneva Convention. However, at the beginning of the
Second World War, the basic documents that determined legal procedures for
casualties of war were as follows:

- Hague Convention on the laws and customs of ground warfare, 5 October
  1907.
- Geneva Convention, concerning the treatment of prisoners of war, 27 July
  1929.

Taking into account that the Soviet Union and Japan did not subscribe to the
Geneva Convention, its relationship with other governments in this area was
regulated on the basis of the Hague convention of 1907.

Within the bounds of the primary convention of 1929, two important aid
establishments, the International Red Cross Committee and the Protecting
Powers Inspectorate,[11] facilitated inspection visits to prisoner of war camps.
The inspection visit facility applied to both Axis and Allied camps; in effect,
both sides wishing to ensure that their prisoners of war were provided with
the protection of the treaty.

Article thirty-nine of the treaty was seemingly no more than one minor
component, yet it became much more than that, and had a great impact upon
the vast majority, if not all, prisoners of war. It quotes:

> Prisoners of war shall be allowed to receive shipments of books individually,
> which may be subject to censorship. Representatives of the protecting powers
> and authorised aid societies may send books and collections of books to the
> libraries of prisoners' camps. The transmission of these shipments to libraries
> may not be delayed under the pretext of censorship difficulties.

Some 160,000 British and Commonwealth servicemen were incarcerated in
around fifty prisoner of war camps in Germany during the Second World War.[12]
Camp conditions varied according to the camp's geographical location. Most
accommodation comprised of wooden huts, with basic stone or wooden floor-

ing. Clearly, the nature of detaining the prisoners of war required that measures to prevent escape were a priority. Camps that were built on the ground that were considered easy for tunneling adopted the principle of constructing the barrack accommodation on brick pillars. This allowed continual observation of the ground underneath each hut, so as to aid a tunneling deterrent that remained consistent wherever appropriate throughout the war. The German PoW camps were identified as the following: Stalag (Stammlager), permanent camps for non-commissioned officers and enlisted men; Stalag Luft (Luftwaffestammlager), permanent camps for air force personnel; Oflag (Offizierslager), permanent camps for officers. These all required watchtowers and barbed wire fencing, and in many instances, multiple wire compounds were erected inside one another. Other camps, such as III-D in Central Berlin, housed selected prisoners of war who had been identified either as possible sympathisers towards the German Reich, or simply overtly anti-Communist. These camps were still identified as Stalag, but were far removed from the massive barbed wire encased compounds and guard towers that had been constructed in Poland, Austria, and Germany.

Germany generally complied with the 1929 Geneva Convention in its treatment of British and Allied servicemen in PoW camps. After the declaration of war against Germany by the United States of America in December 1941, prisoner of war camps began to see an influx of USAAF captured aircrews. The estimated total of American prisoners placed in the camp structure was to reach 95,000 by 1945. The Geneva Convention forbade work of any kind for officer prisoners, with non-commissioned officer prisoners being restricted to supervisory work. However, private soldiers or equivalent ranks in all three services could be made to work, provided the work was not connected with the war effort. PoW work parties were seen by prisoners as an opportunity to escape the boredom of camp life, and in addition, provided opportunities to gather information for possible escape attempts. It was also commonplace for officers to swap identities in order to undertake work parties. Two key priorities for Allied prisoners of war were obtaining sufficient food and ensuring they had warm clothing for the harsh winters in Eastern Europe. These problems were addressed by the International Red Cross (IRC) during the entire period of the war, and to their credit, food and clothing consistently remained their two primary objectives.

At the beginning of the Second World War, the International Red Cross Committee in Geneva became involved in providing books to prisoners of war, as well as civilian internees. The IRC began to coordinate this type of relief through various religious and lay organisations, which had already been active on their own. In October 1939, the World Committee of the YMCA in Geneva, Switzerland, established the War Prisoners Aid in order to satisfy the recreational, educational, and moral needs of war prisoners. The American War Prisoners Aid of the YMCA became the major agency for acquiring books and sending them to the ever-growing number of prisoner of war camps across Germany.

Following the first shipment of books by that organisation, an ever-increasing yet ever-inadequate flow of books was being sent to the numerous camps being constructed or expanded. Neutral YMCA officials from Geneva received permission to visit prisoner of war camps, and talk with the men in order to determine what more could be done to help them. Prisoners' feedback via letters advised that there was a great need for books. Many requests for technical reference material came from the camps, which had not been anticipated by any of the organisations. In late autumn of 1940, the Indoor Recreations section of the Prisoner of War Department of the British Red Cross Society, and the Order of St John of Jerusalem were established, both accepting the responsibility for regular consignments of books. By December 1941, the Indoor Recreations section had sent over 71,000 volumes, and between October 1940 and March 1945[13] they had sent more than 239,500 books directly to the prison camp libraries or to the reserve at Geneva. In addition, a small but significant gift of books arrived in each prisoner of war camp at Christmas, sent by the King and Queen.

In amongst other tasks, the British Military Intelligence Section 9 (MI9) specialised in providing assistance to British and other Allied servicemen, both behind enemy lines and in prison camps. This included facilitating the escape of prisoners of war and helping others evade capture in order to travel safely to friendly or neutral states. MI5, whose job it was to keep Britain free from enemy agents, pointed out that the Germans were using the guise of repatriated or escaped prisoners of war to infiltrate Britain.

MI9 was very much aware of the many volunteer and humanitarian activities providing for prisoners of war. In some instances, they positively exploited them within the boundaries of the Geneva Convention. For the first two years of the war, MI9 used the standard mail service that went into the camps in order to send newsletters on the war's progress. They saw an opportunity to sustain prisoners' morale, and at the same time exploit the mail process in the hope of lowering the morale of the censors. This important department was instrumental in a great many ways, particularly in creating the secret codes that facilitated wireless communication direct to the prison camps' secret radios.

The available statistics give an insight into the commitment of the Red Cross in providing food parcels to all Allied prisoners of war. These were seen as the most important aspect of providing comfort and enhancing the prisoners' quality of life while in captivity. The British, Canadian, and Australian Red Cross packed and shipped 16.5 million food parcels between 1941 and 1945; the cost of the food parcels totaling £30,070,933. This huge sum of money was raised by the three primary Commonwealth Red Cross organisations in Canada, United Kingdom, and Australia. While it must be accepted that the food parcels formed the lifeline of connectivity with prisoners, it could also be argued that the book parcels provided just as much support to each man. The British Red Cross food parcels were carefully chosen to give the best dietetic value and to supply elements that were lacking from the basic prison camp diets. The parcels weighed around 11 lbs, and contained, according to availability, some or all of the following items:

- ¼-lb packet of tea
- Tin of cocoa powder
- Bar of milk or plain chocolate
- Tinned pudding
- Tin of meat roll
- Tin of processed cheese
- Tin of condensed milk
- Tin of dried eggs
- Tin of sardines or herrings
- Tin of preserve
- Tin of margarine
- Tin of sugar
- Tin of vegetables
- Tin of biscuits
- Bar of soap

Volunteers staffed seventeen centres around the UK, and at its peak packed up to 163,000 parcels each week. A House of Commons question on the subject of food parcels was tabled on 30 July 1942. It was responded to by Duncan Sandys, who advised:

> An average 100,000 food parcels a week are being dispatched from this country to Geneva, and this rate is being still further increased. In addition, an average of another 60,000 parcels are being despatched weekly from Canada. There is still some congestion at Lisbon, but the number of parcels transported from there to Geneva has in recent months appreciably increased.

The Joint War Organisation had eight ships under permanent charter, with others standing by to transport the parcels on the first stages of their journey to the prison camps. The majority of these ships operated a shuttle service between Lisbon in neutral Portugal, and Marseilles in the south of France. At Marseilles, the parcels were transported by rail network to Geneva, where the International Committee of the Red Cross arranged for their distribution to prison camps in Germany and elsewhere.

It was possible for relatives to contact the honourable secretary, Invalid Comforts section at 14 Carlton House, London, to apply for permission to send special needs parcels, which were additional to the other parcel privileges. The senior officers of any prisoner of war camp were also able to communicate with this special section to request items such as spectacles, dentures, surgical appliances, or other personal items. The Invalid Comforts section dispatched consignments of ordinary drugs, cod liver oil, malt, and convalescence foods to all known hospitals that held Allied prisoners of war. These comfort parcels became a valued addition to the neediest groups of Allied prisoners.

As the war progressed, Germany not only constructed new labour camps, but also expanded many established larger camps in order to accommodate the ever-increasing numbers of prisoners of war. The Kriegsmarine (German Navy) opened its first purpose-built camp for naval prisoners in 1941. The Luftwaffe wanted to create one large camp for the RAF and another for the USAAF, although this never materialised. Immediate requests for additional books became a natural sequence of events, and in order to deal with these continuing developments, a stockpile of 50,000 English language books were to be held in Geneva. This proved to be a solution to another problem that had onset these organisations. Book request forms were being sent to the numerous camps, with prisoners returning them with very specific and unexpected requirements. When requests were received by the Educational Books section, in many instances they could be selected from the Geneva stockpile, packed, and sent on to the individual concerned. The prisoner concerned was required to return an acknowledgment card; a method of ensuring the completion of such requests. While this infrastructure was effective and efficient, there were obviously many requests that were unobtainable, although incredible effort was always put in place in trying to provide the requested material. The countries' libraries became rich picking grounds, and they quite happily contributed.

In early 1942, the World Committee of the YMCA founded the Men of Science Prisoners of War Service. This service was identified and developed to provide books for prisoners who wished to study, and for those who wanted to gain levels of certified qualifications. Many young men had left their studies and volunteered for military service. For these academics frustrated in the prisoner of war camps, university libraries and professors helped to locate specially requested books. An example of such efforts:

File No. 121-S. Canadian Legion War Services Inc. Education Services.
Reply to Royal Canadian Air Force prisoner of war:

In accordance with the information contained in your letter of 26 August, we are ordering from the publishers a book on diesel maintenance; you will be advised when this goes forward. Meantime we are sending the Canadian Legion course in diesel engineering. It is a very good course. We shall advise you when the book becomes available.

The ever-optimistic Flight Lieutenant Charles Marshall, in Stalag Luft III, had been shot down over Essen in April 1942. He sought the option to learn the German language; a most useful tool to acquire should the opportunity to escape present itself. Remarkably, the Germans allowed the subject to be openly taught within the camp, and Marshall achieved two certificates of competency awarded by the Royal Society for Encouragement of Arts in London. One was for a first class in German language examination.

After the war, some notable individuals had achieved various qualifications while serving as a prisoner in Germany. The photo reconnaissance Spitfire pilot Anthony Barber, captured in 1942, took a law degree in his camp, and achieved a first class honour facilitated through the International Red Cross. After his liberation, he practiced as a barrister, and later ventured into politics, to ultimately be appointed as Chancellor of the Exchequer in Edward Heath's Government.

The War Prisoners Aid reported that 98,962 popular books and textbooks had been shipped to Geneva in 1943. In addition to books, the Red Cross undertook 29,829 PoW requests in 1943 for a multitude of items. The following material was delivered in 48,606 parcels:

- 522,345 books
- 8,504 footballs
- 4,623 boxing gloves
- 118,277 indoor games
- 5,593 musical instruments
- 276,436 painting drawing and educational items
- 29 motion picture projectors and films

The Geneva office reported that, during the last full year of operation in 1944, 108,682 books were shipped to Allied prison camps in Germany. In addition, in the first three months of 1944, the Red Cross delivered a gross 143 tons of leisure time material to the camps. Libraries, as would be expected, were always the busiest center of any PoW camp, with books frequently providing the route into other activities. There were many copies of plays, which were studied and transformed into productions for the enjoyment of endless sittings in camp theatres. Most camps flourished with amateur dramatic societies, and the abbreviation of 'CADS' was applied to those who patronised the theatres.

Some of the most important communication routes to be established with the prisoner of war camps were those of the individual church groups, women's voluntary services, and manufacturers' donations. The War Office had appointed the MI9 Intelligence Officer Clayton Hutton, who used these groups for very special purposes. These alternative routes of communication were vital, as the Geneva Convention imposed restrictions in relation to the Red Cross, and in particular Red Cross parcels. To contravene the restrictions would not have been acceptable in any circumstances. Hutton was an inventor with an amazing ability in creativity. He was specifically recruited by MI9 to give assistance to prisoners of war by developing and supplying them with gadgets to assist breaking out of the camps and finding their way to freedom. 'Clutty', as he became known, was provided with the highest War Office authority, and he used this to access senior military ranking officers and obtain authorisation for the purchase of essential materials, regardless of wartime restrictions or rationing. The treasury became difficult in their red tape requirements for receipts, and stipulated that they wanted one for every single item or service acquired by Clayton. Fortunately, the Ministry of Supply, under direct orders from the War Office, resolved any such problems for him. A rather strange code was developed to maintain security. For instance, the purchase of the silk needed to manufacture the incredibly detailed escape maps that could be sewn into uniforms was referred to on the invoices as 'eggs and bacon'; none of the materials ever bore any resemblance to the actual goods or services. Hutton's MI9 appointment and successes led to him working in his own small section of IS9 known as Z, the intelligence school arm within the MI9 network.

In late 1940, MI9 circulated to the Royal Air Force details for the insertion of escape items into operational flying gear. With no personal cost to any pilot or crew member, maps and compasses would be sewn into their flying tunics. Each tunic or battledress was labeled by a tailor, and in addition, a reference number to that particular item was supplied to the station's Intelligence Officer. This enabled individual escape items in each garment to be identifiable by the reference number supplied. MI9 advised that Messrs. Glandfield & Sons of Brick Lane, London, were the company appointed to undertake this secret work, and that they would endeavor to return each garment within 24 hours.

One of Hutton's inventions was an escape pen; an ordinary fountain pen with a secret. Any escape from a prisoner of war camp was likely to require the prisoner to wear civilian clothing that resembled the average German labourer. To support an escape, the rubber ink bag within the pen was divided into three sections. The first contained standard ink to pass any inspection by the German security, and the two remaining sections held strong brown and blue dye. The clip of the pen was magnetised and designed to swing to the north, while concealed within the top of the pen was a miniature compass. The pen barrel was slightly larger than a genuine article, as it also held a tissue paper map wrapped between the inner and outer cylinders.

It was known that prisoners' personal parcels were examined with utmost vigor by the camp security, but 'Clutty' strongly suspected that gifts from donors to nonspecific prisoners were unlikely to be so scrutinized, so he therefore set up a number of fictitious organisations across the country. The majority were allocated addresses of bombed-out blitz buildings. Printers were provided with letter headings that held quotations and clues, such as, 'knock and it shall be opened unto you', 'seek and ye shall find'. Additionally, telephone calls were diverted by the telephone exchange, as was any mail posted to the spoof addresses.

The use of these spoof venues allowed for the escape inventions to be slipped into the camps without contravention of any laws or written rules. At first, all parcels were completely genuine, and then a few items containing concealments would be integrated into the system. These were incorporated into clothing, games equipment, and even playing cards. Sandwiched between each card would have been small sections of maps, so that when the pack was broken down it revealed a large area of mapping. Books were also used. The covers were removed and rebound with maps and foreign money hidden beneath the new endpapers. A letter from the donor was included with each parcel providing cryptic clues:

Dear Friend,

I am sure you will be sorry to hear that my beautiful vicarage was bombed a month ago by the enemy. Everything was destroyed except my library. As my wife and I feel that it will be some considerable time before we have another home of our own, we have decided that little purpose would be served by putting the books into storage. We are therefore sending them out to the prisoner of war camps, hoping that they will do something to sustain morale of those who, like yourself, are enduring Babylonish captivity.

Please let me know that you have received this parcel safely, and that you are one of those who believe, with Andrew Lang, in The Love of Books, the Golden Key that Opens the Enchanted Door.

Yours most sincerely.

Consignments were packed with old newspapers relative to the spoof address, providing another means of disguising the central packing unit used by the War Office. The cards returned from the camps provided proof that the parcels were being accepted. Soon, chess pieces with left-hand threaded rooks were being dispatched, each holding a map, compass, or other escape material. Board game bases, such as snakes and ladders, were used to conceal money, maps, needles, and thread.

The International Red Cross was charged with corresponding between the prisoners of war and their families throughout the Second World War. The task imposed upon them was enormous by any scale of the imagination, yet it was of the utmost importance, for it provided up-to-date information and allowed direct contact between the camps and families. Instructions on censorship and the materials allowed to be sent to the camps had to be followed with strict discipline. The American Red Cross, in its printed prisoners of war bulletins, provided excellent guidance; it was possible to send one parcel of books to any one prisoner of war every thirty days, providing the parcel weighed no more than 5 lbs. This service was facilitated by the Censors Office in New York. In

Canada, family members of a prisoner of war were given a list of Government registered firms where they could directly order books. All books were subject to rigid censorship control, and material containing anything likely to assist in an escape was prohibited. These included navigational reference books, sailing instructions, map making, wireless and radio information, and chemistry books. No books could have pencil or ink markings in them, and all had to pass the restrictions imposed by the German censor. A whole set of regulations, some standard throughout the Reich and others varying from camp to camp, had to be observed. Parcels sent by relatives were stored in the camp and censored individually. If the books were approved, they were then issued to the prisoner. The Germans did not permit books written or including material by Jewish authors. Once accepted, most books were rubber stamped by the censor, and it appears that green ink became the norm for this particular process, although it was no means the rule. Blue ink was always used for the censoring stamps upon prisoners' personal letters and postcards.

The wartime logs for British prisoners of war frequently became the most treasured books to be held by a prisoner. The books were first distributed in 1944; sadly not available to all prisoners, despite additional funds becoming available for further printing in 1944. The book was small; 113 pages available for writing purposes, and a central section consisting of 12 thick card pages suitable for watercolour sketching and painting. In addition, 4 cellophane envelopes were stuck upon the last pages, designed to hold keepsakes or items of special importance to the book's owner. In many instances, the individual quality of artwork to be found within these unique books is truly incredible. Even more importantly, the wartime logs used by the men who kept detailed diaries provide an unrivaled insight into the personal world of each man's life as a prisoner of war. Strangely, the Canadian equivalent of the wartime logbook was produced in a larger format than the British example. Easily identified by the Canadian maple leaf, this book had the dedication, 'a remembrance from home through the Canadian YMCA' printed on the opening page. The distribution process of these logs was such that no real correlation between nation and log type existed. Many RAF prisoners held the RCAF example, and visa-versa.

The following letter was printed by the YMCA and attached within the initial book distribution:

War Prisoners Aid of the YMCA, introductory letter – October 1944.

Dear Friend,

When the folks at home ask us to choose and send you something special on their behalf, they confront us with a not too easy problem. The wartime log is one solution – others may be coming your way before long.

These blank pages offer many possibilities. Not everyone will want to keep a diary or even a journal – occasional notes on the story of his wartime experiences. If you are a writer, here is space for a short story. If you are an artist (some people are), you may want to cover these pages with sketches of your camp, caricatures of its important personalities, whether residents or authorities. If you are a poet, major or minor, confide your lyrics to these pages. If you feel the circumstances cramp your style in correspondence, you might write here letters unmailable now, but safely kept to be carried with you on your return. This book might serve to list the most striking concoctions of the camp kitchen, the records of a camp Olympics, or a selection of the best jokes cracked in camp. One man has suggested using the autograph of one of his companions (plus his fingerprints?) to head each page, followed by free and frank remarks about the man himself. The written text might be a commentary on such photographs as you may have to mount on the special pages for that purpose. The mounting corners are in an envelope in the pocket of the back cover. Incidentally, this pocket might be used for clippings you want to preserve, or, together with the small envelopes on the last page, to contain authentic souvenirs of life in camp.

You might want to do something altogether different with this book. Whatever you do, let it be a visible link between yourself and folks at home, one more reminder that their thoughts are with you constantly. If it brings you this assurance, the log will have served its purpose.

Yours very sincerely.

War Prisoners Aid of the YMCA.

As aviators, Allied aircrews became the responsibility of the German Luftwaffe, and were held in the Stalag Luft camp system. It must be remembered that the early air force prisoners of war were swept up within the general melee of prisoners from across all the armed services, and initially held within the Wehrmacht *army* prisoner of war camps. In the main, this was the normal procedure while awaiting space in the Stalag Luft camp structure. Initially, the Germans constructed Stalag Luft I as the main aircrew camp, but even after unplanned expansion, it proved insufficient to hold the numbers required.

Germany consistently underestimated the sheer number of prisoners they would take as the war progressed. This was the root cause of the many cases of cramped and appalling conditions, and the lack of food experienced by Allied prisoners of war during the Second World War. The German prisoner management was designed to avoid Allied officers mixing with the lower ranks if at all possible.

Allied prisoners of war in Stalag Luft I. Standing far right is a British RAF observer wearing the early 'observer' navigator's wing. Standing far left is Petr Uruba, a Czechoslovakian pilot from 311 Squadron. In 1941, his crew was captured after they became disorientated over Europe. The weather conditions had created unexpected headwinds that resulted in navigational errors, causing them to unintentionally land on a Luftwaffe airfield in France. Uruba had been flying as second pilot in the squadron's Wellington bomber. It was a most unsatisfactory set of circumstances, but by no means a unique one. This gallant Czech pilot was later moved to other prison camps, including Colditz in 1944. (*PhDr J. Rajlich*)

4

Principal German Camps

Dulag Luft

Derived from Durchgangslager, or entrance camp, Dulag Luft was the Luftwaffe's interrogation center at Oberursel. The processing of aviator prisoners of war commenced here on 15 December 1939. All Allied aircrews were transported to the Dulag Luft after their capture. Pilots and aircrew were then detained in single cells, and interviewed by specialist interrogators who had previously lived in the United Kingdom. The interrogators spoke excellent English, and used their knowledge to gain the confidence of the prisoners in an effort to establish whatever information may become available through them.

As the war waged on, the intelligence centre developed rapidly. Several technical means were also deployed for interrogation, including microphone recording. This concept of specific interrogation of Allied airmen by the Luftwaffe proved beneficial for the quest to gather intelligence and general information, and over the years of operation, small pieces of information were pieced together to provide an accumulative effect of intelligence gathering. The Germans were exceptional in processing information; a classic example being the dog tag identification discs held by every prisoner of war.[14] The numbering on the identity discs gave them clues as to the training undertaken by each individual. The Germans found it possible to reconstruct the system used in the distribution of personnel numbering, and had quickly realised that the Royal Air Force crews were given numbers in alphabetical order when they had finished their training. By inserting the designation of the school in the corresponding groups of numbers, it was possible to determine the training school at which the prisoner of war had concluded his training, and eventually establish the capacity of each school. With a significant number of men being processed, this one area alone allowed the interrogators to predict and divulge information thought impossible for the enemy to know. This was just one of the several unsettling experiences laid before a newly captured aviator, for the Germans had several other intelligence methods to deploy. Techniques were used to identify anyone who may be likely to divulge information that may be of use to the Luftwaffe, although thankfully, these individuals were extremely rare.

During 1940, with some 600 Allied airmen having passed through the interrogation center, the staffing was increased to four primary interrogators, with roughly fifty support staff from 1941. It was a consistently busy place, requiring the interrogators to be prompt in their assessments. In 1942, further holding cell capacity was constructed, followed by yet more holding capacity in 1943. From late 1943 onwards, RAF and Commonwealth prisoners of war were processed in a consistent way. Officers went from Dulag Luft to Stalag Luft I at Barth, or to Stalag Luft III at Sagan, and NCOs went to Stalag 344 at Lamsdorf, to Stalag IV-B at Muhlberg, or to the new camp Stalag Luft VI at Heydekrug, East Prussia. At the close of 1943, the interrogation camp had processed many thousands of Allied airmen. Despite the improvements in their systems, it was found that the compound at Oberursel was far too small to act as a holding centre for prisoners after their interrogation. The transit camp was therefore transferred in September from Oberursel to a new site in the centre of Frankfurt-on-Main. This was not without issues, as the new camp was considered by the International Red Cross Committee to be at danger from an air attack, sufficient to contravene article nine of the Geneva Convention. The British Government made an official complaint through the protecting power in December 1943 regarding the holding of prisoners in the new camp, but to no avail. In early 1944, the interrogation camp processed its heaviest contingent of Allied airmen, a reflection upon the significant losses being experienced within Bomber Command at that time. The prisoner numbers reached a peak in July 1944 when over 3,000 men were processed. As predicted, during a bombing raid on Frankfurt, the camp was badly damaged, forcing a further move to Wetzlar, where the holding centre remained for the duration of the war. The Dulag Luft interrogation structure was operational throughout the war, with the facility finally ceasing operations on 15 April 1945.[15]

The comprehensive Allied prisoner of war debriefing processes, undertaken in 1945, revealed detailed evidence that the Dulag Luft interrogators had amassed a huge amount of information through their interrogations. Frequently, the interrogators would intentionally divulge information to many of their subjects; in some instances information of extraordinary detail. Squadron Leader George Davies DSO, shot down in 1944 while flying with the Pathfinder force, reported the following in his debriefing on 11 May 1945: 'The enemy appeared to have the complete story of 156 Squadron. Even to name the newly appointed commanding officer. A few small errors, but they also had a mass of information upon Pathfinder force techniques.'

The Dulag Luft prisoner identification card was larger than those adopted within most of the Stalag Luft camps. When Squadron Leader Davis was captured, having been shot down over St Dizier, he was allocated prisoner of war number 4,900, photographed, and had his thumb print applied to the

Above: Dulag Luft in Oberusal, Frankfurt.

Right: Dulag Luft prisoner identity form.

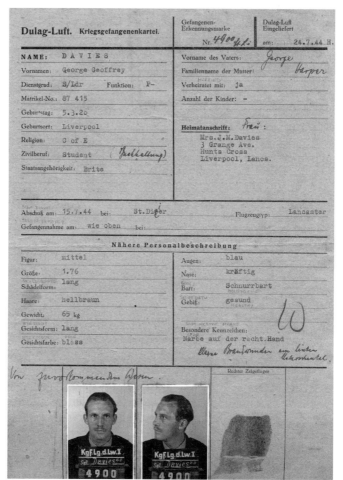

identification card. It is thought that the Dulag Luft card was duplicated and transferred with each prisoner, remaining with the prisoner's records throughout his prisoner of war service. The efficiency of the Luftwaffe's system of prisoner processing saw Squadron Leader Davies resting in his allocated bunk in Stalag Luft I within thirteen days of having been shot down.

Stalag VIII-B

This well-established camp in Lamsdorf, Upper Silesia, had always held considerable numbers of RAF personnel. Frequently deployed as a holding camp, in 1942 it was consuming airmen, primarily from Bomber Command, on a regular basis; essentially, all casualties from the gathering growth of Allied air force activity over France and Germany. By 1943, the famous camp for Allied airmen in Sagan, Stalag Luft III, had become so overcrowded that an estimated 1,000 men, mostly non-commissioned aircrew, were transferred to Lamsdorf. A part of the camp was separated by building new barbed wire fences, thus a camp within a camp was created. It developed and retained a large and fairly good library during its service as a prisoner of war camp.[16] Lamsdorf was never to become a dedicated airman's camp during its long existence.

The German authorities quickly instigated means to thwart the increasing number of escape attempts being committed by the troublesome airmen within the prisoner of war camps. In a decree on 14 December 1943 (number 978/43), the Reichsfuehrer and the Reichsminister of the Interior authorised the criminal police to pay a reward of up to 100 marks for assistance in apprehending fugitive prisoners of war or other wanted persons. In situations where more than one person participated in the capture, the reward was to be divided proportionately. Should the amount of 100 marks not suffice to properly reward all the participants for their cooperation, the matter of increasing the amount was to be submitted for approval to the Reichsfuehrer and the Reichsminister of the Interior. This inspired decree created a significant enhancement in general security across Germany. By the clever deployment of a simple reward scheme, it created even greater difficulty for the men to move through Germany, and directly contributed to many escaping and evading prisoners of war being apprehended during 1944 and 1945.

Stalag Luft I

Built in Barth on the Baltic Coast of north Germany, Stalag Luft I began accepting both officer and non-commissioned officer ranks from the RAF in mid-1940. Initially, the camp consisted of two individual compounds. In common with all the camps, prisoner numbers consistently grew, and the idea on escape became a priority for a great many men. Within the camp, the escape committee became a major component of the daily, and frequently dull, routines. Stalag Luft I has a long history of escape attempts. Its geographical location was seen as ideal, for if prisoners were able to get out of the camp, they did not have to travel very far in order to reach the coast; the town of Barth being a seaport not far from Denmark. In the majority of the other camps you would have to negotiate through Germany before you could hope to find friendly hands. The camp also had an effective library. Many books arrived in personal parcels, which were passed around or donated to the libraries after the recipient had read them. These books accounted for the massive additional numbers of general reading material that circulated within all camps across Germany. In 1943, the camp became a facility for officers only; the NCOs were moved to Stalag Luft VI. In December, the RAF and Commonwealth airmen were subsequently condensed into one compound, and the remaining compound was eventually filled with USAAF airmen. Further compound construction took place as the result of a huge surge of additional American airmen during late 1943 and early 1944. The entire camp benefited from the growth of USAAF airmen. American magazines became available in the camp library and provided great enjoyment, being eagerly read and re-read until they fell apart. The camp produced and distributed its own news sheet, which was highly popular. They also received the German newspaper *OK*, which was especially printed in English. Some suspicion existed, as the newspaper was thought to have been provided for propaganda purposes. This was most certainly the intention of the German authorities, but in fact, they merely supplemented the prisoners' meager, almost non-existent rations of toilet paper. The prisoner population reached over 8,000 men in 1945.

Stalag Luft III

Located near the small town of Sagan, Silesia, Stalag Luft III was made famous by the Great Escape. This camp first opened in March/April 1942 and figured in many movements of captured aviators during its existence. The infamous Wooden Horse escape took place at this camp in 1943. Stalag Luft III was made up of several individual compounds within a massive camp infrastructure. The large north compound was added during March 1943. In September, the south compound opened, and in early 1944, the west compound was added. Each compound had at least two libraries; one for reference material and one for general library lending. Many Allied aircrew personnel had been students, engaged upon serious studies prior to volunteering to serve in the Royal Air Force Volunteer Reserve. The opportunity to continue with those studies while serving as a prisoner of war became important to these unfortunate individuals. Most of the libraries were capable of seating about eighty men.

In addition to books, the War Prisoners Aid also shipped wood intended to build bookcases, and tried to supply book repair and binding materials. No doubt the escape committee reduced the wood available to the library to a minimum, as wood was required for shoring the escape tunnels, and was harvested from any source possible. Following the daily morning roll call, there would always be a rush for the best seats and books in the library. Reference books were generally not allowed out of the reading room. In the first year after the camp opened, prisoners in the east and centre compounds alone had access to 8,000 books; an indication of the standards that had been achieved in the majority of Stalag Luft camps across Germany. Book spines broke down rapidly because of their frequent use, and the personal wartime logs suffered in the same way, as frequent, daily handling caused the card and linen spine construction split.

The reference library in the central compound of Stalag Luft III was generally full from ten o'clock in the morning until ten o'clock at night. Swedish lawyer Henry Söderberg was the representative of the YMCA, and held responsibility for the region of Germany in which Stalag Luft III was located. Söderberg visited the camp regularly, and went to great efforts to procure the items requested by the men. As a result, each compound had established a band and orchestra. In addition, Söderberg supplied sports equipment that met the different British and American national tastes.

Chaplains also had the necessary religious items to enable them to hold regular services. In June 1942, French, Polish, Belgian, Dutch, Canadian, Australian, Lithuanian, Norwegian, New Zealand, South African, Greek, and Czechoslovakian aircrew personnel were imprisoned within the camp, which by 1944 accommodated over 10,000 prisoners of war. At that time, the six compounds were holding primarily American and British airmen; the vast majority of which were officers. Towards the end of the war, the camp was subjected to orders from Hitler to avoid the possibility of the camp falling into Russian capture. This resulted in a 200 mile forced march to the PoW camp at Mooseburg. The prisoners were suffering from a lack of food, and with inadequate clothing for the severe cold, many of the men suffered terribly, some collapsing and needing help in order to avoid freezing to death in the snow. Several personal accounts of men who took part in the great marches are examined within this book. Stalag Luft III, or Belaria, a sub-camp created to accommodate the ever growing establishment in the main camp, was also exposed to the horrors of the evacuation into central Germany.

Stalag Luft VI

Built in Heydekrug, East Prussia, Stalag Luft VI was the northernmost PoW camp within the confines of the German Reich, housing 9,000 British and American airmen. Only a few miles from the Baltic Coast (in what is now Lithuania), it was isolated and remote, and the winters were long and severe. Stalag Luft VI was built on a sandy location a few miles south-east of the small town. The camp consisted of ten single-story brick barracks and twelve wooden huts, with access to the camp over an unpaved road through the woods. The town itself was on a railway spur line that was part of a single track between Tilset and the seaport of Memel. In June 1943, an influx of RAF British airmen arrived, having been transferred from Sagan into Luft VI. By October of that year, they were joined by a further selection of RAF airmen from Barth. The Americans arrived in February 1944, and as was normal practice, segregated from the RAF prisoners. The prisoners made the most of the recreational activities available through the sports equipment provided by the YMCA. Educational courses were also available, with instruction in subjects ranging from banking, foreign languages, and book keeping. Entertainment was provided by a band, a choir, and a dramatic group that produced shows in the camp theatre. The library held 6,000 books, but was never capable of meeting the needs of this sprawling camp, which grew to over 10,000 occupants. When the Russian front approached the camp in July 1944, orders were given to move the prisoners to other camps nearer to central Germany. Most of the men were moved by train to Stalag XX-A, Poland, but some 900 were taken to *Klaipėda,* where they were forced to board a merchant ship for a sixty hour journey to Swinemünde. After a further train journey, the prisoners were brutally force marched from Kiefheide; many men were bayoneted or shot before they reached the end destination of Stalag Luft IV. In October 1944, this action was reported by the protecting powers and the Red Cross delegates as a violation of the Geneva Convention.

Stalag Luft IV

Gross Tychow was located near the small village of Kiefheider, Pomerania. Built in 1944, towards the end of its first year the camp accommodated over 7,000 American PoWs, alongside approximately 1,000 British personnel. For some considerable time, there was a lack of support facilities supplied to this camp, particularly reading material, but eventually a supply began to arrive, enabling a limited library to be created. This camp was by any standards a poor one, with prisoners subjected to the most basic conditions. Fleas and lice were in abundance, with grossly inadequate washing facilities. Gross Tychow had four primary compounds, with a central corridor running through its entire length. This camp always contained a high level of American prisoners, but a large contingent of RAF arrived from Stalag Luft VI and remained there until the camp received orders to be evacuated in order to avoid the Russian advance on 6 February 1945.

Stalag Luft VII

The camp was constructed in Bankau by the Luftwaffe in order to help with the overcrowding of other prisoner of war camps, which was primarily due to the increases in Allied aviators being captured in 1943 and early 1944. The deep penetration air raids into Europe presented little opportunity for aircrews to reach anywhere close to home if they suffered mechanical or air combat damage. Rather strangely, the camp was built in relatively close proximity to the Eastern Front. From June 1944, Stalag Luft VII saw consistent numbers of prisoners arriving from the Luftwaffe interrogation centre, as well as other established camps. Denied basic comforts, if that is what one could class as being available in established camps, Bankau was basic in every aspect. Again, one of the most important activities that overcame boredom was being able to read. Unfortunately, books at Bankau were precious commodities. Reading had always helped the prisoners occupy their time and keep their minds active, so the alternative of the wartime logs would have played a huge role in combating the prisoners' boredom. The wartime logs provided avenues of activity previously impossible, with books being handed to gifted artists in the camps, along with requests to paint or draw views that were meaningful to the books' owners. A trade in precious provisions, mostly cigarettes, paid for the artists' services. Fellow camp mates would supply contact addresses between each other for the endlessly discussed slap-up meals that they visualized themselves enjoying once they were free. They would speak of these almost daily, and in many cases, lists of restaurant menus would be meticulously recorded. The wartime logs within Bankau originated from the logs issued to other camps.

When the American and British PoWs eventually left the prisoner of war camps, approximately 1 million reading books were left behind. Not so with the wartime logs. These nearly always became deeply treasured items and never left the owners possession, even being safely carried on the long marches when prisoners were forced to vacate the camps and trudge endless miles in a westerly direction to avoid the Soviet advances.

The time to march away from Stalag Luft VII arrived just seven months after it had opened. In January 1945, as the Russians advanced westwards, the Luftwaffe guards and over 15,000 prisoners marched in the same direction towards central Germany. The torturous march ended on 8 February, when just under 15,000 Allied prisoners of war entered Stalag III-A, central Germany.

The German military also provided separate compounds to hold RAF prisoners within the larger camps of Stalag IV-B, Muhlberg, and Stalag VIII-B, Lamsdorf.

Stalag IV-B

Situated in Muhlberg, this long-standing camp close to the Swiss Frontier had been in operation since 1940. It grew to consist of ten very large individual compounds, with aviators being contained in compound D. The camp was commanded by the Wehrmacht, and the guards saw all RAF prisoners as 'terror flyers' who bombed and killed German families. It was not a good camp to be in for any member of the Allied Air Force; guards were quite happy to shoot compound D occupants at any opportunity. Towards the end of the war, Muhlberg held in excess of 1,500 RAF and Commonwealth prisoners. The compound had one communal latrine, which was frequently depicted in sketches in prisoners' wartime logs. It was a windowless, doorless, brick construction, with two rows of twenty holes that facilitated all human waste. Each week, the Germans detailed Russian prisoners to pump the foul waste into a tank fixed upon a cart. Once the tank was full, the Russians pulled the cart out of the camp and spread the waste onto the adjoining fields. The Russians grew vegetables in the fields, which were then picked and consumed in the cookhouse. Very little, if any, food was ever provided to the Russian compound. It is estimated that Muhlberg had the capacity of up to 15,000 men.

A most tragic incident involving the death of a Canadian pilot took place at Muhlberg on 30 April 1944. Herbert David Mallory of 434 Squadron had been shot down over Nuremberg in August 1943. He was in the camp exercise yard when a Luftwaffe JU88 aircraft took an exceptionally low pass over the compound. There was a nearby Luftwaffe aerodrome, from which aircraft were frequently seen making low flying passes over the camp. This particular German pilot wanted to frighten the prisoners of war, and intentionally performed an incredibly low pass. Two fellow Canadians witnessed the aircraft coming out of nowhere from behind Warrant Officer Mallory and decapitating him instantly with a propeller blade. Other men were also blown from their feet by the aircrafts motion, with some quite badly injured. The camp fence was struck by the aircraft as it passed, and it was remarkable that the aircraft did not crash into the camp and cause more lives to be lost. Warrant Officer Mallory, service number R113624, was just twenty-two years of age, from Woodstock in New Brunswick, Canada. He is buried in the Berlin War Cemetery, Charlottenburg.[17]

Stalag VIII-B, later Stalag 344

This camp originated from a First World War prison camp and was situated in Lamsdorf, between Breslau and Krakow. The camp held separate compounds for definitive groups, which included those men from the British Army, Canadian Army, and Indian service personnel. The Germans even chose to separate the Royal Air Force and Royal Australian Air Force personnel. Generally, aviators were considered by the Germans as requiring higher security, and therefore significant numbers of RAF were held in this camp. Stalag VIII-B's notoriety is centred upon an order to bind the hands of the RAF prisoners in retaliation for a number of speculative reasons, one of which is the Allied raid upon Dieppe in 1942.

During the raid, the British and Allied combined commando forces secured a number of German prisoners and temporarily tied their hands behind their backs. This decision was made beacuse the small raiding party was limited in men, and it reduced the requirement of closely having to guard the German soldiers. The German High Command chose to create a great amount of propaganda over the tying up of prisoners, claiming it was 'contrary to the Geneva Convention'.

Because of this tying up episode, the Germans took reprisals that focused upon the RAF prisoners in Lamsdorf. From 8 October 1942, they endured daily hand binding from 7 a.m. to 7 p.m. for over a years duration. Ironically, the Germans initially chose to use Red Cross parcel string. Prison life for these men was terribly difficult, as they were inhibited from engaging in the mundane, yet normal, activities of passing time. For instance, these men were unable to even put on their coats to walk to the wire; a previously underappreciated exercise that was typically carried out several times a day. Respite at midday saw the restraints temporarily released for a meal and ablutions. The binding or handcuffing of the RAF prisoners of war was a blatant contravention to the Geneva Convention. Prisoners that that were found guilty of releasing themselves from the binding faced immediate retribution. They would be marched to the guard house and made to stand facing a wall for the remainder of the day, with verbal abuse inflicted on them on a regular basis. Handcuffs replaced the string on 20 November 1942, and it was only on 18 November 1943 that the tying up practice ceased altogether.

As further retaliation for the Dieppe raid, Adolf Hitler issued a series of orders on October 18 1942. The Commando Order identified the commandoes as bandits, and as such they could be shot on sight. That order led to the execution of American soldiers dropped into Czechoslovakia by parachute, and Canadian forces being killed by the Second SS Panzer Division in Normandy, in June 1944. Hitler's orders provided the grounds for loose interpretation. Terrible fates befell some airmen who parachuted into German cities, and in some cases, 'terror flyers' were brutally attacked and beaten to death by both civilian and military offenders.

On 17 June 1944, the chief of the German Security Police stated in a top secret letter addressed to the Supreme Command of the Armed Forces, that 'he had instructed the Commander of the SIPO[18] and SD[19] in Paris to treat parachutists in English uniform as members of commando operations in accordance with Hitler's order of 18 October 1942'.[20]

5

German Prisoner of War Camp Rules and Regulations

Camp Regulations Nr. 1 D. L. W. Barth, 1 January 1945

These camp regulations are based on the provisions of the Geneva Convention of 1929. All prior regulations are hereby cancelled:

I. Camp Management.

1. The language of the Camp is German.
2. The Camp is under the command of the Kommandant, who gives the instructions and orders, which are necessary to maintain order in the Camp.
3. To carry out the numerous tasks, the Kommandant is assisted by the Senior Officer (Gruppenleiter) of the Camp Administration (Lagerfuhrung), who is his permanent representative at the same time. He controls the execution of the instructions and orders given by the Kommandant.
4. For this purpose the Gruppenleiter of the Lagerfuhrung has at his disposal:
    a) Lageroffiziere (Camp Officers).
    b) Lagerfeldwebel (Camp Sergents).
    c) Lagerpersonal (including interpreters).
   The Lageroffizier sees to it that the current duties of the camp personnel within the compound under his command are carried out. He is also responsible for the maintenance of discipline and order. He has to immediately report to the Gruppenleiter of the Lagerfuhrung about any particular abuses and occurrences.
5. Every German soldier, irrespective of his rank, is superior to all PoW when he is on duty. The orders given by the German superiors must be obeyed under all circumstances.
6. In accordance with the proposal of the PoW, the Kommandant appoints as Senior Officer one of the PoW, who is fit for the task of a Senior Compound Officer according to rank and age. It is the task of the Senior Compound Officer and of the block commanders appointed by him, to see to it that the orders given by the German authorities are carried out.
7. At the same time, the Senior Compound Officer is the Man of Confidence

of the PoW.

8. There are two notice boards in every block:

    a) One for orders and notices of the German authorities.

    b) One for the notices of the Senior Compound Officer and Block Commander.

II. Camp Discipline.

1. It is expected that military discipline is strictly maintained.

2. All PoW are to salute the German officers and military officials who are equal or superior in rank.

III. Roll Calls.

1. As a rule there are two roll calls, one in the morning, one in the evening. In addition to these roll calls, the Gruppenleiter of the Lagerfuhrung will order extra roll calls at hours not known before. During bad weather, the Lageroffiziere may allow that the roll calls take place inside the blocks. The hours for the regular roll calls are always fixed by the Lagerfuhrung in accordance with the season.

2. All PoW have to be on parade, with the exception of the kitchen personnel and those who are 'sick in room' or in hospital, if they are in possession of a certificate from the German camp doctor.

3. The PoW are to stand on parade in proper clothing. Shorts may be worn during the warm season.

4. According to the season, the time is fixed by the Lagerfuhrung for the last post, and in connection with it for closing and opening of block doors and shutters.

5. When air raid warning is given, the PoW are to immediately proceed to their blocks or to stay in the rooms (shower bath, sick bay etc.), in which they are present at the beginning of the alarm. Block doors and windows must be closed by the PoW. PoW who are outside their compound are taken back as fast as possible by the soldiers who accompany them.

6. In case of fire breaking out, the guard in the nearest look-out box must immediately be notified of it. The fire must be fought at once by the PoW by means of the fire extinguishing equipment at hand, till the camp fire brigade arrives, whom they have to assist most energetically. The fire extinguishing equipment must always be kept in order, for which the block commanders are responsible.

IV. The Following is Prohibited.

1. To touch the warning wire and trespass upon the area between the warning wire and barbed-wire fence. Balls that have fallen into this forbidden zone while playing may be fetched out once a day in the presence of a guard.

2. Singing and playing of national anthem.

3. Hoisting or hanging of national flags and emblems.

4. To be in possession of any kind of arms or such like instruments.
5. To wear a beard.[21]
6. Unauthorized changing of quarters without previous permission. All requests re above must be directed to the Lagerführung through the Senior Compound Officer with corresponding reasons.
7. To remain in the block doorway or by the open windows during air raid alarm.
8. To hand laundry, blankets etc. over the warning wire or leave same in the open air over night.
9. Rubbish, thick paper, solid articles etc. are not to be thrown into the W.Cs. or into the night latrines.
10. To throw swill water, sand, and rubbish into the latrine pits.
11. To throw Red Cross cardboard boxes into the incinerators.
12. To damage or destroy equipment or articles that are property of the Reich. Articles which have been destroyed will not be replaced; The PoW have to pay for same the full amount of the actual price.

V. Punishments.

In the following cases, PoW will be punished by disciplinary measures or by Court martial:
1. For any violation of the above cases mentioned under paragraph III.
2. For lack of respect towards German officers.
3. For non-observance of instructions and orders that have been given, or for preventing the execution of same.
4. For hindering the German personnel in carrying out their duty.
5. For laying obstacles of any kind below the barrack floors.
6. For insulting any personnel of the German Wehrmacht or authorities, verbally, by action or in writing.
7. For attempting to bribe or incite German personnel to rebellion.
8. For wilful damaging or destroying of equipment or articles belonging to the Reich.
9. Wilful wasting or spoiling of foodstuff of any kind.
10. Staying away from roll call without special permission.
11. Improper behaviour during roll call and during other specially appointed occasions (inappropriate clothing, smoking, reading etc.)
12. For scribbling, damaging or tearing off German orders and notices.

VI. Use of Firearms.

Firearms will be used:
1. To ward off a bodily attack.
2. To enforce the execution of a given order.
3. Against PoW who are met outside their quarters after lock-up.
4. Against PoW who are within the forbidden zone or who are attempting to

enter it (touching the warning wire),

5. Against PoW who during an air raid warning are found outside their billets in the open air or standing in the block doorway or by the open windows.
6. Against PoW who are about to escape.

VII. Hygienic Precautionary Measures.

1. Living quarters and rooms are to be kept in a clean state. They must be thoroughly cleaned at regular periods.
2. Blankets must be repeatedly aired and dusted. Palliasses (straw mattresses) must be shaken up.
3. The rooms must be aired several times a day by opening the windows.
4. Food refuse must be immediately thrown into the receptacles provided for same.
5. Ashes, sweepings, and other rubbish are to be thrown into the incinerators, and not be thrown outside same.
6. The area around the blocks must be kept orderly and free of rubbish.
7. Empty cans are to be taken daily into the crates provided for them.
8. Night latrines must be emptied daily before the morning roll call.

VIII. PoW Mail.

1. Incoming mail will be distributed immediately after receipt.
2. Three letters and four postcards may monthly be written by every American or British officer PoW, two letters and four postcards by every American or British NCO and man on forms provided.
3. In urgent cases airmail letters and telegrams may be sent.
4. Private parcels will be regularly issued after being examined by the Abwehr Dept.

IX. Red Cross Parcels.

1. There will be a regular issue to the amount of a days ration.
2. Only so many full cans will be given out as empty have been returned.

X. Canteen.

The PoW may run their own canteen.

Gez. Warnstedt Oberst und Kommandant

PoW Camp Organisations

During the Second World War, a number of Allied prisoner of war camps created and developed excellent internal command structures, with a prime objective to manage and create escape attempts. The German authorities ran and organised the camp functions under a formal disciplined basis, and so to was the internal camp organisation, which was headed up by the most senior ranking officer present, who tended to be either American or British.

Appointments or responsibilities cascaded down from the senior officer in an identical way to an operational base. One primary exception existed, as rank did not in itself influence or dictate roles. Rather, it was the individual's abilities, and their skills in particular areas, that were seen as the influencing factors.

Men, such as the legendary Roger Bushell of the infamous Great Escape, commanded respect and motivated those around them regardless of rank. The camps required these strong personalities to head up the escape structure, and they would always work immediately alongside the camp's intelligence officer. These two posts carried immense responsibilities, which commanded direct areas of accountability. The intelligence officer oversaw twelve positions that all inter-linked, including analysing the wireless news from the BBC, combined with coded letters entering and leaving the camp, and the responsibility for compasses, forgery of documents, maps, rubber stamps, and photographs that sat alongside the very specific escape intelligence position. This post in particular gathered all intelligence from newly arrived prisoners and recaptured prisoners. The latter were always debriefed to absorb as much information as possible regarding any commute away from the camp; they were considered to be a most valued source of potential intelligence. The last area of general information required was that of the railway movements. Many camps were situated close to rail links, so the hours of observation via noise alone enabled timetables to be constructed with a reasonable level of competency and accuracy.

The head of escape services had a more complex structure of responsibilities. Security was always of immense importance, and each block had an appointed head that was responsible for the general management of such matters, with each reporting to the security officer who held key responsibilities for the camp security, for instance, monitoring the German activity within the camp, and guard accountability.

Escape proposals fell into four main areas; wire schemes, tunnel schemes, gate walk out schemes, and transportation exit schemes. Each one was headed by an individual who assessed and assisted the escape committee's process of acceptance or rejection of any plan. Tunnel schemes were passed to the tunnel committee, which resulted in complex and time consuming projects involving tunnelling. This demanded significant support in a great many areas, such as tunnel construction, engineering, and soil disposal. The position of supplies officer had a direct impact upon any tunnel plan. They would secure wood, tools, and many other requirements that were fundamental to progress. Carpentry alone was a massive, on-going task, which demanded ingenuity to maintain. The supplies officer also had the onerous task of managing the creation of escape clothing and securing camp resources, such as food stores, for those participating in any plan.

While this overview provides a simple account of the evolution that took place within the camps, the process of planning and executing escapes was in itself very complex, and without doubt, the camp community thrived on such aspirations. Unfortunately, luck was a part that was so frequently required in plans of escape; one that frequently failed to deliver for these gallant men.

6

Warrant Officer
Sydney Eric Hamblin

Born in 1919, Sydney Hamblin came from Glamorgan, South Wales. As a young eighteen-year-old, Sydney chose to enlist into the Royal Air Force. Joining the ranks as a boy mechanic on 8 September 1937, he was allocated the service number 543883. Hamblin's recruitment was prior to the now well renowned RAF Halton Apprentice structure. He studied in the west wing at RAF Cranwell, rapidly adjusting to service life, which he thoroughly enjoyed.

The opportunity to volunteer for flying duty presented itself to Hamblin when the RAF Expansion Scheme sought direct recruitment from within the ground trades.[22] The position of observer or air gunner was regarded as a part-time role, alongside ground crew duties. It therefore proved to be an exciting time for Hamblin, and he was able to demonstrate all the skills required while gaining experience in various aircraft types. The additional allowances of pay as an under-training recruit within aircrew would have been most appreciated, as ground crew were poorly paid in comparison to aircrew personnel.

Hamblin was successful in his official training as an air gunner, and deservedly achieved full-time aircrew status. The RAF had recognised the need for developing the trade of air gunners, but very few students received courses, so in the main, training was undertaken on a squadron, or at Armament Training Stations. Those young men lucky enough to gain selection for an air gunner's course attended a four week, structured programme. Hamblin was promoted to sergeant and gained his qualification as an air gunner in April 1939.

From the declaration of war with Germany on 3 September 1939, Hamblin was at the front line of offensive operations. Serving with 103 Squadron, he departed England and flew to be based in France as part of the Advanced Air Strike Force. The French Air Force was neither robust nor strong, as it had experienced political and inter-service rivalry. Nevertheless, the Air Force was equipped with modern aircraft, and her pilots flew with gallant efforts of bravery. Patrols were being flown across the French borders, supported by the RAF. On 20 September, three RAF Fairey Battle aircraft were protecting the French north-east boarder when they were attacked by German ME109 fighters. Although two Battles were shot down, Sergeant Letchford, the rear gunner in Battle K9243, had the honour of claiming the first enemy aircraft to be destroyed by the RAF over France. History describes this period as the phony war, and it led towards the aggressive invasion by German forces into Holland and Belgium in early 1940, and then to the Battle for France. Sergeant Hamblin was flying with Flying Officer Vipan, who had already captained his Battle aircraft on a total of seven daylight raids and nine night operations. In May 1940, the raids undertaken to attack the bridges over the Meuse in an effort to delay the German advance were particularly harrowing, and costly in airmen's lives. Shortly after, on 12 June 1940, Hamblin was one of the fortunate few to be evacuated from France. That same day, the first Victoria Cross medals to be achieved by the RAF were posthumously awarded to Flying Officer Garland and Sergeant Gray for their attacks on bridges over the Albert Canal, Belgium. 103 Squadron had lost many aircraft and much personal equipment was left behind, including Hamblin's flying logbook.[23]

Hamblin recommenced operational flying from England, once again in the crew of Flying Officer Vipan, flying in the Fairey Battle aircraft. Bombing raids against the German forces were undertaken, with targets in Holland and France. The Fairey Battle was regarded as an outdated and vulnerable aircraft, as evidenced by the significant losses incurred during the early engagements with the Luftwaffe. 103 Squadron were fortunate to be re-equipped with the Wellington Bomber, and Hamblin attended the Central Gunnery School, RAF Warmwell, where he qualified as a gunnery leader. This was a position of responsibility for him, as the entire strength of air gunner personnel serving in 103 Squadron came under his direction. When operations commenced in the

Above left: Drawing of Sydney Hamblin.

Above right: Drawing of 103 Squadron Crest.

Wellington aircraft in 1941, Sydney became part of Squadron Leader Mellor's crew. The Squadron Leader had his own personal aircraft named *Sierra Leone*. On 21 March, his crew was on a raid to bomb the submarine base at Lorient. The Luftwaffe in turn bombed Plymouth that night. Hamblin and his crew had an uneventful trip, but returning from that operation, *Sierra Leone* was attacked from below by a Luftwaffe night fighter. The Wellington Bomber's hydraulics was badly damaged. Hamblin, sitting in the rear gunner's turret, returned fire, causing the night fighter to break away from the attack. *Sierra Leone* managed to return to base, but as a result of the hydraulics damage, almost no braking capacity existed, and due to the damaged flaps, the aircraft ran out of runway and crashed into the aerodromes bomb dump, resulting in a complete write off. Remarkably, the crew sustained no injuries and they received two days leave to recover from the ordeal. Squadron Leader Mellor swiftly took delivery of his own *Sierra Leone II* and resumed operations.

Unfortunately, *Sierra Leone II* was herself subject to a night fighter attack on 30 March 1941. Sid Finn's book, *The Black Swan*, provides a graphic account:

At base, an unexpected reception awaited the returning aircraft. A JU88 night fighter had joined the circuit. Barratt's (Flying Officer Barratt) aircraft came under fire just as it was about to land. It was not hit, but the flare path was sprayed with cannon shells. The next attack was on Mellor's aircraft, which was hit in the wings, engine, and fuel tanks. The rear gunner was not in his turret at the time. The enemy aircraft pressed home the attack and the Wellington finally crashed about a mile from the airfield. Flying Officer Roberts, from within the crew, recalls: 'I was flying as a wireless operator on this trip and the gunners were Stewart up front and Hamblin in the rear turret. As we were approaching Newton, a voice on the intercom said, "Can I come out of the turret now?" It was standard practice for the front gunner to vacate his turret during landing. Mellor assumed it to be Stewart and agreed. So after carefully unloading his guns, Hamblin got out of the rear turret. Seconds later, all hell broke loose. There was a loud slamming, rattling noise, sparks flying off armored plating, the smell of cordite, and utter confusion. The aircraft dived and turned to evade the attack. Mellor called the rear gunner, got no reply, told me to take a look. In the dark I fell over Hamblin on the way aft, wrenched open the turret doors and saw the JU88 coming in dead astern for another attack, didn't bother to get into the turret, just squeezed the triggers. Nothing happened. Then we hit the telegraph pole and I cracked my head on the turret. At the time, Squadron Leader Mellor was not at the controls. His second pilot, on his first operation with the squadron, was doing the flying.'

Sierra Leone II had crashed at East Bridgeford. Several crew members suffered cuts and bruises, but nothing serious. Just fifteen days later, Sydney Hamblin climbed into the rear turret of Wellington R1538, and once more with Squadron Leader Mellor, attacked the target of Kiel, followed two nights later by a long trek to bomb Berlin.

In May 1941, Hamblin joined the crew of a New Zealander, Flying Officer Eccles. Their first raid to Emden in Germany passed by without any problem, but they were to only fly together once more. On 15 May, Hannover was to be the target; never an easy operation, but with a total of thirty-two operations recorded for Hamblin, he was looking forward to a rest from operations. His total of operations was regarded as a complete tour of duty within Bomber Command, and posting onto a training duty for Hamblin was imminent. Unfortunately, Wellington R1494 received a direct hit from flak over Bremen. Catastrophic damage resulted in the aircraft crashing in flames on the Dutch boarder. The front gunner Sergeant Maclean, and Flying Officer Eccles RNZAF both died in the incident. Hamblin managed to escape from the aircraft, and successfully avoided capture for two days. However, his luck ran out when at Winschoten, Holland, where he was detained and secured as a prisoner of war. Hamblin was taken to the interrogation centre at Dulag Luft, where he was imprisoned in solitary confinement from 17 to 30 May. His prisoner of war number was 2, a rather unique number to be allocated in 1941.

It is at this point that Hamblin's journey within the German prison camp structure can be examined in some detail. His YMCA wartime log, which has survived to this day, contains detailed information regarding events from his personal incarceration. The painting of a red cross features immediately within the first few pages. Twenty-two Allied countries are recorded around the cross, which holds the inscription, 'Thank God for a Red Cross.' Hamblin wanted to illustrate the deep appreciation that all the Allied countries felt for the support provided to prisoners of war by the Red Cross organisation, and for the food parcels received from the Commonwealth and Americans. These food parcels contained different produce that was of immense benefit to the prisoners of war. When full parcels were received, it brought forth a series of mutual exchanges between the prisoners in accordance with each man's personal preferences.

Appropriately, the blue ink, precise roll of honour script follows. It records details of Hamblin's capture and the subsequent prisoner of war camps in which he was detained. His movements and various camp confinements provide detailed evidence of the German prisoner management. Prisoners of war were transported around occupied Europe like pieces of a jigsaw; it would appear that Hamblin was in no way an exception to such movements.

The prisoners themselves may well have been moved with fellow roommates, but in many instances, conditions worsened with such transfers; overcrowding and food shortages were almost always encountered. The cattle trucks used to transport the prisoners were an undesirable form of transportation, with essentially no basic human needs being fulfilled.

Hamblin's first movement, direct from the Dulag Luft interrogation centre, was into Oflag XVIIIB in Wolfsberg, Austria. This camp was built to accom-

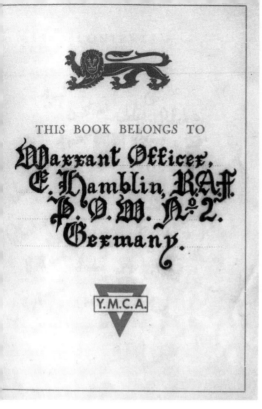

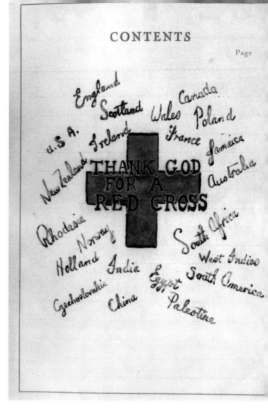

THIS BOOK BELONGS TO

Warrant Officer, E. Hamblin, R.A.F. P.O.W. No. 2. Germany.

Y.M.C.A.

CONTENTS

Page

England
Scotland
Wales
Canada
Poland
U.S.A.
New Zealand
Ireland
France
Jamaica
Australia
Rhodesia
Norway
South Africa
Holland
India
West Indies
Czechoslovakia
China
Egypt
South America
Palestine

THANK GOD FOR A RED CROSS

Clockwise from top left: The first page illustrated with the unusually low prisoner of war number allocated to Eric Hamblin; dedication drawn to the work of the Red Cross; Red Cross food parcel content listed in detail; illustrated scroll with details of the prison camps where Hamblin was detained.

Roll of Honour

First captured, 0100hrs, May 16th 1941 Winschoten, Holland.

Aircraft Vickers Wellington. Hit by A.A. fire, Crashed in flames. List of P.O.W. camps.

Dulag Luft, Germany.
Wolfsberg XVIIIa, Austria.
Lodz, Poland. 3 Camps.
Lansdorf VIIIb, Germany.
Sargan, Luft III, Germany.
Heydekrug, Luft VI, E. Prussia.
Thorne, 357, Poland.
Fallingbostel, Germany.

CONTENTS OF RED CROSS PARCELS.

9

CANADIAN PARCEL.

1 BAR CHOCOLATE 5 OZS.
1 PKT RAISONS 8 OZS.
1 SMALL PKT PRUNES
1 LB TIN JAM OR MARMALADE
1 LB TIN BUTTER
1 PKT BISCUITS (13)
1 TIN CORNED BEEF 12 OZS.
1 TIN SALMON 8 OZS
1 SMALL TIN OF SARDINES
1 SMALL PKT SALT AND PEPPER MIXED
1 PKT CHEESE 4 OZS.
1 PKT TEA OR COFFEE 4 OZS.
1 LB TIN OF POWDERED MILK (KLIM OR COW BELL)
1 BAR OF SOAP.
1 TIN OF KAM 12B

NEW ZEALAND PARCEL.

1 LB TIN OF JAM
1 LB TIN OF HONEY
1 LB BUTTER
1 TIN OF CHOCOLATE ¼ LB
1 PKT TEA 2 OZS
1 PKT BROWN SUGAR ½ LB
1 TIN OF VEAL ½ LB
1 TIN OF PEAS
1 TIN OF MILK (NESTLE'S CAFÉ AU LAIT)
1 LB CHEESE
1 TIN OF CORNED BEEF 12 O
1 TIN OF MIXED MEAT.

AMERICAN PARCEL.

100 CIGARETTES
2 TABLETS OF SOAP
2 BARS OF CHOCOLATE 4 OZS EACH
1 TIN OF ROSE PÂTÉ OR JAM
1 LB OF OLEO MARGARINE, OR
½ LB OF PEANUT BUTTER.
1 TIN OF SPAM 12 OZS
1 TIN OF CORNED BEEF 12 OZS
1 TIN OF SALMON OR SARDINES
1 LB TIN OF POWDERED MILK
½ LB CUBED SUGAR
1 TIN OF COFFEE
1 LB OF PRUNES, OR RAISINS.
1 TIN OF ORANGE JUICE
1 PKT OF VITIMINS
1 PKT OF BISCUITS

BRITISH OR SCOTISH PARCELS

1 OR 2 TINS OF BISCUITS (SERVICE OR HEALTHY LIF
1 BAR OF SOAP
1 TIN OF NESTLES CONDENSED MIL
1 PKT OF TEA OR COCOA
1 TIN OF STEW, STEAK AND KID OR COTTAGE PIE.
1 TIN OF MIXED VEGITABLES
1 TIN OF FISH, SAUSAGES OR B
1 TIN OF MEAT ROLL
¼ LB BUTTER OR MARGARINE
1 BAR OF CHOCOLATE 4 O
1 BAR OF SUGAR 3 O
1 TIN OF CHEESE 2 O
1 TIN OF EGG POWDER
1 TIN OF PUDDING, OR PANCAKE M
1 TIN OF JAM OR SURUP.
1 TIN OF PORRIDGE
1 PKT SWEETS.

modate Polish prisoners captured in 1939. The camp was later re-designated in early 1941 as Stalag XVIII-A, intended to hold both French and Belgian PoW. Hamblin arrived on 5 June 1941, but departed shortly after on 18 June. It would appear that this was no more than a holding camp for him.

The next movement was to the transit camp Dulag 240 in Lodz, Poland. For Hamblin, this was another short and temporary detention. He was only at that camp from 19 June to 1 July. Lodz was a Polish ghetto, a name that history now associates with the mass murder of Jews. In 1941 and 1942, almost 40,000 Jews were deported to the Lodz ghetto; 20,000 from Germany, Austria, the Protectorate of Bohemia, and Luxembourg. In addition, almost 20,000 from the smaller provincial towns, and an estimated 5,000 Roma (Gypsies) from Austria were deported to the ghetto. In January 1942, German authorities began to deport Jews from Lodz to Chelmno extermination camp. By September 1942, they had deported over 70,000 Jews and about 5,000 Roma. Between September 1942 and May 1944, there were no major deportations from Lodz. The ghetto resembled a forced labour camp, and the conditions were worse than could ever be described in writing. In the spring of 1944, the Nazis decided to destroy the Lodz ghetto. They deported the 70,000 surviving ghetto residents to the Auschwitz-Birkenau extermination camp in August 1944.

On 2 July 1941, Hamblin entered Stalag VIII-B in Lamsdorf. He was to be held in that camp for nine months, amongst a fellow group of Royal Air Force non-commissioned officers.

Hamblin can be seen in a photograph taken on 11 April 1942, identified as RAF prisoners of war, along with thirty-two other airmen who had all been captured during May 1941. This group of aviators had been collectively grouped together by the Germans. Within the group are several combinations from entire crews, which would clearly indicate that these men were processed collectively at the Dulag Luft interrogation centre and transported as a group through the transit camps onto Stalag VIII-B.

The reverse of the photograph has been signed by every individual, along with the date on which they became a prisoner of war. Flight Sergeant Sydney Hamblin can be seen front row, fourth from the left, immediately next to the kneeling pilot. Hamblin retained this photograph, attaching it to his wartime log. Note the wooden clogs being worn by two of the prisoners.

In early May 1942, Hamblin departed Lamsdorf, bound for the infamous Stalag Luft III camp in Sagan. Unknown to him at that time, the war in the Far East was going badly for the Allies. On the same day he walked into Stalag Luft III, 6 May 1942, the Japanese captured the Philippine Island Corregidor, and took in excess of 11,000 American and Filipino personnel as prisoners.

Every intake to a camp of Allied prisoners brought with it the expectation of information. Newly captured airmen would be questioned at length in order to establish how the war was going and whether victory was in sight. Unfortunately in the early years, good news was not very forthcoming. The

(Detail in italic may contain errors). Front row, right to left: Sgt C. A. Stickland 10 sqd 8/5/41, Sgt E. A. C. Lee 207 sqd 2/5/41, Sgt F. J. Smith 107 sqd 21/5/41, F/Sgt S. E. Panton 207 sqd 2/5/41, Sgt A. S. Duncan 207 sqd 2/5/41, Sgt P. Addison 40 sqd 15/5/41, Sgt A. Morris 77 sqd 17/5/41 MBE 1946 for PoW activities, F/Sgt S. E. T. Hamblin 103 sqd 15/5/41, *Spittles 7/5/41*, Sgt D. J. Harvey 97 sqd 10/5/41, *Edwards 8/5/41*. Middle row, right to left: *Cols 8/5/41* Sgt W. Chantler 97 sqd 10/5/41, Sgt H. Gillies 214 sqd 10/5/41, Sgt M. Newlyn 10 sqd 8/5/41, Sgt B. Tillotson 214 sqd 9/5/41, Sgt J. Fry 214 Sqd 9/5/41, Sgt H. Hale 139 Sqd 8/5/41, F/Sgt J. Shaw 40 sqd 11/5/41, Sgt A. Morgan 115 sqd 10/5/41, Sgt G. W. Hogg 115 sqd 10/5/41, Sgt D. Frazer 115 sqd 10/5/41, *Gardman 8/5/41*, F/Sgt J. Bryce 97 sqd 10/5/41. Back row, right to left: Sgt R. G. Ratcliffe 107 sqd 21/5/41, Sgt J. W. Middleton 139 sqd 7/5/41, *Holiday 12/5/41*, Sgt C. N. Barron 207 sqd 2/5/41, Sgt R. Anderson 97 sqd 10/5/41, Sgt E. Sykes 97 sqd 11/5/41, *Dickens 8/5/41*, *Baines 10/5/41*, F/Sgt T. Wady 304 sqd 8/5/41

other important opportunity availed to the prisoners was to scan the intake of men for a friendly face; perhaps someone they had served with in training, on station, or even from home. The chance for Hamblin to meet up with such contacts increased dramatically with his importation into the aviators camp Luft III.

Each and every airman in the camp had a story to tell in relation to the events that befell them in the air over the occupied countries, whether they had been shot down by anti-aircraft guns or night fighters, parachuted out, crash landed, or initially evaded capture. Every story would be one touching on life or death events. For those prisoners fortunate enough to have a wartime log, the story would be recalled on its pages almost without exception. Hamblin chose to document his story in the form of poetry and thought provoking dialog within a superb watercolour illustration, entitled, 'How it Happened'.

It becomes obvious from Hamblin's words that their critically damaged air-

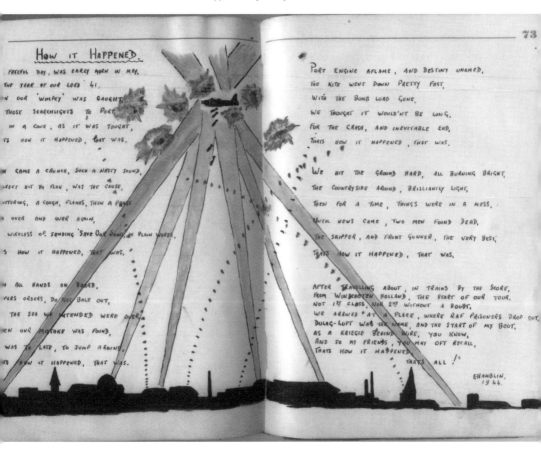

Detailed illustrated account of how Hamblin was shot down.

craft was presumed to have been over the English Channel. The captain had chose to ditch the aircraft, but unbeknown to him and the crew, they were still over Holland. The operational records of 103 Squadron recorded the following:

> Pilot Officer Eccles reported the failure of one engine on the return trip, finally landing in the sea at a position plotted by ground stations as forty miles from the English Coast. No sign was seen of the crew or wreckage by searching aircraft, which consisted of five machines over a period of two days. Personnel were finally reported as missing.

The commanding officer of 103 Squadron would have sent letters to the next of kin, indicating that the crew were listed as missing on operations over Europe. Following the report on Hamblin's crew, six families would have become focused on finding out what had happened to their loved ones. Official correspondence from the Air Ministry would follow, but no answers were forthcoming until the International Red Cross dispatched information processed by the Luftwaffe.

After many months, four of the six families received official notification that their sons were safe and being held as prisoners of war in Germany.

Hamblin's mother, Mrs S. Hamblin of Glen-Doig, 35a St Nicholas Road, Barry, Glamorgan, England, received a small 'kriegsgefenenpost' postcard, censored by gepruft 26 at Dulag Luft. It was written in pencil by Hamblin and dated 19 May 1941. It simply read:

> Dear Mother,
>
> I expect it's been a bit of a shock to you about the whole affair, still one thing I'm alive and kicking. The only thing to hope for now is that this war will soon be over and done with. Has Dad managed to get my car away from camp, also my belongings? You can put the car away for the duration. Well Mum, if it's possible try and send a parcel of food etc. through the International Red Cross. Don't forget these people do all the work now. Don't worry about me if you don't receive any letters. I was very lucky to get away alive, so we have that to be thankful for. By the way, I am growing a nice beard. Well cheerio now give my love to Dad and all.
>
> Best of luck xxxxx

Hamblin settled in well at Sagan. The camp was well run and provided as best as it possibly could for all those held within its barbed wire boundaries. Hamblin was most fortunate to be in the camp with Warrant Officer James 'Dixie' Deans, and took part in the nominations to elect Deans as camp leader in June 1942.[24] It was to transpire that Hamblin and Deans would remain in each other's company for the duration of imprisonment; a most fortunate development for Hamblin's Kriegie war service.

On 10 September 1940, Sergeant Pilot J. A. G. Deans of 77 Squadron took off on an ill-fated flight from RAF Linton-on-Ouse in Whitley Bomber P5042 to attack Bremen. His aircraft was hit by flak and subsequently crash landed at Venebrugge, Holland, where Deans was captured and imprisoned.

Once settled into Stalag Luft III, Deans became crucially involved in a wide range of tasks, from maintaining morale to organising trading among PoW to facilitate the bribery of the guards, which yielded much valuable escape material, such as maps, train timetables, compasses, tools, photographic film, and chemicals. The escape committee's planning was a heavy responsibility in which Deans was actively engaged. Weekly meetings with the Germans were a regular event, and he was seen as the leader in every respect; a role that he was impressively good at. He also organised the use of secret radios, constructed from parts that has been attained by bribing the guards. Gaining access to a reception to hear the BBC news service was one of the most significant means to increase morale amongst the men.

The revered and respected actions that Deans took to support his fellow men sit prominently within the written history of the prisoner of war camps from the Second World War. He went on to achieve the accolade of an MBE for his services whilst a prisoner. After the war, evidence confirmed that he was responsible for saving the lives of many prisoners of war and supplying the intelligence network with immense levels of information. His was a personality that is referred to in endless situations, and his contributions are consistently evidenced in the lives touched upon in this book alone; a statement that can be replicated many hundredfold. 'Dixie' Deans went on to become the first president of the RAF Ex-PoW Association.

Another important member of the camp at that time was Pilot Officer Howard Goolding-Cundall. Goolding-Cundall had been a civilian scientist employed at the Telecommunication Research Establishment,[25] and as part of his job, he was required to fly on special signals investigation flights over France with the RAF. To facilitate this, he was provided with an honorary commission into the RAF on 18 September 1941. On the night of 5 November 1941, the Wellington aircraft T2565 in which he was flying had to be abandoned when its starboard propeller fell off. This resulted in the crew of seven men all successfully escaping by parachute. Goolding-Cundall evaded capture for fourteen days before he was arrested in a small boat attempting to sail across the English Channel. Two of his crew, Pilot Officer Leslie Bull and Pilot Officer William Grisman, were captured and imprisoned in Stalag Luft I. After a very short period of time, they were moved into Stalag Luft III, where all three men met once again.

Warrant Officer James 'Dixie' Deans at Stalag Luft III.

In the camp, Goolding-Cundall became the secret wireless maintenance officer. The Germans were ignorant of the fact that they had a radar communication scientist in their camp and that he was using his expertise to send secret messages within his letters back to England. Leslie Bull DFC and William Grisman took part in the Great Escape, having been active participants in the tunnelling. It was Leslie Bull who opened the exit hatch of the tunnel 'Harry' on the night of 24/25 March 1944. He had been the tunnel's shift boss, and accepted the honour of being the first prisoner to exit the tunnel, thereby experiencing the shock and disappointment of seeing the tunnel come up short of its expected location. Both men became victims of the order to execute fifty of the captured participants. Leslie Bull was murdered on 29 March, and William Grisman on 6 April.

Stalag Luft III had gifted personnel who engaged in model making, and arts and craft construction. The most basic and crude materials were used to produce incredibly detailed and precisely scaled models.

Those same construction skills were sought by the men in the handicraft section. They were craftsmen, capable of creating incredibly detailed and precisely accurate devices to be used in escapes. The carving of rubber ink Luftwaffe stamps used to endorse false documentation is a classic example, along with the casting of replica insignia for German uniforms used in escape attempts. Lead was collected from tin can seals, which was patiently gathered over several months before being melted down and cast into superbly detailed carved moulds. Within any camp, there was likely to be men who had a trade or skill that could be adapted into the industry of escape. In Stalag Luft III, there was a problem to be solved in relation to the stiff linen covers required to contain some of the essential escape documentation required for the Great Escape. A prisoner within the camp, D. W. Lusty,[26] a rear gunner from 78 Squadron, had some previous experience in the publishing trade. He was recruited to try and recreate the production of the covers. Using tracing paper, cardboard, and other materials, Lusty created superb linen replicas from the handicraft supplies provided by the YMCA.

Sport was also an important part of camp life. In the summer months, sports days were organised, and became highly competitive events in the camps. Individual events were supported by team and barrack competitions, many of which had cups or trophies built from whatever was available. Some of the more prestigious race events had cups presented and engraved appropriately by the YMCA. The photograph in Sydney Hamblin's log provides an opportunity to see the relay running race being watched by an entire contingent of prisoners sitting on the roof.

Camp commandants evidenced such successful events with photographs and availed them to the delegates of the protecting powers. It was envisaged that every camp would be inspected around three times a year. Reports submitted by the protecting powers were only sent to the home government while the International Red Cross inspection reports were submitted to both the

Above: Examples of handicraft skills –
metal castings of Polish Air Force insignia.

Right: Model of a glider.

home governments and the detaining powers.[27] The reports always followed a specific format and scoring terminology.

Escaping from the camp was always a priority, but to be successful, meticulous planning and an element of good luck were mandatory conditions. Stalag Luft III, Sagan, is a name synonymous with prison camp escapes. The Wooden Horse and the Great Escape have been immortalised through film, but there were other escapes equally as daring, such as that of Flying Officer Pat Leeson, who tried to march out of the camp dressed as a German chimney sweep while the actual sweep was still working in the camp. This attempt failed, as did his next one just a few weeks later when he tried a similar tactic, impersonating a German interpreter who was escorting two prisoners to a dentist.

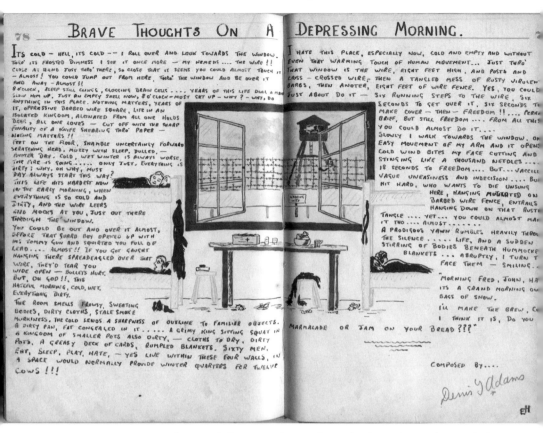

An impressive compilation of the painted view from the barrack window and the 'Brave thoughts on a depressing morning' composed by Dennis Adams.

In the summer of 1942, prisoners had started in excess of sixty tunnels,[28] with very few reaching successful conclusions. Nevertheless, each tunnel represented hope to the men. Hamblin was in the camp during that particularly active period, but unfortunately, no evidence exists to indicate that he was engaged in these efforts. However, his obvious closeness to Deans may well be seen as a positive indication towards these activities. The escape committee had to seek committed men who had the drive, strength, and ability to escape, and not all prisoners had such qualities. Large tunnel digging projects involved a great many men, with guards needing to be constantly monitored while the spoil was distributed across the camp.

Hamblin's time at Sagen came to an end on 6 June 1943, when he was included within the selection of 2,500 prisoners to be relocated to the PoW camp Stalag Luft VI in Heydekrug, East Prussia. A long cattle truck train journey northwards saw him march into the camp on 12 June. Heydekrug was a camp that had no direct mail access. All mail was received via Stalag Luft III, thereby creating massive backlogs of correspondence, which seriously affected

'Sports day' photographed for propaganda purposes with the men clearly enjoying the event.

the morale within the camp. The camp was never completed as such, with construction and expansion always present. At that time of year, the weather was probably quite pleasant, with full summer ahead of the men. But the harshness of the winter in Prussia was soon to be experienced, and in fact, this move was one of the worst for these men. Hamblin experienced the cold winter of 1943, which created the continual need to try and keep warm. Only the support of the Red Cross food parcels made survival possible. By then, Dulag Luft was sending new prisoners directly to Heydekrug, and in November 1943, there were 3,000 British ranks in the camp. By March 1944, it had grown to four compounds and a compliment of 5,000 men, which included airmen from most Allied countries, and over 100 New Zealanders. This resulted in the camp becoming seriously overcrowded during 1944. Marquees were erected and used to accommodate the overspill of men.

Prisoners with prior records of escape were segregated to a special barrack known as the black room. As was usual in the camps, a committee controlled all attempts at escape, with several being successful in getting men out of the

The front cover of the YMCA wartime logbook.

camp. In some instances, the use of an escape route designed to support escapees enabled successful runs to Allied lines.

It is quite probable that Hamblin received his wartime log while at Heydekrug in 1944. The YMCA was impressively efficient in the distribution of these books at the time. The delivery of these logbooks would have been incorporated into the rather diverse and comprehensive list of requests from this rapidly expanding camp.

Hamblin spent a full year in Heydekrug camp. In July 1944, he became part of another large movement of prisoners, this time being transported by cattle truck to Thorn in Poland. It was a long journey that took them through Germany, with just one stop for sanitary reasons before terminating at Fallingbostel, the correct camp title being Stalag XI-B.[29] This horrid camp complex sprawled out over several ancient, sunken forts and additional large, barbed wire compounds. With an ever-increasing population of up to 96,000 prisoners of war, conditions deteriorated. The RAF NCOs gained the assistance of 'Dixie' Deans, who once settled, took a commanding stance within the air force sector of the camp. Ironically, Hamblin was now not far from Bremen, the target he had been bombing on that fateful night in 1941 when he had crash landed.

Hamblin painted a picture in his log which provides an opportunity to view his personal perspective of camp life. For over three years, all he had been looking at were high barbed wire fences and guard towers. The Wehrmacht stated that no applicable instructions existed for the construction of watchtowers. It depended upon the topographic and climatic conditions, but watchtowers had to provide the best possible field of view and fire. The functional shape of

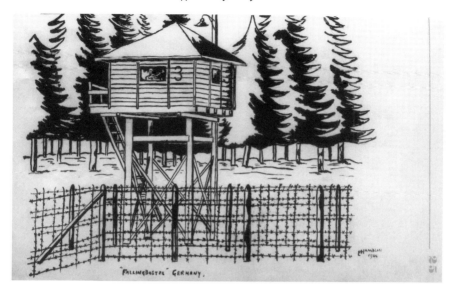

One of the views of Fallingbostel camp drawn by Eric Hamblin.

the watchtower was to be determined by the camp commandant. There were however, instructions in relation to the wire; it was stated that the wire entanglement between the inner and outer fences must be so constructed that an escaping prisoner of war will be able neither to climb over them, nor to crawl under them. Anchor posts should only be slightly out of the ground, and the wire fences must be carefully inspected for reasons of security, with existing defects corrected.

Hamblin passed his log to one of his friends, Flight Sergeant Bernard Millett, who had accompanied him on the journey to his new camp. Conversations on how they came to be prisoners revealed that Millett's crew had tried to continue flying in their Halifax HX348 after two of its four engines had been hit by flak over Flensburg. He was the navigator, and had been attempting to plot the way to Berlin when they were forced to make a crash landing near Trappe, Denmark. The front section of the bomber was badly crushed, but the belly landing was regarded as successful, as nobody was injured. Millett and the crew made off from the crash scene, but ultimately they were all detained within 24 hours. The crew all met up once more at the Dulag Luft camp and fortunately remained together.

On 23 August 1944, Bernard Millett sketched the comical representation of his crew continuing their operation on one engine.

On many occasions, the phrase 'keep your chin up', an old English term indicating that one should keep one's spirits up, had been written in Hamblin's letters received from home. It proved to be a slight bone of contention, which was reflected in Hamblin's painting on the subject. His comical representation was very much appreciated by his fellow roommates.

Bernard Millett's crash-landed Halifax. (*Soren Flensted*)

Above left: Comical sketch from Eric's logbook, drawn by Bernard Millett.

Above right: 'Chins Up' – the archetypal British quote frequently written in his post from home.

With RAF promotion procedures still being applied to men that were now prisoners of war, Hamblin received notification that he had been made a warrant officer. Many prisoners kept meticulous records of pay in their wartime logs; every salary payment was carefully noted, and increases in pay due to promotion were estimated and calculated to provide a running total. With so much time on their hands, such thoughts frequently occupied the men's minds, and resulted in these detailed records being compiled in the logs.

Sydney Hamblin made two special friends, both Spitfire pilots, during his long term of imprisonment. Both men are featured within Hamblin's YMCA log. The two pilots had come down over enemy territory in similar circumstances, having both been escorting Blenheim Bombers on raids in 1941. On 3 July, Sergeant R. J. Thoburn of 266 Squadron was shot down by Luftwaffe fighters while escorting Blenheims to attack Mazingarbe. The MkIIa Spitfire P8173 he was flying had been purchased in November 1940 with the donation of £5,520 11s 9d from the Alton Urban and Rural District Spitfire Fund in Hampshire.[30] Thoburn had been wounded and later captured in very similar circumstances to Hamblin, and had been allocated another extraordinarily low PoW identity; number 6. The second Spitfire pilot was Sergeant Denchfield 610 Squadron.

With the winter of 1944 exceptionally harsh, and temperatures consistently far below normal, the entire prisoner of war network in Germany was becoming unstable, with unpredictable events unfolding. Through the illicit radios, daily reports on the war's progress were enabling prisoners to be aware of the invasion in France, and realistic prospects of freedom existed in their minds. Consistent daylight bombing raids by the USAAF and night operations by the RAF presented opportunities for the prisoners at Fallingbostel to hear and see the Allied aerial forces at work. The Russian advance from the west was forcing a mass of prisoners westwards into central Germany, while the Western Front was grinding slowly eastwards. Vast numbers of Allied prisoners of war were converging on already overpopulated camps. The German morale was at its lowest, with officers and guards entering 1945 with the fairly obvious expectation that the war would be ending in Allied victory. Hitler was resolute in not allowing the prisoners of war the opportunity of liberation, and he continued to instruct camp officials to remove the Allies and march them at force towards central Germany. Sydney Hamblin was able to create a full account of his movements from capture to his last camp in Fallingbostel. Painted in watercolour, it was a work of art with fine details that recorded his passage across the European frontiers that had been lost with the German invasion across Europe.

On 6 April 1945, 'Dixie' Deans instructed the prisoners in Fallingbostel to leave, following orders from the camp commandant. Food parcels were made available, and whatever supplies possible were to be carried. Expecting a long walk, they only went as far as the nearby railway station, where they were ushered once again into the cattle trucks; a particularly dangerous way to travel at

4. FOSTER ROAD.
CHISWICK.
LONDON, W.4.

Above and below: Sgt Thoburn has drawn himself flying the donated Spitfire, which carried the Squadron identification letter 'C' alongside 266 Squadron's code of 'UO'. This type of caricature is frequently found within prisoners' log books. Hamblin's holds several, illustrating Blenheims and Lancasters, each signed by the artist-pilot. The second Spitfire pilot was Sergeant H. D. Denchfield, shot down over St Omer whilst escorting a Blenheim on 5 February 1941. Operating with 610 Squadron, Denchfield had been engaged in the Battle of Britain, but ran out of luck when flying his Spitfire N3249 and became a prisoner of war. In 1944, while imprisoned in Fallingbostel, Denchfield painted a most impressive contemporary-style watercolour in Hamblin's wartime log. His signature was applied with the date, 26 September 1944.

Oh God! Even the beds turn 'barbary'!

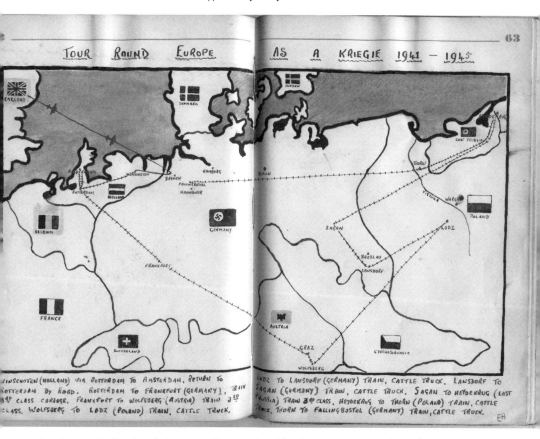

An impressively detailed map, illustrated with the movements through Europe between 1941-45.

that time, as the RAF was likely to attack almost any moving communication target. Some transports had the white lettering 'PoW' painted on the roofs of the trucks in order to avoid such instances. The train left at mid-morning the following day, travelling for four days with a lot of stopping and starting, no doubt as a result of Allied attention upon transportation targets. Eventually, the train reached the end of its journey and stopped in open countryside near the hamlet of Leiston. Here Hamblin, in company with a Flight Sergeant Javis, found the opportunity to escape from the transport. Remaining together, they walked for several days and nights, foraging for food to survive until they met up with American forces on 19 April 1945. Both men were by that time looking the worse for wear, but the German prisoner of war identity tags would have satisfied the initially cautious approach of the American soldiers.

Sydney Hamblin had carried his wartime log with him during his imprisonment and transit across occupied Poland and Germany. It is an important and impressive example of its type. The concept developed by the YMCA could not have been better represented, both in content or presentation.

7

Wing Commander Douglas Bader

One of the most infamous RAF pilots and prisoners of war from the Second World War is Wing Commander Douglas Bader. Bader is remembered as an iconic PoW, possibly due to his false legs and his link with Colditz Castle (Oflag IVC).

On 9 August 1941, whilst flying in combat with 616 Squadron, Douglas Bader was forced to bale out of his aircraft after colliding with a Luftwaffe Me109 fighter of JG26 near Le Touquet, France. Unfortunately, one of his artificial legs became stuck fast in his Spitfire. With steely determination, Bader managed to escape, with his other artificial leg damaged but still attached. Having received injuries during the ordeal of escaping and parachuting to the ground, Bader was captured and hospitalised by the Germans for a short period in St Omer.

Bader was highly respected by the Luftwaffe, and being in a rather uncomfortable position without his second leg, he asked the Luftwaffe if they might arrange for the RAF to drop in his spare leg, which was kept on the base in England. In a rare case of collaboration, the Luftwaffe agreed to Bader's request and radioed the RAF to arrange the delivery.[31] On 13 August, several RAF radio stations received a broadcast from Ushant.[32] The wireless operator at 13 Group recorded the message sent on 500 KC, timed at 1.15 p.m. The German text translates:

> Wing Commander Douglas Bader has been taken prisoner. He requests a new artificial leg. The dropping by parachute is agreed from the German side. Date and time [of the drop] by radio. The location of the drop will then be specified from this side. Aircraft making the drop will be given free passage.

The Luftwaffe offer of safe passage was not accepted, for the RAF incorporated the sortie to St Omer into an operational bombing mission. Nevertheless, the replacement leg was duly delivered. The box was marked, 'Please deliver to the commanding officer, German Air Force, St Omer, Longuenesse airfield.'

With the help of a French nurse, Bader, now fully equipped with two tin legs, was able to escape from the hospital in St Omer, but he was found almost immediately, and later sent to a prisoner of war camp. This initial prison camp become one of several in which he was held: Oflag XC, Lubeck, from 30 September to 1 October 1941; Oflag VI-B, Dossel, from 5 October 1941 to 11 May 1942; Stalag Luft III, Sagan, from 13 May to 7 July 1942; Stalag VIII-B, Lamsdorf, from 7 July to 2 August 1942; Stalag VIII-B, Lamsdorf, from 4 August to 18 August 1942; Oflag IVC, Colditz, from 18 August 1942 to 15 April 1945.

Douglas Bader's detention at Oflag VI-B in north-west Germany was as a result of the collation of British officers by the Germans. It was a most basic camp, and Douglas made reference to this fact in his postwar recollections. It appears his removal, and that of other British officers from Oflag VI-B, was only as a result of a policy to infill the camp with a high percentage of Polish officers in mid-1942. Many of the Polish prisoners were held from the initial invasion of their country by Germany in 1939, and included some of the remnants of the Polish Air Force. Some 3,000 men, mostly Polish, remained in the camp until it was liberated in April 1945.

Polish officers in Dossel in 1945. This was Wing Commander Bader's original PoW camp. (*US Signal Corp*)

8

Flying Officer Patrick Nickless

Patrick Nickless originated from Devon. Having chosen a career in banking, he was employed with the National Provincial Bank, Tottenham Court Road, London. Nickless volunteered for flying service in the Royal Air Force, but was not accepted until September 1940. The training for pilots was extensive, and two years later, Patrick passed out as a qualified pilot selected for service within 247 Squadron, Fighter Command. This would have been every young man's wish at this time in aviation history.

Sergeant Patrick Nickless arrived on 247 Squadron, based in Exeter, Devon, on 6 September 1942. Fate or good fortune had brought him back to the family farm in Drewsteignton, which was no more than a few miles away from the airfield. The Squadron at that time was flying Hurricanes, having been heavily engaged in night fighter operations over Southern England. Nickless arrived at a time when the squadron was becoming non-operational, due to the requirements of both rest and training. Shortly after his arrival on the squadron, Nickless received a new posting to 111 Squadron, better known as Treble One Squadron, flying Spitfires in North Africa.

Treble One arrived in North Africa in early November 1942, with Nickless being thrust into hostile activity almost immediately. Flying from Maison Blanche, an aerodrome a few miles from Algiers, the squadron immediately became engaged in harbour protection and providing fighter cover for convoys. The Luftwaffe was exceptionally active in the area, bombing shipping, airfields, and harbours, and aerial combat took place on a daily basis. Nickless claimed a quarter kill of a JU88 Bomber on 29 November, followed on 6 December by him damaging a ME109 Fighter during an extensive aerial battle. As one of only two squadrons operating in the most advanced aerodromes in Tunisia, Treble One Squadron was consistently being attacked both in the air and on the ground. Intense activity continued through to April 1943, when the following entry was typed by the adjutant in the squadron record book, recording the loss of freedom for Nickless: 'Our score for the month is ten and a half enemy aircraft destroyed, seven probably destroyed and fourteen damaged. This score avenges in some measure the loss of F/Sgt Nickless, Sgt Spranger, F/O Clark, and F/O Fowler.'

Patrick Nickless, September 1942. Nickless stands in the back row, third from left.

Sgt Ken Plumridge was flying with Patrick Nickless on 5 April 1943 when the squadron were tasked with a sweep over Tunis Bay. The twelve Spitfires were hoping to located German JU52 aircraft that were frequently passing between the Axis forces. Plumridge recalls the events that unfolded:

> I was indeed on that do involving E Boats in the gulf of Hammemet. The battle was hoting up and it was decided to make a sweep of the Tunis area. We cruised at 20,000 ft when the W.C. took us down to attack the E Boats. We dived down, line astern, the Germans had a pretty heavy concentration of ack ack of all calibres, putting up a hefty barrage. Now and again during the dive my kite was rocked by near misses. I was diving very steeply. There was spray all around the boats from the attacking aircraft in front of me. I pulled up sharply out of the dive and shoved sights on the first E Boat, giving a long burst of cannon and machine gun fire. I had a quick sight of the superstructure as I flew over the boat and put a short burst on the second boat. Enemy aircraft were being reported as one shot past me at right angles overhead. I had used up all my ammo and all hell was being let loose. Gun batteries from the coast joined in, and I found myself flying through columns of water. The top cover had taken on the German 109 Fighters. I weaved violently at sea level and turned for land. Above me I saw a Spitfire going down in flames, and then a 109. With no ammo and only fifteen gallons of fuel, time I went home. I landed with just seven gallons of fuel remaining.

The Spitfire in flames was being flown by Patrick Nickless, and he was seen to abandon his burning aircraft and safely deploy his parachute,[33] descending down towards inevitable captivity.

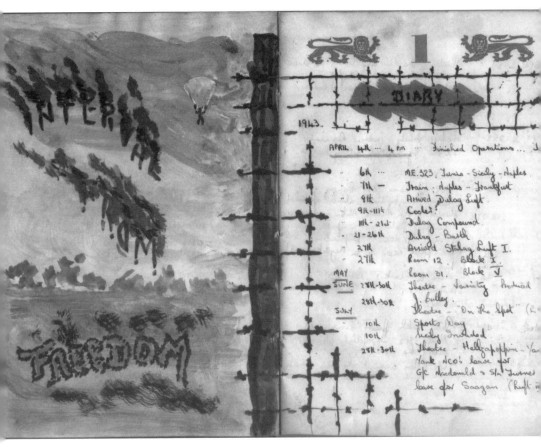

The introductory pages illustrating Patrick Nickless parachuting into imprisonment.

The wartime log of Nickless provides a diary of events from 4 p.m. on 4 April 1943 to Wednesday 9 May 1945; his entire period of service as a prisoner of war. Patrick penned an illustration in his log, depicting him landing by parachute and losing his freedom into the barbed wire cage. He wrote:

4 April: finished operations–Tunis.
6 April: Luftwaffe ME323 transport aircraft from Tunis–Sicily.
7 April: train from Naples–Frankfurt.
9 April: arrived Dulag Luft interrogation centre.
9-11 April: detained in solitary isolation at Dulag Luft.
11-21 April: Dulag Luft–compound.
21-26 April: Dulag Luft–Barth.

Food rations at the interrogation camp were two slices of black bread and jam, with ersatz coffee in the morning, watery soup of a vegetable base at midday, and two slices of bread at night. No Red Cross food supplies were available and water was provided upon request to a guard. The Red Cross, YMCA, and protecting powers were frustrated in their attempts to undertake welfare visits to this particular camp.

21 April: arrived Stalag Luft I, room 12, block 1.
May: moved to room 31, block 5.

Nickless created a drawing of his own compound. Three other large barbed wire compounds were situated running in a line northwards, making one enormous camp structure. A Luftwaffe flak school was also sited just south of the camp, well within sight of Nickless' barrack block.

Flak was an abbreviation for 'fliegerabwehrkanonen', German for 'anti-aircraft guns'. At the beginning of the war, the flak arm of the Luftwaffe consisted of nearly 1 million men, which was about two thirds of the total Luftwaffe strength. In 1944, it had increased to approximately 1,250,000 men and women, which accounted for approximately half the total Luftwaffe. As the war progressed, the men in the static, home defence flak units were moved to the mobile field flak units. These able bodied men were replaced by old men serving in the Home Guard, teenage school boys, and youths in the labour service. Female auxiliaries also served, and were supported by younger generation females as well. The most common heavy flak weapon was the 88 mm, which could fire fifteen to twenty rounds a minute at a maximum altitude of

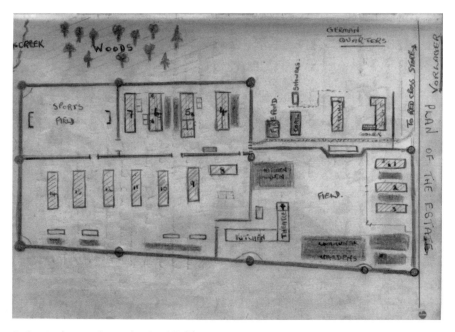

Stalag Luft I, as drawn by Pat Nickless.

The flak school next to Stalag Luft in Barth.

35,000 feet. The flak 88 required ten people to operate it; later in the war this would be reduced to eight people.

The flak school next to Stalag Luft I, Barth, was engaged in training many operatives for the defence of Germany. It was a large complex covering a substantial area of land. The female flak school students had been issued with instruction books, in which they were referred to as 'flakettes'. In 1945, when the establishment was abandoned by the Luftwaffe, prisoners from the camp sought keepsakes in the partly demolished building that had been blown up by the retreating Germans.

Flak was a primary reason for many Bomber Command aircraft losses. In 1943, the Luftwaffe introduced the controlled fragmentation rounds of flak shells. These had grooves cut on the inside face of the casings, and when the charge detonated, the case broke up into a smaller number of larger fragments. This fragmentation round was far more effective against heavy bombers than the regular, high explosive rounds. Near the end of the war the Germans developed the incendiary shrapnel, a thin-walled projectile containing numerous small pellets. When the shells detonated, the pellets were blown outwards and forwards at incredible velocity. The pellets were designed to pierce the skin of the aircraft in order to enter the fuel tanks and start fires. These incendiary shrapnel rounds proved to be far more effective than the controlled fragmentation rounds. It is ironic that the Luftwaffe was teaching the skill to shoot down RAF aircraft in such close proximity to the prisoner of war camp. Past students from the flak school at Barth may well have been responsible for some of the actual prisoners of war held in the adjacent prisoner of war camp.

In his wartime log, Nickless recorded the movement of Group Captain Macdonald and Squadron Leader Turner to Sagan Luft III at the end of July. The group captain was the senior British officer, and had been responsible for a lot of good work in the camp. One item in particular was the camp publication, in which he wrote the following foreword:

> I do not intend to write a foreword to *Luft* each month, but I feel the camp would like me to express our appreciation to the editors and staff of our magazine for the excellence of the first number produced last month.
>
> Although we have a duplicator, the actual process of running off the copies is by no means as simple as it sounds, and the editing, typing, and binding, not forgetting the hand painting of the 100 first copies, entailed much hard work for all the staff.
>
> We have now moved into the other compound, and with our theatre well on the way towards completion, and the expert musicians newly arrived from Sagan, I hope this will be the sign for plenty of activity from the entertainments branch.
>
> We are opening very soon a reference library and quiet room in the church building. This has proved extremely popular in other camps, and I hope everyone here will help to ensure that this room is not misused, but kept for quiet private reading or study.
>
> As the commandant has kindly given permission for us to send a copy of our magazine to the British Red Cross in England, and also to Sagan, I take this opportunity of letting them know we are in good heart, and sending them our best wishes.
>
> J. C. MacDonald
> Group Captain
> Senior British Officer

Group Captain John Charles Macdonald 26183 had been engaged on the very first offensive operation of the war against Germany. On some of the initial raids he was dropping leaflets. On the night of 19 March 1940, he dropped his first bomb load in a raid upon the seaplane base at Hornum. He was flying a Whitley, N1380. This operation allowed him to claim to be the first pilot to drop bombs on German soil in the Second World War. He was awarded the Distinguished Flying Cross and a bar to that medal for his outstanding early war exploits. On 2 July 1942, he was flying with 105 Squadron when his aircraft was severely damaged by flak during a raid against Flensburg. The damage sustained resulted in him crash landing in Germany. Almost immediately captured, he was to serve three years in captivity, which was not without incident. Macdonald was removed from his post as senior British officer at Stalag Luft

I for refusing to give the commandant the name of an escaped prisoner. Group Captain Macdonald later became senior British officer at the Belaria compound at Stalag Luft III until the camp was liberated in 1945. After the war, he returned to active service in the RAF where he rose to the rank of air commodore.

The camp theatre, as mentioned in the circulation by the group captain, proved to be a great success. Alongside other entries in his logbook, Nickless recorded several diverse theatre performances between July and October 1943:

> 28-30 July: theatre: *Hellgopoppin* Yank NCO's production.
>
> 3-5 Sepember: theatre: *The Man who Came to Dinner.*
>
> 2 October: the two accommodation huts in Rugby field almost finished.
>
> 25-27 October: theatre: *Ten minute Alibi*, ended in a farce owing to move of NOCs.
>
> 27 October: first party of NCOs go to Heydekrug.
>
> 28 October: move to Block 1, in the far corner next to German quarters in Room 3. In company with Hurford, Neary, Lindsay, Lambert, Wilkinson, and Wilcox.
>
> 29 October: last party of NCOs go to Hedykrug.
>
> 11 November: first batch of officers arrive, 10 p.m. air raid, blocks 1 and 2 are filled at intervals during the month. Wing Commander Hilton[34] was amongst the new arrivals.

Patrick Nickless recorded Wing Commander Fred Hilton's arrival, a man who swiftly assumed the position of senior British officer at Stalag Luft I. The events surrounding the removal of group captain Macdonald were still reeling within the camp.

> 15 December: move to block 4, with a view of the pine forests, room 5 with F/L Young, F/O Lambert, F/O Smyth, F/O Nickless, F/L Halliwell, and two yanks.
>
> 25 December: Christmas Dinner with room 6 Canadians
>
> 23 February 1944: the compound library was moved into the common room within block 5 due to the recently received books requiring additional space.

Prisoners' mail and books were two of the most important factors within the life of a Kriegie. The extra space created by the move to block 5 enabled the internal system to function with greater efficiency. Patrick Nickless depicts the sorry state of the camp library in Stalag Luft I prior to its expansion and stock holding of books.

The expansion of the library was a welcome improvement to the men in the camp. As an avid reader, Nickless felt it was worthy of inclusion within his wartime log, and in addition, he pasted a book receipt sent direct to him from

'Penguin Books' prisoner of war post label, retained and stuck into the YMCA log.

Empty shelves in the library.

SET DESIGNED BY J. VAUGHAN FOR PRODUCTION OF "BUSMANS' HONEYMOON"

Sketch and colouring of the theatre set 'Busman's Honeymoon'.

30 May: Americans move to north compound.

15 June: theatre re-opens the result of a YMCA visit.

12 July: tents start going up as not enough accommodation available.

Nickless was involved in the construction and painting of the stage set, which had been designed by Sergeant J. Vaughn for the theatre production, *Busman's Holiday* (5 to 11 September). Sgt Vaughn of 9 Squadron found himself in the camp, after being shot down on 18 February 1943 during an attack on Wilhelmshaven. Vaughn became a leading light in the camp's theatre production team. The theatre activities were regarded as a mainstay of morale within the camp, and a great deal of effort was taken in an attempt to create good productions that were thoroughly enjoyed and appreciated. Normally, the front row seats were set aside for any visiting dignitaries, such as YMCA and Red Cross officials. The bulk of the remaining tickets were allocated by allotment to the respective barracks. Theatre creativity was significant in any prisoner of war camp that was fortunate to have such a facility, but obviously it had to continue around the normal, mundane events of daily life, one of which was the predictable and tiresome roll calls.

1 September 1944: 'Roll Call Thoughts' by F/O. Ruff RCAF.

We've stood in the rain, the snow and the sleet, We've stood there for hours with nothing to eat. And why have we stood there, so 'browned off' and mad? Because Unterofficer Noyes just couldn't add. We've dug nice long tunnels through miles of sand. Made fancy clothes and hid in tin cans. But why have we failed to leave 'Kriegie' Land? Because Henry, the 'Butcher Boy' is always on hand.[36] We don't like this camp, so windy, so bleak, and the barking of watch-dogs that bother our sleep. Oh, Major Von Muller, please give us a break; just call off your blood-hounds and let us escape!

The author of 'Roll Call Thoughts', Flying Officer Ruff, had served with 428 Squadron. His Halifax Bomber, serial number LK969, took off from Middleton St George late on 25 November 1943. The aircraft was shot down at a height of 19,000 feet over Frankfurt by a night fighter. The sudden attack set the starboard inner engine on fire, and the fighter's second pass struck the outer starboard engine; it had been a classic night fighter attack, expertly executed by a most competent Luftwaffe pilot. One member of the crew was killed during the attack, but the rest of the crew survived, managing to escape by parachute only to be swiftly captured and taken prisoners of war. Squadron Leader J. R. Beggs was held in Stalag IXC with Flight Sergeant J. P. McMaster. Sergeant F. Moore was held in Stalag IV-B, with Sergeant T. C. Qualey and Sergeant G. W. Redwood. Redwood also spent time at Stalag Luft III, while Flying Officer G. M. Ruff was held in Stalag Luft I.

In September 1944, Nickless added some of his own artwork to his wartime log. His skill is clearly demonstrated in this detailed piece of work.

Above left: Hpt Von Muller erected a memorial cross to the 52nd escape tunnel detected.

Above right: Pat Nickless was a proficient artist.

From October 1944, his log entries were as follows:

> October: roll call now at 4 p.m. Germans give permission to pass between
> blocks in separate compounds until 8 p.m. Weather fairly cold now. New
> Library times of attendance for our block now between 6 p.m. and 8 p.m.
> 24 December: Geisler moved to block 11, and R. J, Allen comes in, 'Pal of
> mine from school – what a place to meet again!'

Flying Officer Allen DFC had been captured on 24 September 1944. His
Lancaster had been carrying a tallboy bomb for an attack on the Dortmund
Ems Canal when he was shot down by night fighters. F/O Allen had been
operational with the famous 617 Dambusters Squadron based at RAF
Woodhall, Spa. Allen was a most experienced man and flying on his second
tour of operations.

> January 1945: ice rink organised. Communal skates allowed out by the
> Germans.

Dulag Luft saw another group captain through their doors. Group Captain
'Ginger' Weir[37] had been in the crew of a Lancaster on 21 November 1944,
attacking the Mittelland Canal. RAF Fulbeck's irrepressible Station Commander
'Ginger' Weir was at the controls when his aircraft suddenly exploded, completely
disintegrating and causing the subsequent destruction of an adjacent aircraft while
directly over their target area. The only survivor from the Lancaster was the group
captain, who apparently fell from the explosion with his parachute operating in
unknown circumstances. When he regained consciousness, he found himself lying
on his back on the muddy bottom reaches of the breached and drained Mittelland
Canal. Later detained and taken into custody, Weir was the second group captain
to be interrogated at Dulag Luft within a few months. On his arrival at Stalag
Luft I, Group Captain Weir later took over as the senior British officer. The reason
for that is explained by the following entry recorded by Nickless:

> January 1945: Col. Spicer sentenced to death by German court martial
> for inciting men to mutiny. Group Captain Marwood-Elton and Wing
> Commander Ferrers still in civilian clink, and sentenced to three years
> and nine months respectively.

Col. Henry Russell Spicer was the USAAF commanding officer in compound
2. On 31 October 1944, the German camp commander made him responsible
in ordering the return of a metal bar that had been reported missing. It must
be assumed that the Germans saw this as a serious matter for the security of
the camp. Spicer chose to address the entire compound, advising of the missing metal bar and requiring its immediate return. Spicer then rallied his men

The volleyball net in the yard at
Stalag Luft I.

with a speech about the Germans still being the enemy, and that some prisoners were acting too friendly with an army that were responsible for serious acts of murder upon British soldiers. It was a speech that resulted in his court martial and subsequent sentence to death. That sentence was to be carried out following an immediately imposed, six month period of solitary confinement in the camp's solitary cooler cell.

The reference Nickless made in his wartime log about Group Captain Marwood-Elton related to him taking exception to the order published by Camp Commandant Oberst Scherer in April 1944. Scherer required Marwood-Elton to order his men to acknowledge his officer's 'Heil Hitler' salutes. Failing to comply with that order resulted in Scherer arresting Marwood-Elton and securing him for trial by court martial; his actions being seen as an incitement of mutiny.

Wing Commander Ferrers was arrested that same day, but on an unrelated matter. Both men were removed from the camp and detained in Stralsund. On 15 November, Marwood-Elton and Ferrers appeared in court. Both were found guilty of the charges laid upon them. Marwood-Elton was immediately sentenced to three years imprisonment, and Ferrers nine months imprisonment. Both were unceremoniously transported directly to the civil prison in Stettin. These events provide an explanation for Group Captain Weir talking over as the senior British officer in January. However, in mid-March 1945, Group Captain Marwood-Elton and Wing Commander Ferrers returned under armed guard to Stalag Luft I. Both men joined Col. Spicer USAAF in the solitary confinement cell block.

Nickless continued to occupy room 14 in barrack block 6, and drew a

Pat's bunk in Room 14 Block 6.

rough sketch of his room in his logbook. Room 14 had ten bunks, which were allocated to Flight Lieutenant J. W. Bridger 42740, Flight Lieutenant R. S. Matthews 119127, Flying Officer F. J. Eisberg 161585, Flying Officer R. Dryden RCAF J24224, Flying Officer P. H. Todd 149553, Flying Officer R. E. Cooper 171628, Flying Officer Olaf Lambert 142017, Nickless, and Flying Officer R. J. Allen 52101. The first few months of 1945 had been very hard, and weather conditions had prevented any potato deliveries, resulting in the men being on at least half quantities. Despite the ever present hunger, morale was relatively high in the camp. This was primarily due to the hidden radios that continued to report news of the Allied onslaught on Germany. Amongst the men, sweepstakes were underway, with predictions of when the war would finish. Most bets were in the form of 'IOU' declarations to be honoured after the men had been repatriated.

In January 1945, Oberst Warnstedt took over the command of Stalag Luft I. This man adopted a far more offensive attitude than his predecessor Oberst Scherer, particularly in relation to the guard's duties and the deployment of their firearms. Warnstedt clearly wanted to run the camp using the threat of lethal force.

In mid-February, Nickless recorded the fact that the camp's food supply had been reduced to a bare minimum. The prisoners were told that Red Cross parcels were expected at any time, but until they arrived, it was going to be seriously difficult to provide food across the camp. Adding to that situation was the unexpected arrival of 1,500 non-commissioned men; prisoners who had been evacuated from a camp near Thorn.

In his log, Nickless recalls back to October 1943, when several of his friends had been removed from Stalag Luft I. He hoped that the new contingent of prisoners may have seen the return of those same men. Nickless had avoided the transfer away from Stalag Luft I due to his commission to the rank of pilot officer. Despite extensive searching, Nickless failed to find any of his lost friends, and nobody had any news of them. As prisoners were provided the opportunity to seek an audience with a member of the protecting powers, it was possible that they may have been in a position to pass on any messages between camps.

Switzerland and Sweden acted as protecting powers during the Second World War, empowered by the Geneva Convention and its provision to undertake inspections. The protecting powers' inspector, Monsieur Bovey, visited the camp on 22 February 1945. At that time, he reported that the camp establishment was in excess of 8,000 prisoners: 7,202 Americans, 759 British, 260 Canadians, 59 Australians, 49 South Africans, 30 New Zealanders, 5 Rhodesians, and 3 Irish. Some new arrivals had not been recorded in those calculations.

Amongst those significant numbers of men, they all recognised that almost every item of consumables had a value in relation to cigarettes. Cigarettes created 'foodacco prices'. Nickless listed the respective values in his logbook. Sugar was valued according to the respective country and supplier: American sugar equalled 60 cigarettes, Canadian equalled 50, and English 25. A single tin of 'klim' milk was worth 100 cigarettes, while a tin of condensed milk was 80. The most expensive item was chocolate; Canadian milk chocolate was valued at 160 cigarettes, but the English equivalent was only 120. Biscuits were always sought after, with the English service biscuit worth 40 cigarettes, American 'K' biscuits 40, and the Canadian biscuit a more desirable 50. A biscuit known as 'healthy life' was a particular favourite, which commanded a high value of 75 cigarettes. These biscuits were infrequently seen in food parcels. Rather interestingly, a small tin of sardines was only worth 15 cigarettes, representing the cheapest food commodity to exchange. Clearly there was a stock market approach to these valuations, and bartering was a way of life in the camp. Nickless made the following comments in his log:

Fifty cigarettes nearly always issued with a food parcel. English parcels are packed at various centres such as Bermondsey, North Row, Birmingham, Leicester, Wood Green, and the essentials are in all types and variations. One can almost count on getting a pudding in a North Row, or a pancake mixture in a Leicester parcel. The meats vary. Sausages replaced the meat roll, and different types of stew or a pie for the larger tin of meat. American parcels boost you up on milk, chocolate, margarine and sugar. Any meat was a little more solid, but less variety. Jam is only half the amount than in an English parcel. Canadian parcels [are] very similar to the American, advantages lie with the

Cooking stove from Stalag Luft I, block 5.

biscuits, delicious when soaked, swelling to twice their size, fried and served with jam. The coffee is fine ground and good but not very economical.

When food was scarce, it became a constant source of conversation, and menus were written and re-written time and time again.

On 25 February, Patrick Nickless was advised that a small consignment of Red Cross food parcels had arrived in the camp, however, the consignment was less than a quarter of that required to fulfil the needs of the men. The influx of new prisoners by far outweighed any benefit of such a supply, and the hunger Nickless was experiencing continued. During March, the situation deteriorated further and he recorded in his log, 'Now on reduced German rations: A few slices of bread a day and a glop.' The reference to 'glop' was a small ladle of fluid that was supposed to be soup; it apparently bore very little resemblance to soup!

'The Romance of a Bucket'

It's only an old wooden bucket, that stands near the stove on the floor, and the uses to which we adopt it, I'm sure you would really deplore.

Three times a day after eating we wash up our dishes 'My life' the grease on the bucket when finished I'm sure you could cut with a knife.

And then every Monday is bath day, we just use the old wooden bucket and manage the best that we may. We squat on our haunches beside it and lather our bodies with soap, then re-fill the pail with clean water and rinse it all off us, 'we hope'.

On Tuesday we all do our washing, the bucket of course, plays its part. To look at that washing when finished would sadden a laundry man's heart.

Twice every week comes inspection, I don't think I need to say more. But the bucket we use for our washing is used too for scrubbing the floor.

With conditions like these we're expected to keep ourselves tidy and clean, we try hard, you know, notwithstanding, but I guess you can see what I mean.

Anon., PoW.

Towards the end of February 1945, Germany commenced the distribution of a propaganda pamphlet urging British prisoners to join Germany in the fight against Communist Russia:

Soldiers of the British Commonwealth and soldiers of the United States of America.

The great Bolshevik offensive has now crossed the frontiers of Germany [...] Extraordinary events demand extraordinary measures and decisions [...] The Fate of Your Country is at stake! [...] This means the fate of your wives, of your children, your home [...] Whether you are willing to fight in the front line or in the service corps, we make you this solemn promise: whoever as a soldier of his own nation is willing to join the common front for the common cause, will be freed immediately after the victory of the present offensive and can return to his own country via Switzerland.

All that we have to ask from you is the word of the gentleman not to fight directly or indirectly for the cause of Bolshevik-Communism as long as this war continues [...] At this moment we do not ask you to think about Germany. We ask you to think about your own country [...] You will receive the privileges of our own men for we expect you to share their duty.

Are you ready for the culture of West or the barbaric Asiatic East?

Make your decision now!

This was clearly a flawed strategy, yet it was still proposed to many Allied prisoners of war. The Russian threat was accentuated to a level conceived by the failing Third Reich's propaganda machine, and it has to be regarded as one of their last, dismal failures.

On the morning of 18 March, an air raid alert took place, with the men responding as required by immediately returning to their own barrack, or if not practical, into the closest barrack. Approximately forty-five minutes after the alert had been sounded, the South African Pilot Lt George Whitehouse left his barrack[38] carrying a basin of used water. Quite possibly forgetting the previous alert, he was shot through his body while carrying the basin to the vegetable plot. Whitehouse was immediately recovered from where he fell and treated in the hospital, where his life was saved by some impressive surgery. Lieutenant Whitehouse SAAF 206733 had been originally captured by the Germans in Italy after escaping by parachute from his Marauder aircraft, which had been struck by anti-aircraft flak. On that occasion, Whitehouse witnessed one of his crew members fall to his death after his parachute failed to open properly, and another whose parachute did work correctly, causing him to fall into the sea and drown.[39]

During the same air raid alert, and only a few minutes after the shooting of Lt Whitehouse, Second Lieutenant Elroy Wyman USAAF decided to return to his own barrack. Within a few feet of having left the barrack he realised that the all clear had still not been sounded as nobody was about. Wyman turned to return back to the doorway but as he reached it, he was shot in the head.[40]

Both casualties were treated by Captain W. M. Nichols Royal Army Medical Corp. He was an officer with past expertise in neurosurgery, but had been captured in the withdrawal of the Allied forces at Dunkirk in 1940. From that time, he experienced several moves within various hospitals and prisoner of war camps, arriving in Stalag Luft I in January 1943. Working in collaboration with the German doctor Gunther Obst, they created an effective surgery and hospital in the camp. Unfortunately for Captain Nichols, the excellent partnership with Obst was broken when he was removed from his post by the German authorities. Quite possibly, this was retribution for his close working relationship with the British doctor.

Captain Nichols was responsible for saving the life of the SAAF Pilot George Whitehouse, but the gunshot wound to the head of Elroy Wyman had proven

Captain Nichols RAMC. (*Judy Cameron*)

to be fatal. George Whitehouse recovered and was subsequently repatriated to his native South Africa. His gratitude to Captain Nichols was expressed in the regular exchange of Christmas cards for many years after the war.

Captain Nichols had served in the pre-war Territorial Army. That service led to the award of the Territorial Decoration medal. His service as a medical doctor in the field forces, and the distinguished service within various prisoner of war camps was recognised by the award of an MBE in December 1945.

On 28 March 1945, a substantial delivery of 30,000 Red Cross parcels arrived at the prison camp. It was the most welcome sight possible for the starving men. 'Food, glorious food' was penned inside Nickless' log. On 5 April, potatoes, coal, and further parcels arrived in the camp. Within a short period of time, the conditions had completely turned around, but not before Nickless had suffered. He was committed to the sick bay for seven days, and issued special food rations by the doctor.

Rumours of unrest within the guards came to the fore with evidence that the Germans had commenced demolishing the flak school on 29 May. The prisoners were aware that their time as Kriegies was coming to an end, but they were apprehensive, not knowing what was going to happen as events unfolded around them. It was presumed that the Russians would soon be upon them. On the night of 30 May 1945, at 2 a.m., freedom finally came. Patrick made a note in his log:

Germans crept away with Red Cross parcels. They silently left the camp in Allied hands. Rapid reorganisation and Red Cross parcels issued for complete week. Queer to get the tins unpunctured.[41] Nil water – a few explanations during the day.

Group Captain Weir instigated the release of Group Captain Marwood-Elton, Wing Commander Ferrers, and Colonel Spicer from their cells, and water and electricity supplies were returned to the camp. Nickless made the note:

The civilians are scattering, Russians arrive at 10.30 a.m.

Wednesday 2 June: camp gates thrown wide open. Bags of disorganisation. Peninsular area opened to us. Barth and the flak school placed out of bounds. Chaps packing up their things and going west with Russians to make for our lines.

Thursday 3: wandered around, boys crossing creek in boats in search of booze. Got chickens, eggs, and fish.

Friday 4: fairly quiet day, wandered about listen to stories about our chaps experiences 'mit der Ruskies'. Civilians terrified of them – rape and looting done by shock troops that have moved on. Communists now set up in Barth. BBC radio switched on all the time now.

Saturday 5: law and order being restored. Russians in full control. Barth airfield now serviceable, work done by our bods, water and light spasmodic.

RAF Group Captain Cecil Weir, seen standing left, easily identifiable with his pilots wings worn on his tunic. Leaning into the picture adjacent to Weir is Flight Lieutenant DeLarge,[42] who acted as interpreter. He is addressing Major General Borisov. The Russian liberators of Stalag Luft I are wearing their military orders and medals; this was normal practice for the Russians throughout the war. Colonel Hubert Zemke, the Senior American Officer, is sitting on the right wearing an open shirt collar, with another interpreter on hand sitting slightly behind him. This photograph is thought to have been taken in the camp commandant's office when official business concerning the repatriation process was conducted and subsequent diplomatic agreements were reached.

Allied guard of honour held for the Russian liberators at the main entrance to Stalag Luft I. The armbands being worn are those made and issued for the selected men of the camp who acted as the Field Force, those men had been appointed by the senior camp leaders. The FF armbands identified the men as being in charge of the camp following the German withdrawal and prior to the arrival of the Russian Army. The two main-gate guard boxes can just be seen with the guard tower overlooking the entire location; countless times the Allied prisoners had devised escape plans through those gates.

The Russians enjoyed the honour expressed to them at the gate parade by the Allied prisoners, but Colonel Zemke requested through the Russian command that Colonel Zhovanik, who was in command of the district of Bath, detail his soldiers to patrol the camp's gates and perimeter. Zemke's reasoning for his request was that Russian soldiers and officers were passing through the camp with some frequency, and no control existed. Colonel Zhovanik assigned his troops to conduct security outside the camp. In addition, patrols were established by the camp administration, utilising the Field Force, which had assumed responsibility for camp security following the German withdrawal. The Red Army patrols were entrusted with the specific mission of not admitting any unauthorised personnel into the camp. Colonel Zemke and his assistant Group Captain Weir regulated any exit from the camp. The American and British prisoners conducted internal patrols and security of the warehouses holding the Red Cross supplies.

Barrack 5 at Stalag Luft I had a rather dowdy environment, primarily created by the lack of natural light. Pinned on the outside of the door was the following message:

Knock, but be prepared to listen as well as talk! We have known gallant men who have bailed out of every type of aircraft, under every type of circumstances, with every type of chute, from every altitude, with any number of props feathered. We will have eaten better and worse food than you. We know better stories, and have known more women and more generals. We can be more dignified or more undignified than anybody else in the whole camp. You are very welcome, come in friend.

Patrick Nickless had been a prisoner of war for just over two years, and most unusually, he had been held in one single camp for that entire duration. On Wednesday 9 May, Nickless and his fellow room mates were marched away from Stalag Luft I. The security gate, which had so often been shut and guarded, now represented true freedom, and he was soon to walk out and not look back. Tucked into his logbook was his camp identification card that he had liberated from the administration offices after the Germans withdrew from the camp. On the card, his mug shot photograph displaying his prisoner number 1023.

Celebrations of victory in Europe the previous night had resulted in a display of pyrotechnics, pistol flares fired up into the sky, and bonfires, resulting in some pastern 'goon' boxes going up in smoke. Safe in Nickless' pocket were the ten, well-thumbed letters received from his family during his incarceration, along with a few theatre production programmes produced for several plays undertaken in the camp. Nickless clearly remembered these with fondness. Also securely packed in his small bag was his YMCA wartime log, which had become one of the most important items for him during his camp life. Many pages documented facts that he felt were worthy of recording at the time,

A view of the Red Cross parcel store that had been constructed in the German quarters. The hand-drawn carts used to distribute the food parcels can be seen, as well as other larger carts, with a water bowser also identifiable. The buildings were German barracks, and the camp wire posts identify the prisoner's boundary adjacent to the German quarters.

The camp sick quarters with the German Luftwaffe flak school in the distance. This extensive construction appears to have an open courtyard to walk through. The flak school looks to be fairly close to the prison camp when viewed from this perspective. Of note is the fact that the roof of the sick quarters has been clearly identified with the International Red Cross symbol. A collection of prisoners can be seen in the compound furthest away, whilst a pedal cyclist is riding along the path away from the sick quarters.

A view across the camp from the guard tower or postern box, which interestingly shows the length of the barrack blocks. Note the single-brick partition wall in the first barrack block. The partition wall proved to be an ideal location to construct long term hides for escape materials; single bricks were often removed with false brick fronts added. The large, single apex roofed building and the central guard tower indicate this position to be looking northwards towards the northern compounds of the camp.

The view from barrack block 5, looking into the German quarters. The Red Cross store building is easily recognised from this perspective. The postern box can be seen, which immediately overlooked Patrick Nickess' accommodation block. The wet ditch is from the worn pathway walked daily by the prisoners. The warning wire and posts can be clearly seen.

The observation point provided to the German guards from within the postern tower close to Nickess' barrack block. This perspective provides an opportunity to see how the prisoners exploited the blind spots created by these viewpoints. However, this postern box provided the guards with an unmolested view of the barbed wire fence line and the internal warning wire.

Inside barrack 5, Stalag Luft I. Some drawings are pinned on the wall in an effort to try and brighten up the dull room. Warrant Officer Lambert can be seen doing some domestic chores on the stove. Note the assorted cloths hanging up, acting as a reminder that every single usable item was retained and utilised during prison camp life.

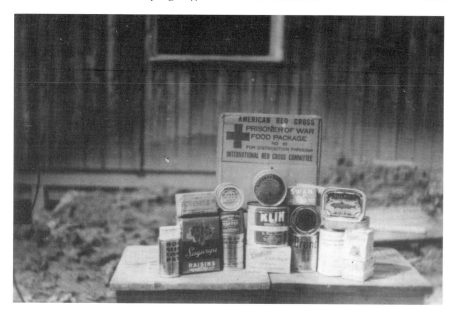

The American Red Cross parcel contents, displaying the infamous 'klim' milk tin. Nickless clearly wanted to bring home a reminder of the food parcels that had been of such importance during his period of imprisonment. Carefully placing the contents on a table, he took the photograph outside his barrack block.

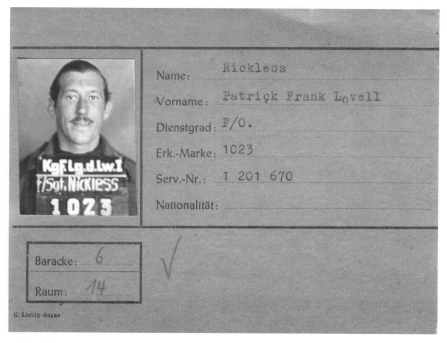

Luftwaffe prisoners' registration form, liberated by Pat Nickless.

including three entire pages of publications, authors, and critique upon each book that he had read. Without any doubt, books had provided a release from the men's relentless desire to fill as many hours as possible in the days when time appeared to stand still.

Nickless recorded that the march to the airfield was an enjoyable, longed-for experience, with the sweet, fresh air and the view uninterrupted by the endless expanses of barbed wire. Barth aerodrome was a welcome sight, with the men mingling in small groups along the grass verge adjacent to the large concrete runway. Looking across the aerodrome, Nickless sighted several abandoned enemy aircraft, which had been strewn across the airfield. The withdrawing Luftwaffe establishment had destroyed as much of their material and facilities as possible. For the released prisoners, the sight before them was a most tangible representation of the crushed and recently defeated enemy.

Some men sought the opportunity to try and scavenge keepsakes from the abandoned aircraft prior to the arrival of an American B-17. When it did arrive, little encouragement was needed to climb aboard, and once settled they set off en route to Brussels. This was to be in preparation for the final leg of their journey to the United Kingdom. The remaining camp personnel and all of the supplies and materials within the camp had been left under the command of the Russian Major General Borisov.

Having regained freedom, Nickless had no need to make any further entries in his wartime log. Therefore, on Thursday 10 May 1945, no more than the date had been written at the top of the page. Life as a prisoner of war had finally ceased for the Spitfire pilot Patrick Nickless.

Captain Nichols, the camp doctor, remained behind in the camp, assisting in the treatment of those prisoners that were not fit enough to leave. On 13 May, he eventually departed with the sick and wounded patients that he had been treating. Amongst the entire contingent of personnel leaving were three girls wearing nurse's uniforms. They were not in fact nurses, but three young German staff who had risked a great deal by providing help to Captain Nichols during his service in the camp. The Russians forbade any German civilians to be allowed to leave, but fearing for their lives, Captain Nichols had no wish to leave them to the mercy of the Russian Army. The disguised nurses were smuggled out successfully and finally reached England, where Captain Nichols had to vouch for their credentials. It is known that the three women returned safely to Germany and maintained contact with their saviour for many years.[43]

A Military Intelligence Service analysis,[44] dated 1 November 1945, indicates that 7,717 American and 1,427 British and Commonwealth prisoners of war from Stalag Luft I had returned to their respective military controls by late May 1945. This was an increase of 777 men from the statistics provided by the protecting powers' report three months previously.

Warrant Officer John Sheridan

John Joseph Charles Sheridan was raised in Langley Prairie, British Columbia, Canada. He volunteered for service in the Royal Canadian Air Force, and commenced his training in his home country during May 1941. Sheridan was later selected for the aircrew positions of a wireless operator and air gunner. The gunnery school training took place in MacDonald, where Sheridan quickly completed the course in early 1942. He was then posted to England to complete his qualifications for his primary role at the RAF Radio School, Madley, Hereford.

Having been shipped half way across the world, Sheridan was keen to write to his parents as often as possible. His letters explaining the quaint thatched cottages and rows of identical houses could not have depicted a wider contrast to Langley Prairie. The intensity of training as a wireless operator was something that Sheridan had not expected. The commitment to study, and the hours upon hours attached to the headset and transmitter appeared to be relentless, and he was delighted to pass the skills testing and examinations that qualified him to wear the wireless operators' half wing on his tunic. Throughout his time in England, Sheridan wrote home every week without exception, and his mother fondly kept every single piece of correspondence. He wrote about going to Scotland for the final part of his training at Elgin, Morayshire. Letters had become seriously delayed between Canada and England, and as time progressed Sheridan became frustrated. He wrote:

> I can't understand you not receiving my letters, have sent some airmail as it is faster than aerographs as a rule. I sent three in one week. I am on a RAF squadron, didn't get to a Canadian one this time,[45] maybe the next one will be though. This is supposed to be an English one but it has mainly New Zealanders and Canadians and every other kind of guys.

As Sheridan's training drew to a close, his competency had been tested, and he was now part of a complete crew in Bomber Command. On 21 September 1942 he wrote of his exploits, 'We are flying in the biggest bombers we have;

now they sure are some kite, big as a house.' Clearly, the letter situation was still a problem in his mind. His mother wrote, 'I am very glad to hear from you but I am mad at you, how do you expect my letters to be anything but the same old stuff when I have to write every week. Some of your letters take over a month to arrive.' But letters were soon to be far from Sheridan's thoughts. He advised that he was with 218 Squadron somewhere in England, with whom offensive operations were soon to start in the squadron's Short Stirling Bombers.

Sherdian was at last ready to fly his first operation over occupied Europe; a mine laying sortie to drop a large sea mine in the mouth of the Gironde estuary, Southern France. These operations were coded as 'gardening' sorties, and regarded as excellent opportunities for novice crews to undertake, as they had to experience both navigation and low level flying in order to plant the mines precisely. There was always the ever-present danger of enemy flak ships protecting harbours and estuaries from mining operations. These heavily armed units were positioned to take advantage of the predictable approaches such aircraft were likely to take.

Sheridan's crew of seven men, consisting of three Canadians, one New Zealander, and three British, took off from RAF Downham Market just before 5 p.m. on 6 November 1942. Stirling R9185 left the runway safely, and gaining height slowly, headed towards France. John Sheridan had commenced his operational tour of duty, and would need to complete approximately twenty-nine further operations to fulfil the tour. That same night, nineteen Stirlings from three different squadrons were going to plant mines, frequently referred to as 'vegetables'. One aircraft from each of the participating squadrons failed to

A Stirling bomber being made ready for operations.

return, and twenty-one young men never returned to the safety of their squadron. Sergeant John Sheridan was one of them; he never even completed one full operation. Stirling R9185 had crashed around 7.15 p.m. near St Brieuc, France, more than likely as the result of damage inflicted upon the aircraft by a German armed trawler or flak ship assigned to protecting that area of coastline. Two of the Canadian crew members were killed in the crash, and their bodies later buried in the town's cemetery. The remaining five crew members survived the incident to become prisoners of war. Sergeant Hyde from New Zealand, the aircraft's pilot, had managed to evaded capture until the end of December. As a prisoner of war, Hyde was later court martialed by the Germans for being part of an audacious escape plot attempting to steal a Luftwaffe aircraft. He was sentenced to two years imprisonment. After the war, recognition of his acts undertaken as a prisoner of war resulted in the award of the MBE.

Following John Sheridan's capture, he was taken in transit to the Dulag Luft interrogation centre. John was a Catholic of some conviction, and his thoughts were very much with his family in Langley Prairie. On 10 November, the Canadian National Telegram Service delivered a small typed message to his home, issued by the RCAF casualty officer.

The telegram read:

M-9452 regret to inform you advice has been received from the Royal Canadian Air Force casualty officer overseas that your son Sergeant John Joseph Charles Sheridan is reported missing as the result of air operations on November sixth nineteen forty two stop In the best interests of the possible

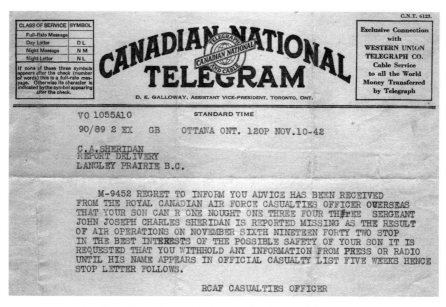

Telegram sent by Canadian National Telegram Service, 10 November 1942.

safety of your son it is requested that you withhold any information from press or radio until his name appears in official casualty list five weeks hence stop letter follows RCAF Casualties Officer.

Following receipt of that first telegram, Sheridan's mother collated and retained every single piece of correspondence relating to her son. The story of her son's life as a prisoner of war is uniquely described through the plethora of official and non-official letters. At the time, the postage system was erratic and inconsistent. As a result, the story of events taken from the original documents is recorded by date, but may not necessarily indicate the sequence in which they were received. The author's following collection of correspondence from the Sheridan family provides a vivid story of the anguish and frustration experienced by one mother in Canada. It is a sobering thought that these circumstances were replicated many thousandfold during the war:

8 November: the Wing Commander from 218 Squadron, Downham Market, writes a personal letter to Canada:

No message was received from your son's aircraft after takeoff, but there is always the possibility that he and the rest of the crew are prisoners of war. News of their whereabouts will reach us in time through the International Red Cross, but such information may take as long as three months.

11 November: Air Commodore, Air Officer in charge of Air Ministry records, despatches the following:

I am commanded by the Air Council to express to you their grave concern on learning from the casualties officer of the RCAF that your son has been reported missing – The Stirling aircraft of which your son was the wireless operator and air gunner failed to return to its base on 6 November 1942 from an operational flight. This does not necessarily mean that he is killed or wounded, and if he is a prisoner of war, he should be able to communicate with you in due course. Meanwhile enquiries will be made through the International Red Cross Society.

12 November: a personal letter was sent from the chief chaplain, Group Captain McCarthy, from RCAF Overseas Headquarters, London. The next day, a letter confirming the previous telegram information was sent from RCAF Casualties Officer, Ottawa. In addition, the department advised that within the crew were the following: Sergeant A. G. Cummings, next of kin Mr A. Cummings 4607, Blenheim Street, Vancouver, B.C.; Sergeant E. C. Kehl, next of kin (wife), 352 Foley Street, Port Arthur, Ontario. The letter states, 'This is all the information that we have at these Headquarters, but your son's commanding officers are writing you a letter, which you should receive shortly,

and which will give you all available details.'

17 November: a condolence card was sent by the Minister of National Defence for Air, stating, 'The Government and people of Canada join me in expressing the hope that more favourable news will be forthcoming in the near future.'

3 December: an RCAF Western Air Command letter was sent by the squadron leader command chaplain:

> It is indeed a regret on the part of the air officer commanding Western Air Command to learn that your son Sergeant John Joseph Charles Sheridan is reported missing. Our earnest prayers and hopes will be for the safe finding of your son.

10 December: the Canadian National Telegram sent the following at 12.12 a.m.:

> M-9934 pleased to inform you advice received from the International Red Cross society quoting German information states that your son Sergeant John Joseph Charles Sheridan is now a prisoner of war stop letter follows. RCAF Casualty Officer.

10 December: letter sent from the RCAF Casualties Officer:

> It is a pleasure to convey this further information, as I feel it will relieve to some extent the great anxiety endured – Your eagerness to despatch letters and parcels to your son is realised, and to assist in that connection, detailed information and instructions will be forwarded to you buy the Department of National War Service, Ottawa.

15 December: letter received from the parents of Sergeant Cummings. At that time, the death of their son was unknown. A second letter the following day advised that their son had been classified as 'missing believed killed'.

17 December: the Department of National War Service, Ottawa, sent a letter advising that they may write to John via British Prisoner of War RCAF C/O International Red Cross, Geneva, Switzerland. In addition, the following advice and directions were provided:

> You will note that the next of kin may forward a personal parcel to a prisoner of war once every three months. Cigarettes, tobacco, books, cards, games, music are not considered personal parcels, and may be sent at any time by anyone through the duly licensed dealers.

Within the letter were listed the firms permitted to forward books and similar, and in addition, those permitted to forward tobacco products.

Doolittle, had been tried and executed by the Japanese, who alleged that they had intentionally bombed non-military installations and fired on civilians. A strong note of protest was sent by the United States of America through the Swiss Minister in Tokyo. Prime Minister Winston Churchill sent a message to General Arnold, Chief of the USAAF, informing him of British indignation at the barbarity of the Japanese. The executed men were Lt D. Hallmark, Lt W. Farrow, and Sgt H. Spatz.

22 April: letter sent from the Canadian Red Cross Society:

> From the information received it is apparent that your son is at Stalag Luft I, via Stalag Luft III. We believe that via Stalag Luft III is because it is a censor camp, and mail for a number of camps is sent that way. With regard to the next of kin parcel, we are sorry that there is no other way that you can send a blanket, and while we realise it takes up most of the weight in the parcel, we think it wise to send one. Blankets are provided by the British Red Cross, but we receive quite a few letters from the boys at Stalag Luft requesting blankets.

6 May: the Canadian Red Cross Society wrote again, enclosing a printed map produced by the society showing all known prisoner of war camps in Germany and Italy. These were sent to every registered next of kin across Canada, with a note advising that information regarding new camps would be given once they had been built and that the recipient should keep the map updated accordingly.

24 May: the Sheridan family received correspondence from the Department of National War Service, who gave details on the procedures required for despatching quarterly parcels to prisoners of war:

> As regard personal parcels it is important that no articles should be included which would give excuse to the enemy to withhold delivery. Consequently all such parcels are examined and a note is made of their content, which are checked on your P/W No. 3 forms.

28 June: letter sent by the Canadian Red Cross Society:

> We are happy to inform you as the next of kin that a capture parcel has been forwarded from our Canadian Red Cross Office overseas. The parcel contains two pairs of socks, one each of the following: sweater, scarf, helmet cap, gloves, set of underwear, pair of pyjamas, bath towel, hussif, blanket, wash cloth razor, tooth powder and brush, shaving brush, soap, comb, two cakes of soap, three handkerchiefs, hand towel, chocolate, and chewing gum.

19 August: letter sent from the Department of National War Service:

Capture postcard.

> I am returning herewith a prohibited item which was removed from a personal parcel which carried your address, and addressed to Sgt J. J. Sheridan No. 902 Stalag Luft I. Article returned paragraph fifty-two and fifty-three prohibited articles.

27 August: letter sent from the Royal Canadian Air Force, Ottawa:

> It is a pleasure to advise you that your son has been appointed flight sergeant, temporary paid, effective 16 Aug 1942, and warrant officer, Class two, temporary paid effective 16 February 1943. Pay adjustments will be credited to his deferred pay account. Notification of these appointments is being forwarded to the Department of External Affairs, Ottawa, for transmission to your son.

28 August: letter sent from the Canadian Red Cross Society:

> We have now received an acknowledgement card from your son in respect of a captured parcel. We are sending this card to you as we believe that you wish to have it in your possession.

1 September: letter sent from the Canadian Legion War Services Inc. Educational Services:

> In accordance with the information provided, we are ordering the reference book from the publishers. This service is made available to Canadian prison-

The repatriation ship *Gripsholm*, as seen in the American National Dairy advertisements, 1944.

In May 1944, the ship employed for the repatriation voyage to Canada carried 627 eligible prisoners of war, several of which were RCAF personnel, including Warrant Officer Douglas Castling. Repatriation also provided an important, but unofficial, means to transfer intelligence. If the candidate was suitable, the camp leaders would provide information thought to be valuable to the war effort. This information would be memorised and later passed onto the respective departments of the War Office. When Castling arrived in his native country, the medical orthopaedists at Shaughnessy Hospital commented that the false limb made in the camp was equal in quality to that of current manufacture. He had worn the false leg for eight months with no adverse medical complications.

During the Second World War, *Gripsholm* made twelve round trips to various parts of the world, and carried a total of 27,712 displaced or repatriated persons. It is not beyond possibility that Red Cross food parcels carried by *Gripsholm* were destined for the camp holding John Sheridan. Correspondence regarding his fate continues:

2 August: Department of National War Service issued personal parcel labels. Mrs Sheridan posted her seventh parcel: Sugar 2 lbs, coffee 1 lb, chocolate 3 lbs, Bananas dried 1 lb, oxo cubes, onions and beans dried, eggs dried, tooth powder, razor blades.

23 October: letter sent from the Canadian Red Cross Society:

We have received word through the International Red Cross, Geneva, that your son is now located at Stalag Luft IV. Letters should be addressed to:

Stalag Luft IV, via Stalag Luft III. Parcels need not go to Stalag Luft III for censorship, and should be addressed directly to Stalag Luft IV.

Unbeknown to anyone involved in the correspondence with John Sheridan, Stalag Luft IV was to be forcibly evacuated on 6 February 1945. The commandant ordered the prisoners to leave under armed guard with little, if any, notice given, despite the obvious circumstances of the advancing eastern approach of the Russians. More than 6,000 prisoners began a forced march towards the west in what were atrocious sub-zero weather conditions. The continent of prisoners was experiencing some of the worst freezing conditions in many years. In the main, the prisoners were not adequately clothed; it was common to see prisoners wearing clogs and no socks. Conditions on the march were completely deplorable, and as a result of these conditions and the near starvation diet, disease became rampant. A major problem was frostbite. Many cases resulted in the most horrid of injuries to feet and hands, and even core body sections were affected from sleeping on the frozen ground. Shelter was frequently impossible to find for such large numbers of men during the overnight stops. Typhus fever spread by body lice, and dysentery, pneumonia, and other diseases were present in a great many men. Those men with even the most minor of medical experience helped the small number of doctors, but almost no medicine was available. John Sheridan had sustained an injury when a guard used a rifle butt to enforce the pace. The use of rifle butts was common place, and capable of inflicting serious injury. Sheridan needed some assistance from his fellow friends in recovering from the assault.

Survival for these fragile men depended on factors such as having a coat or additional clothing, preventing the common place foot blistering from escalating into open puss wounds, or just not falling ill. Clearly, avoiding serious diseases remained a priority, although basic hygiene was almost impossible. In many cases, it was simply a case of the stronger helping the weaker.

After walking all day with frequent pauses to care for stragglers, the doctors and spiritual leaders then spent the night caring for the ill. These men carried on with such little rest, in almost impossible conditions, and must be seen as truly inspiring individuals. Allied air attack or the shock blasts from bombing operations frequently killed field livestock; in many cases, it was not known how long the carcass had lain dead. These were butchered, and provided the energy to survive for a great many men. As the march continued, the guards became less insistent on achieving the relentless consumption of miles. In addition to the precious watch repair kit that Sheridan stored in one of his pockets, he carried something that was very dear to him; a small copy of the Missal, containing the mass for all Sundays. It was his wartime log, read and re-read many times over. The front endpapers held pencil notes of his imprisonment and a few details of his friends in the camps. He wrote, 'Stalag Luft IV, Tychow. 19 August 1944 until 6 February 1945. At 10 o'clock we started marching.'

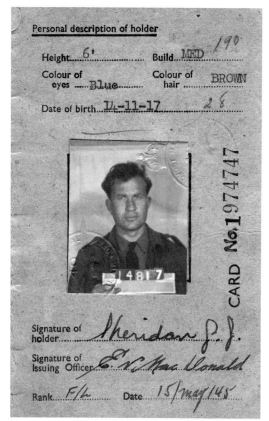

Personal description of holder

Height....*6'*........... Build...MED..../90'

Colour of
eyes .....Blue........... Colour of
hair ....BROWN

Date of birth...14-11-17.......28

CARD No.1974747

Signature of
holder.......*Sheridan J. J.*

Signature of
Issuing Officer...*E. V. MacDonald*

Rank....*F/L*.......Date....*15/may/45*

Identity card of J. J. Sheridan, 14
May 1945.

letters and in red, 'LIBERATED'. This is a particularly pleasant task in the
case of lads with whose parents we have corresponded. We almost feel we
know the boys personally.

For Sheridan, the war was over. He took part in just the one raid in the
Short Sterling R9185. That aircraft had been built under contract number
763825/38, by Short Brothers (Rochester), air tested, and taken on charge with
218 Squadron in September 1942. On 25 October, R9185 became operational
within the squadron. The immense materials, man hours in construction, and
financial costs to the Air Ministry was repaid with just 15 hours in the air,
after failing to return on 6 November 1942.

Warrant Officer John Sheridan arrived in Canada during the first week
of June 1945. Secure in his kitbag was a most precious little book; it held
a few written pencil notes on the end pages. His small Missal had been of
utmost importance to him during the endless months of imprisonment. He
had survived, unlike the 55,573 casualties who never returned home from
their Bomber Command operations.

10

Luftwaffe Ferrets

In all of the Stalag Luft prisoner of war camps, the camp commandants appointed responsible German personnel charged with security and intelligence gathering measures. They were required to thwart the prisoners escape attempts, and to frustrate the procurement of devices and materials required to manage or facilitate escape from the camps. The camp commandants knew that escape committees and organisational structures existed. The RAF in particular was renowned for consistent and well managed escape attempts. It was a priority for the German forces to prevent the most valued prisoners of war from escaping and eventually returning to serve in their respective air forces. The close relationships between the men in each room allowed hours of time to plan and dream up escape plans.

Aviators had the ability to attempt many avenues of escape. Tunnels were probably the most ambitious, as materials were always going to be difficult to procure, and each tunnel needed the removed spoil to be distributed around the camp. This task alone became massive, and it always appeared that what was removed from underground grew to be twice the mass once it was spread around the camp grounds. 'Penguins' were employed; these being prisoners with special bags sewn into the trousers, or with yokes across their shoulders and down the legs. Using draw strings, the soil was deposited over their shoes or boots, which then became fairly easy to distribute if the men were tending to the small gardening plots. However, this task was not so easy when the spoil was differing in colour and there was nowhere for it to be hidden. The men also used large greatcoats by securing the sleeves and filling both arms with soil. By carrying the coat over his shoulder, each man was able to move slightly more soil at once; a popular choice with many men who took advantage of the mass movement caused by the regular appell role calls. Every day that a tunnel progressed, the chance of detection grew. Although an average tunnel was dug as small as possible, 1 ton of soil was produced for just 3.5 feet (106 cm) progress. A well organised tunnel plan was most likely to employ around 200 'penguins'. The German 'goons', or guards, were well aware of the men's passion for digging tunnels, and measures specifically designed to detect dig-

Room mates in a typical Stalag Luft camp room.

ging were deployed. Simple, but basic, ground listening, or vibration detecting devices were used. At Sagan for instance, microphones were sunk several feet into the ground and placed approximately at 30 to 35 feet intervals outside of the double wire fence. These devices consisted of a long metal spike that was driven into the ground. Attached onto the spike by a locking mechanism was a small box that contained a microphone, by means of a direct link between the rod and the microphone. It was possible for the simple device to register any vibration created by digging. Each separate device was contained in a small wooden box to protect it from the weather, and each device was connected by wires that linked all of the devices together. In some cases, it was possible to encircle the whole perimeter of camps or compounds.

Another most basic means deployed against tunnelling was achieved by driving heavy vehicles around the compounds; the weight of the vehicle was most likely to collapse any tunnel, although not everywhere was accessible. The monitoring of prisoners' activities to establish frequent transits to or from particular huts would always lead to an extensive 'ferret' search. Frequently, those searches were unproductive for the Germans, and if convinced that tunnelling activities were taking place, they would commence digging anti-tunnelling ditches in an effort to locate any such construction by the prisoners.

The escapes that occurred spontaneously were more difficult to detect. These were opportunistic attempts, with prisoners taking advantage of both predicted and unpredicted events. A classic example would involve deliveries or tradespersons entering and leaving the camp. The German security waited with efficient search and control at the main gates for this type of prisoner activity. The same applied to the planned and executed escape attempts that involved false identities or false authorisation documents. Within the camp, some gifted prisoners had the skill and patience to spend hours upon hours perfecting copies of documents. This was no easy task, as procuring the paper alone was immensely difficult, and then the copy had to be identical to an original. It became common practice to examine all books that arrived in the camp in the hope that some endpapers may have been of the right thickness and quality to use, but the only reliable way to gain access to such material was by theft or bribery. Selected guards were groomed for compliance over many weeks and months. It was possible to use many means of bribery; the prisoners just needed to know what it was that any particular guard had a weakness for. Once exploited, these guards became the key to obtaining almost anything.

It was however a most dangerous practice for any guard. In late 1942, Private First Class Jungmichel, assigned to a guard detail at an officers' prisoner of war camp, entered into personal relations with a Polish officer interned at that camp. He supplied the officer, at the latter's request, with various tools, maps, and other items intended to facilitate the escape of prisoners. Jungmichel was sentenced to death by the Reich court martial for war treason, and the sentence was carried out on 5 Marsh 1943. News of such actions spread through the camps by way of official notices, no doubt designed to deter such activity. Any guard caught engaged in unnecessary conversation with a prisoner of war was likely to be reprimanded severely.

Another official notification distributed to the camps advised that a private first class on guard duty in a certain camp had on several occasions accepted bribes of cigarettes and chocolate from prisoners of war, and permitted them to escape without interference instead of reporting them to his superior at their very first suggestion. He was sentenced to death for dereliction of guard duty, for wilfully releasing prisoners of war, and for accepting bribes.
All guard personnel entrusted with the custody of prisoners of war were to be informed of the above. The announcement was to be repeated at least every three months.[47]

German documentation procedures very often employed the use of rubber stamps. In some instances, one document might have had up to three rubber stamps. To replicate such fake documents each stamp had to be forged. Rubber heels were carved with utmost precision using the most basic of tools. This work, undertaken in huts fitted with the dimmest of light, was truly remarkable, and the detailed results were impeccable. These stamps and seals needed protection, and were hidden away during the day to be recovered at night for continued improvements until the prisoners were complete satisfied with what they had achieved. Ingenuity of thought was needed to maintain the secrecy of the escape material; hiding places themselves had to be extremely well constructed to avoid detection. Other measures were devised to protect escape materials for short term hides. These were hides that could be swiftly utilised in the event of a sudden intrusion by a guard or other unexpected visitor. An example of these hides would be the pinning of documents under a drawing, sketch, or watercolour that was currently being worked upon. These were games of hide and seek with the most significant prizes being sought; the means to escape from the prison camp.

The German intelligence gathering process would frequently identify a particular hut that was suspected of holding escaping operatives. With the knowledge that a complete search would be required, plans would be put into place. Morning appell[48] or parade would have entire sections of the camp lined up and presented in the square or designated location. This was frequently the time for a full barrack search. Guards with dogs were posted around the particular building. Once the prisoners were released from appell, they returned to their barracks to find access denied. Searches were sometimes carried out for 4 or 5 hours. Searches were frequently represented in prisoners' wartime logs. For example, Patrick Nickless depicted a comical account of a search, with items flying out of windows and a 'ferret' poking out from the chimney.

Searches were intensified if guards has reasons to believe that forbidden items, such as a radio, camera, or escape aids were hidden. The guards that specialised in detecting tunnels were known as 'ferrets', and would remove sections of walls, floors, and ceilings. Mattresses would be torn open, stoves moved and cleaned out, as were lockers and shelves. Books were always thought to be good hiding places, so the 'ferrets' opened each one and threw it into the corner of the hut. In the many instances where books were used to hold forged documentation, the book would be split open at its spine and the paper inserted between the binding and the cover, which was then re-glued with the spine returned intact. This type of long term hide was most secure, and almost required the book to be destroyed before it exposed its hidden secret.

The 'ferrets' were diligent, and became most proficient at searching. With every item and concealment that they located, the guards gained experience. The prisoners' means of hiding escape plans required constant development throughout the war. 'Ferret' searches evolved into an efficient and effective means to disrupt, deter, and prevent escape. 'Ferrets' were by and large regarded as elite members of the camp duty strength, and they looked down on the plodding guards who manned the sentry posts or patrolled the wire. The escape committees had to respect the 'ferrets', who were known to secrete themselves under, and even in, barrack blocks. On other occasions, they were

Comic sketch illustrating the Luftwaffe 'Ferrets' searching a barrack.

'Ferrets' inside the barrack.

known to observe the camp from outside the wire, gaining a different perspective of activity. This clearly indicated the intelligence and thought applied to their anti-escape duties.

The Germans constantly tried to find one of the most important pieces of contraband in any of the camps; the prisoners' hidden radios. These most valued and protected devices were only used under complete security in order to hear the BBC broadcast, and then immediately dismantled or hidden. Frequently, each part was assigned to a different prisoner, who had an excellent long term hide where their tiny component was hidden. This security practice was found to be a most effective means to protect the radio and gather consistent news on a regular basis. It was not uncommon for the tame or corruptible German guards to frequently come to find out news of the war.

Covert communication within the camps was impressive. The need to monitor 'ferrets' was of utmost importance to the security of escape activity. At any time when one or more 'ferrets' entered the camp, their whereabouts had to be known. This was only possible by effective communication between the security officers in the camp and the controller who watched the main gate, logging the 'ferrets' in and out. There needed to be a high proportion of security officers on duty at all times, capable of monitoring the entire German presence in their own compound at any time. 'Ferrets' wore a different uniform to the other guards; dark blue coloured overalls. Setting themselves apart from the guards, the special uniform was seen as a sign of authority within the camp ranking structure. For the prisoners engaged in security monitoring, it was of great benefit in helping to plot their movements. The normal section of 'ferrets' consisted of one officer and six men to each compound; they were known to work collectively and independently. This structure was replicated according to the number of compounds in each camp. 'Ferrets' were frequently within the aviator's compound between dawn and dusk, fully committed to their role or duty. They frequently carried long metal rods to prod, poke, and delve into the ground. At any time they could enter a hut, or search anyone at will.

Prison Camp Money

The German word 'lagergeld' literally means 'camp money'. Special camp currency was denominated in Reichsmark. It was distributed to the camps by Oberkommando der Wehrmacht; the High Command of the German military forces. Camp money was issued according to the officer's rank and rate of pay. This process was required to equate the same rates accorded to German officers held in Allied camps. The printing and distribution of the camp money was undertaken in order to comply with the Geneva Convention. Lagergeld was usually issued to officers on a monthly basis, but proved to be a dismal failure, as very little, if anything, was available by way of exchange. Possession of these notes was in many instances worthless, although they did provide a means of currency for the many gambling syndicates that existed within the majority of camps.

> Dieser Gutschein gilt nur als Zahlungsmittel für Kriegsgefangene und darf von ihnen nur innerhalb der Kriegsgefangenenlager oder bei Arbeitskommandos in den ausdrücklich hierfür bezeichneten Verkaufsstellen verausgabt und entgegengenommen werden. Der Umtausch dieses Gutscheines in gesetzliche Zahlungsmittel darf nur bei der zuständigen Rasse der Lagerverwaltung erfolgen. Zuwiderbehandlungen, Nachahmungen und Fälschungen werden bestraft.

English Translation :

> This coupon is valid only as means of payment for PoW and may be used by them only within the PoW camps or on working assignments and redeemed and accepted only in points of sale, which are designated for this purpose. The exchange of this coupon into legal tender may only be carried out by the designated cashiers of the camp administration. Contraventions, limitations and forgeries will be punished.

The International Red Cross assisted in the financial exchanges between Allied and German forces. Compliance with the Geneva Convention in relation to

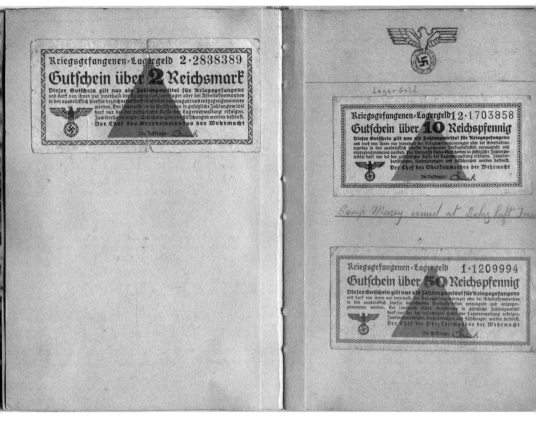

Prison camp money.

pay for prisoners of war was, in the main, well organised. In many respects, cigarettes, tobacco, and food was the 'money' in any camp, and cigarettes in particular were used to purchase German cash from the tame guards. This 'money' was imperative to any escape plan that required the purchase of train tickets or other commodities. The possession of real German currency was strictly forbidden for any prisoner of war.

In 1941, the Air Ministry made prisoners aware that after the war the Government would refund in pounds sterling any lagergeld in possession of or having been credited to prisoners of war. However in practical terms, this was a flawed concept, as men were frequently moved between several camps and little, if any, accountancy existed. In addition, many men gave these notes little credibility. Lagergeld notes of various denominations are frequently found stuck in wartime logs as keepsakes.

12

Warrant Officer
Bernard Howard Nutt

Born in 1923, Bernard Nutt originated from Birmingham. After his formal education, Nutt became an electrical heating engineer. On his eighteenth birthday, he volunteered for service in the Royal Air Force. He passed the initial training and arduous examinations with flying colours, and was successful in his selection for aircrew duties, volunteering to serve as an air gunner. He was likely to see operational service swiftly, as the duration of air gunner training was less than other trades in aircrew postings. However, the standard required was intense, and student air gunners were well aware that tail gunners in Bomber Command were likely to suffer the highest casualty rates.

The following is from a gunnery course manual:

Aim of enemy fighter is to destroy.
Aim of bomber air gunner is to get safely to target and back to base.
Never fire until fired upon; if gun fire, search for fighter; take evasive action.
Always watch your own tail.
Conserve your ammo; if you're fired upon from long range, instruct pilot to use evasive action.
Use good team work with rest of crew.
If on reconnaissance aircraft; your job is to return with information; not to seek combat with enemy aircraft.
All aircraft approaching are considered to be enemy until identified otherwise.
If your own guns fail, or are damaged during an attack, use your ingenuity to outwit the attacker.
To be surprised is to be lost.

Frequently, if an enemy fighter pilot knew he had been identified, or simply the element of surprise had been lost, no attempt would be made to follow the bomber through its normal evasive gyrations. The Luftwaffe night fighters knew that the bomber crews were extremely sensitive to another approach; they would seek out another aircraft, hopeful that it might have a less alert tail gunner. Quite surprisingly, many air gunners within Bomber Command com-

An early enlistment photograph of Bernard Nutt.

pleted their tour of operations without firing a single shot in aerial combat. However, it must be said that the stress they were constantly under was equal to those who took part in the often brief but terrifying life and death battles in the night sky with enemy night fighters.

The gun turrets within a bomber during a night operation were very lonely places. Nutt frequently occupied the mid-upper gunners position, spending the entire operation suspended in a canvas sling seat with his lower body in the draughty fuselage and his head and shoulders in the perspex dome. The rear gunner was even more removed from his fellow crew members; a truly cold and isolated position. Perched at the extreme end of the fuselage, the 'tail-end Charlie' squeezed into the cramped metal and perspex cupola. The rear gunner had so little space that his parachute was behind the twin panel doors in the fuselage. Through the entire operation, the rear gunner knew that the Luftwaffe fighter pilots preferred to attack from the rear and frequently from under the belly of the bomber. Nutt also occupied the tail gunner position, as swapping positions between aerial gunners was not unusual. Any rear gunner knew he was often first in line for enemy night fighter attention, for if the rear gunner could be killed, it considerably reduced the risk to the enemy fighter. From takeoff to landing, the air gunners were constantly rotating their turret, scanning the surrounding blackness for the grey shadow that could instantly become an attacking enemy night fighter. The crew, busy with the many tasks associated with getting the bomber to the target in the forward section of the bomber, placed all their trust in the air gunner's vigilance. Just a few moments of relaxation could mean death for them all.

Nutt gained the respect of his crew, which had formed voluntarily at the operational training unit. The training procedure had drawn to its close and operational duty beckoned. 207 Squadron were equipped with the new MkI Lancaster. Nutt's crew of seven men comprised of six sergeants and the skipper or pilot, who was an officer. The only Commonwealth member was Nutt's fellow air gunner Canadian Sergeant Taylor.

The skipper, Flying Officer 123026 Denys Oliver Street, was completely separated from his other ranks' crew when on station. The rank structure created two separate existences, but off station, at the pub or elsewhere, they were a tightly bonded crew. Street was the son of Sir Arthur Street GCB, KBE, CMG, CIE, MC, a most important figure within the Air Ministry at that time. He had served with distinction in the First World War, later to serve in the Admiralty, and during the inter-war years, as second secretary at the Ministry of Agriculture, before joining the Air Ministry as deputy secretary in 1938. During the Second World War, he was appointed permanent under secretary of the Air Ministry, a post that he occupied throughout the war.

The substantial and consistent casualty rates in Bomber Command would have been most prominent in Sir Arthur Street's mind. Very few people had such an intimate knowledge of the harrowing statistics. His son Denys Street was leading a good crew of young men, all of whom were performing well and accumulating successful operations in their flying logbooks. On 29 March 1943, the crew attended a squadron briefing; the target was Berlin. Any crew seeing the long taped route across Germany to Berlin became filled with thoughts of flak, searchlights, night fighters, and many hours in the air. From that moment onwards, it was difficult to think of little else. The gunnery leader would have probably held a separate briefing for Nutt and his fellow gunners, as would the navigators, who had the responsibility of getting the aircraft all the way to Berlin and back. Lancaster W4931 had been allocated to Flying Officer Street's crew, a fairly new airframe that had only arrived on station on 14 March. That particular aircraft had only participated in one previous raid; coincidently, it had been to Berlin two nights previously.

Bomber Command had committed a total of 329 aircraft to undertake the raid upon Berlin, 162 of which were Lancasters. Nutt was to occupy the mid-upper gunners position. From his turret, he was provided with a view along the entire length of the aircraft's fuselage. Nutt knew that he was going to spend hours scanning the dark skies in an effort to spot the prowling night fighters. He checked the oxygen supply and his communications with the skipper, and checked the scanning or turning mechanism of the turret. The guns would be test fired once they were in the air and the skipper had authorised the gunners to do so. The time was just past 9.30 p.m. when Lancaster W4931 lifted off the runway at RAF Langar. The skipper requested the testing of all guns and settled into the dangerous business of carrying the bomb load to Berlin.

When the bombers approached the target area, the anti-aircraft defences around Berlin were, as expected, very intense. When almost upon the actual target area and flying at a height of around 15,000 feet, Lancaster W4931 was struck by flak. Flying Officer Street fought hard to keep control over the aircraft. They initially lost a lot of height, but Street managed to stabilise at around 8,000 feet. Almost immediately, a night fighter attack took place. No doubt Lancaster W4931 was by then regarded as a lame duck. This time there was to be no escape, and the skipper immediately instructed all crew to bail out, shouting his instructions over the microphone fitted in his oxygen mask. No crew ever wanted to hear such instructions, least of all when over Berlin.

Flying Officer Street explained this well in a letter sent to his father in late 1943:

> I cannot obviously tell you the story of how I became a prisoner of war till later, but we were shot up, and despite all our efforts I had to give the order to bail out. I saw all the crew go out, then jumped myself, and you will be pleased to hear that they are all safe and well. They were all glorious and behaved with great fortitude. I wonder if you would be so kind as to write a letter to their next of kin on my behalf saying they are OK and were absolutely grand.

Sir Arthur Street was able to rest easy with the news that his son was safe, as were his entire crew, all of whom were to spend the rest of the war in a German prison camp. Denys Street's incarceration as a prisoner of war was to become truly historical.

Returning to Nutt, the air gunner had landed in close proximity to his skipper, and by great fortune they met up almost immediately; an omen of how closely these two young men's lives were to be interwoven by destiny. The following account is recorded in Bernard Nutt's wartime log. It provides some detail to the misfortunate events experienced over Berlin:

> 30 March 1943: shot down over Berlin by flak and night fighter. Got captured with the skipper outside Brandenburg, taken to the drome[49] by the town, and put in a cell.
>
> 31 March: left Brandenburg for Dulag Luft I, via Berlin.
>
> 1 April: arrived Dulag Luft, searched once again then put into the cooler. Very bad food. Skipper's twenty-first birthday today.
>
> 5 April: fetched from the cooler to be interrogated by a German officer. Had first smoke for five days.
>
> 6 April: taken into the big camp and met the rest of the crew.
>
> 10 April: left Dulag Luft for Sargan-Stalag Luft III in French third class train carriages.
>
> 12 April: arrived Stalag Luft III welcomed by crowds of RAF PoW. We were the first new chaps they had met for twelve months.

Prisoner of war life in Stalag Luft III commenced well for Nutt. He was security checked and cleared by the appointed British interrogator; a standard proce-

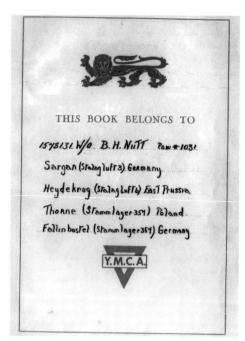

THIS BOOK BELONGS TO

1578131. W/o. B.H. Nutt. Pow # 1031.

Sargan (Stalag luft 3) Germany

Heydekrug (Stalag Luft 6) East Prussia

Thorne. (Stammlager 357) Poland

Fallinbostel (Stammlager 357) Germany

Y.M.C.A.

The initial page within Bernard
Nutt's YMCA log.

dure that was adopted and maintained during the war in the majority of Allied prisoner of war camps. This procedure had previously exposed the German 'stool pigeons', who were introduced by the Germans and designed to gather intelligence for the German authorities. It was a task undertaken by the security officers, and was seen as a high priority. Nutt explored the camp, walking the boundary within the warning wire, or short fence line as it was known. To step over the warning wire was to invite probable death from the machine guns mounted in the guard towers. The camp do's and don'ts were explained to Nutt, with the matter of the warning line being top of the list. To assist with so many prisoners walking or running the boundary line, there was a clearly defined path. Standing on the path, Nutt would have looked at the two 10 feet high barbed wire fences, with coils of further barbed wire between them. Freedom was just the other side of that second barbed wire fence, but Nutt was going to stare at these types of fences for another two full years.

Nutt's first drawing in his wartime log was of a guard tower, or postern box, with its searchlight. The individual barracks or huts at Stalag Luft III were prefabricated wooden structures. The interiors had frequently been left in an unfinished condition, with exposed stud work and no inner wall panelling. Running down the centre of the long barrack was a corridor, with doors leading into separate rooms on either side. Each barrack had a most basic night latrine, a washroom, and a small cooking stove. Each room had a window fitted, with shutters that were closed at night. Ventilation was poor, and each room was filled with the stale smell of tobacco and body odour every morning.

Above: Coils of barbed wire between the high fences.

Left: Bernard Nutt's first drawing of a guard tower, known also as a postern box.

In June, Nutt wrote, 'Officers make a very bold attempt to escape.' The renowned and famous Roger Bushell was responsible for the execution of that escape. Squadron Leader Bushell had become a prisoner of war relatively early on in the war. Shot down in his Spitfire in October 1939, his squadron, 92 Squadron, had lost their commanding officer. Bushell was a natural born leader, who by his demeanour alone, commanded respect from those he served with. For Bushell, escape was always of utmost priority, regardless of where he was in the German prisoner of war structure.

Squadron Leader Bushell and Flying Officer Street, Bernard Nutt's skipper on 207 Squadron, would eventually meet and become friends while in Stalag Luft III. Nutt himself would not be part of that group, having been relocated when Stalag Luft III became an officer's camp.

Returning to Nutt's wartime log entry from June 1943, it was Squadron Leader Bushell who had masterminded the escape attempt. Yet it was prisoners Walter Morison and Lorne Welch who had conceived the idea. Morison was an intimate member of the escape committee, and a close friend of Roger Bushell. The plan was to walk out of the prison escorted by bogus guards during one of the regular delousing sessions. Delousing was a cleaning method used by the Germans to rid prisoners of lice; the horrid blood sucking creatures were responsible for spreading deadly typhus. The only delousing facility was in the old compound, and this was the vital key to the scheme, for to reach the compound, the men had to go right outside the camp and along approximately 100 yards of public road. On one side of road was wire, but on the other was dense pine forest into which the escaped prisoners would hopefully disappear. The delousing party, escorted by German-speaking Kriegies wearing fake Luftwaffe uniforms, reached the forest undetected, allowing twenty-six prisoners to escape in all directions. The escapees made good their respective routes away from the camp. Flying Officer Arthur Garwell DFC, DFM, was amongst the many men detained within the first twenty-four hour period. Garwell found himself threatened with a court martial for acts of sabotage and espionage. It is possible that the German command selected this gallant pilot wearing two distinguished gallantry ribbons as the ideal subject to be jailed for his crimes. Garwell was placed in solitary from 12 June to 8 August 1943.

Only two men avoided immediate recapture; Lorne Welch and Walter Morison. Following a week of rough living, the pair targeted an airbase in Kupper;[50] a base perilously close to the prison camp from which they had boldly escaped. Having observed a suitable aircraft, they committed themselves to stealing it, but in the process of doing so the original crew returned. A dire situation presented itself, as Welch and Morrison's fake Luftwaffe uniforms deceived the aviators, who then issued orders to the two RAF escapees. Morison and Welch managed to assist the crew's successful departure. Very fortunate to have survived that experience, Welch and Morison returned to their observation point. The following day, another aircraft was selected, but bad luck prevented them from starting the engine quickly, and they were finally recaptured. The escapees' true identities were established, and both were taken back to Stalag Luft III. The commandant predictably imposed an immediate six week period in the cooler for both of them.

Both Welch and Morison were threatened with a court martial and execution for the crimes of wearing German uniforms, espionage, and sabotage. At the conclusion of their solitary confinement in the cooler, they were transferred to Oflag IVC, Colditz castle, in July.[51] The author is grateful to Belinda Shear, Walter Morison's daughter, for permission to use the following photograph, taken two days after Morison's capture.

The Luftwaffe uniform worn by Pilot Officer Walter Morison was that of a 'gefreiter' or 'private soldier'. The Germans were very interested in the prisoners' abilities to create such quality disguises. Reportedly, a general wanted to see the escapees wearing the uniforms. Morison and Welch were removed from their cells and paraded in the replica uniforms.

This type of escape required considerable planning and preparation. In this particular incident, some form of clothing disguise would be required for all twenty-six participants. The inventive Clayton Hutton added to his list of escape aids by creating a 'civvy' suit inside the replacement uniforms that were sent to the various camps. The officer's tunic could be recognised by a slightly differing shade of blue. The lining could be removed to expose an undergarment that needed very little effort to be deployed as a working man's suit. These garments were sent to the camps in low numbers, concealed amongst non-adapted uniforms. The most important factor for any escapee was to travel as far away as possible in the shortest time period, thus railway station were always prime venues to negotiate. The presence of security and document

Flight Lieutenant Lorne Welch and Pilot Officer Walter Morison in their replica Luftwaffe uniforms. (*Belinda Shear*)

inspection raised the chances of discovery manyfold. In this particular escape attempt, a significant number of the escapees were detained at or in close proximity to Sagan railway station. They had been free for less than 24 hours.

Within the prisoner of war camps, success was not measured by achieving an ultimate escape and home run, although that was always the objective of every attempt. To conceive a plan and execute it without detection was always a morale boost for the camp. It provided the stimulus to maintain the relentless inspirations needed for escape planning. With every attempt and escape, regardless of its duration, intelligence was gained. Prisoners captured and returned to the camp were able to add to the knowledge base held by the escape committees. It must be remembered that the escape committees and those engaged in escaping may have been a very small proportion of men within any camp. The balance between security, practicability, and possibility were delicately managed. The reputation of the Royal Air Force and their ingenious ability to escape was something acknowledged by the German authorities throughout the Second World War. In addition, it needs to be recognised that each individual compound was a separate unit, and as such, each was commanded by an individual escape committee.

Sergeant Major Hermann Glemnitz was the senior Luftwaffe non-commissioned officer on the security staff at Stalag Luft III. He was in charge of the 'ferrets', and had overall responsiblity for preventing escape within the six compounds. He was a wise and intelligent man, having served as a pilot in the First World War. His 'ferrets' found many escape tunnels being dug out of the six compounds. In essence, he was fighting six independent escape committees. Glemnitz was Roger Bushell's direct combatant.

Nutt recorded in his log, 'Kriegie goes over the wire in daylight,' and, 'another goes wire mad.' This entry relates to the sad events surrounding Sub Lieutenant J. Kiddell RN. Kiddell was suffering from mental illness, and detained in the camp infirmary without the treatment he required, Kiddell made for the wire. Crossing the warning line and reaching the fence, he was shot dead.

Sub Lt John Bartram Kiddell, 825 Squadron, Fleet Air Arm, had been flying in a Swordfish attacking Schiphol Airfield on 2 July 1940. The German war diary of Fliegerhorst[52] Schiphol mentions:

> Shortly before three o'clock an enemy aircraft headed for the dummy airfield, flew several times over a nearby search light and dropped three bombs. The aircraft was shot down by a machine gun located on the dummy airfield. One occupant is dead; the second made PoW and brought to the Luftgau Kommando,[53] Holland. On our side there were no victims or damage.

Leading Airman Burt had been the casualty. The pilot Sub Lt Kiddell, became a prisoner of war held in Stalag Luft III.

Towards the end of June, Bernard Nutt departed Stalag Luft III. He was amongst the second party of non-commissioned officers in transit to the camp at Heydekrug. The timing for him could not have been worse, as he had just received his first mail and parcel from England. The transfer to the camp in East Prussia meant that mail and parcels were likely to be delayed by months before they reached him again. This was a depressing state of affairs, one which he had absolutely no control over. On 10 July, his twentieth birthday, he had been established in his new barrack at Heydekrug. The camp was conceived as a camp for non-commissioned men. The bunks were squeezed in tightly and unusually stacked three high. Nutt's morale was low, having no letters and crammed into a barrack smaller than his previous room. The weather was a bonus, and in August a sports day called Fleiger Jockey day was organised. Nutt participated, and noted barrack C7 won the Klim (milk) Cup, an indication of camp humour.

The infamous 'Dixie' Deans had also been swept up in the swathe of non-commissioned men transported to Heydekrug. Deans was obviously appointed camp leader immediately. The other appointment of some priority was that of the escape committee and its command. Predictably, Deans was engaged in plans that were immediately drawn for a tunnel escape; extracts from Nutt's logbook will make mention of that shortly. Within Heydekrug, there was a contingent of men sent directly from the Dulag Luft interrogation centre. The old sweats from Stalag Luft III were immediately quizzed about escape, letters from home, and parcels. In turn, an equal amount of questioning took place in relation to news of the war from the new types. Amongst the old sweats was a Canadian officer who had swapped identities with a Sergeant D. E. Fair, Royal New Zealand Air Force, in order to access Heydekrug. Flight Lieutenant William Ash was an active tunneller.[54] He assumed that the new camp would be a better option to escape from. He had been a Spitfire pilot shot down in March 1942, and since that date had been involved in many escape plots. After a short time at Heydekrug, Ash had organised a tunnel. About fifty men were engaged in the construction that commenced in June. The entrance was from a wash house, and the tunnel broke cover, approximately 140 feet later, outside the wire a short distance from a small wood. This was a classic tunnel that was completed very swiftly under the direction of Ash. In addition, the escape committee had manufactured all the clothing required, which was quite some task. On a date close to the end of August, a small number of prisoners broke through and escaped. Unfortunately, the tunnel was discovered before the other prisoners could follow. The planning had been excellent, and Ash himself had escaped in the first run of men. He wore civilian clothes, carried some food, and had the vital compass and maps required to navigate the land. Under the guise of a Polish worker, Ash carried an appropriate identity card. Despite successfully making it to Libau (Lithuania), he was later detained on a goods train and taken back to Heydekrug. Placed in the cooler for solitary confinement, his true identity was discovered and he was then sent back to Stalag Luft III. The question of why he was not sent to Oflag IVC (Colditz Castle) like Morison and Welsh inevitably presents itself.

Nutt's logbook makes reference to the events surrounding the tunnel: 'August 1943: tunnel discovered only five out of fifty men away ... Camera identity and finger prints ... Lots of Krieges put in bunker for stealing cards.' The comments relate to the offensive actions taken by the camp commandant after the escape attempt had been discovered. Immediately, an early morning appell was called. The commandant required a full head count to establish if any prisoners had actually escaped. Following an escape, it was a standard procedure for the prison contingent to thwart the guard's attempts to establish if there were missing prisoners. To frustrate the head count, many means were adopted to create duplicate calculations or disrupt the entire counting process. At Heydekrug, the prisoners' disruption made it appear as if there were more prisoners in the camp than there should have been. A second appell was called later in the day, which the guards attempted to control by using several independent men acting as counters and moving the prisoners into a controlled pen or funnel. Due to the prisoners' insistent attempts to frustrate the head count, the guards' calculations were still in excess of the compounds' true numbers. The next day, a more organised count was to be undertaken using the prisoners' personal index cards. Each prisoner's card held their photograph and fingerprint. The previous extract from Nutt's wartime log clearly identifies this procedure. In essence, it should have been a simple, but a lengthy process was to follow, with the remaining cards identifying the prisoners that had escaped. The prisoners realised that the only way to frustrate that process was to steal some cards. By clever manipulation, a few hundred cards were removed from the counting table. Once again, the correct head count had not been achieved, but as indicated by Nutt's log entry, several prisoners were subsequently identified for stealing the record cards and immediately placed in solitary. Nutt noted, 'lots of fun,' and drew a pencil sketch of Commandant Oberst Hoermann Von Hoerbach overseeing the counting mayhem. He has been described as a very fine Prussian gentleman officer, who was strict but very fair during his period of command at Heydekrug.

After the excitement in August, Nutt made no further entry in his log until December. He comments upon Christmas, 'Not too bad considering, homemade brew with rather a big effect. Made a very good Christmas cake but the fruit was stopped because of the brew.' Complete agreement was required between the barrack, or possibly just a room within a barrack, to plan for the distilling of alcohol. The process needed valuable resources, such as fuel to burn in the stove, sufficient dried fruit or any equivalent product that contained sugar, the construction of the condensing unit, and importantly, somewhere to undertake the task of making the drink. Like most things within camp life, the anticipation of the event was almost as good as the end product. Fortunately

While Nutt fails to identify these individuals within his wartime log, the enties encompass the period from May to July 1944. Research into these statements indicates that the Canadian was Sergeant D. E. Kenwall. He had been washing his laundry, and approached the wire to throw water into no-go area. As he did so, a guard shot his arm, which was shattered by the bullet. Kendall's act was regarded as defiance to the warning wire, and possibly part of an escape attempt.

Guards were under instructions issued by the Supreme Command of the Wehrmact on 16 June 1941:

> Regulation 9, item 462: timely use of arms to prevent escapes of prisoners of war: in view of the increasing number of individual and mass escapes of prisoners of war, it is hereby again emphasized that guards will be subject to the severest disciplinary punishment or, when a detailed report is at hand, to court martial, not only for contributing to the escape of prisoners of war through negligence, but also for failure to use their arms in time. The frequently observed hesitancy to make use of firearms must be suppressed by all means. Guard personnel must be instructed in this sense again and again. They must be imbued with the idea that it is better to fire too soon than too late.

> Regulation 32, item 504: use of firearms against prisoners of war: the service regulations for prisoner of war affairs do not provide for any warning shots. Should the occasion for the use of firearms arise, they must be fired with the intent to hit.

These two instructions alone provide some understanding of the situations that became all too regular with the camps. The Yank, as referred to by Nutt, appears to have been Staff Sergeant Nies, who left his hut just prior to curfew being lifted. Carrying his towel and making for the wash house, he was shot and later died.

An explanation for these sad circumstances may well rest in examining the normal night procedures followed by the guards. Stalag Luft VI would be closed down, with the window shutters shut and locked. The barrack doors would then be individually locked. The camp was thus locked down, creating a curfew within the entire camp. At 6 a.m., the doors would be unlocked by the guards. From 6 a.m. onwards, prisoners went about their daily business; the latrines and wash rooms being their first points of call.

Walter Nies woke early and found the barrack door unlocked; it is quite probable that the door had been missed in the locking procedure. He walked from the barrack, progressing towards the latrine, and at 5.30 a.m. he was shot by a guard. Nies was severely injured and immediately treated by the medical officer in the camp infirmary, Captain R. Pollock RAMC. Pollock did what he could with the basic equipment available to him. Nies was later removed to the civilian hospital in Heydekrug. Captain Pollock, known to everyone as 'Paddy' was permitted to attend the hospital, but they were unable to save his

Captain R. Pollock RAMC standing far left. The photograph includes French and RAF prisoners.

life.[56] The guards once more regarded Nies movements as an escape attempt, despite the most obvious set of circumstances.

Finally, the last entry by Bernard Nutt relates to Staff Sergeant Jurist and Sergeant Walker, two Americans who had been attempting to escape in the early hours. Their plan had been to use the transfer of Red Cross parcels carried between the parcel store and the compound as a cover for an escape after the camp had shut down for the night. By an ingenious method of swapping the numbers of men pushing the cart, they confused the guards, who then failed to detect both prisoners being unaccounted for at the store. At nightfall, Jurist and Walker crawled to the first barbed wire fence with their wire cutters. They needed to cut through, then negotiate the coiled wire, a ditch, and then another fence. The men were detected by guards and shots were fired towards both of them. Remaining still and making no further attempt to escape, they awaited developments, probably expecting the guards to approach them. The searchlights were trained on them, and for Walker, the first to stand up, it was an act that saw him shot dead. Not long after the incident, Captain Pollock was provided the opportunity to examine Sergeant Walker's body, which had been recovered to one of the buildings in the outer camp area.

These thought provoking entries written by Bernard Nutt are by no means isolated incidents; the guards at Heydekrug were renowned for being trigger happy. The ever-increasing numbers of prisoners imported into Heydekrug created serious overcrowding, a factor that did little to lessen the tension at that time. In anticipation of Nutt's impending birthday, his fellow barrack mates rallied round and put aside chocolate from their food parcels. They presented him with a present on 10 July, his twenty-first birthday. The hand painted label

The label attached to Bernard Nutt's twenty-first birthday parcel.

attached to his present was retained by Nutt and had great sentiment attached to it. He stuck it prominently on its own page inside his wartime log.

Just a few days after Nutt's birthday, news of Heydekrug being evacuated started to spread around the entire camp. In July 1944, the fortunes of war changed sufficiently enough for Stalag Luft VI to be at risk of liberation by the Eastern Front activity. It was to be a structured withdraw, with the Americans leaving first. The RAF and Commonwealth prisoners were to follow. Bernard Nutt made the entry: 'Moved from Heydekrug, transported in cattle trucks, departed 1900 hours 17 July. Arrived 2000 hours 18 July. Arrived at Thorn Army Camp after 25 hours travelling, the first Army Camp I have seen.' The much respected 'Dixie' Deans was, as ever, at the forefront. Concern was expressed as to how Thorn would be able to accommodate the massive influx of prisoners; it already held some 7,000 soldiers. Little imagination is required to understand the logistics of feeding these huge groups of men. Without the consistent supply of Red Cross food parcels, life would most probably have become unsustainable. Where food parcel stocks were held, significant impor-tation of prisoners was most likely to immediately reduce such stores, resulting in severe rationing that affected all prisoners. Thorn covered a large expanse; the camp accommodation included several Prussian forts, which lay about 100 miles north-west of Warsaw. The forts had been built in the 1800s, and were partially sunk in the ground, creating terrible conditions inside. Almost everywhere there were dank, slimy corridors, with water dripping continu-ously from the roof down the immensely thick walls. Infrequently spaced low wattage bulbs provided the only form of lighting. Apart from the forts, the prisoners slept on straw that was spread on the ground of large tents. Bernard Nutt found himself in far worse conditions than he had left, and he was keen to get out on a work party. The main camp was surrounded by several work camps, and Nutt misguidedly thought that food or fuel would be present, but it was not. He provides no further detail, but records on 25 July that an American was killed for being out late. That same day, Nutt's wartime log received 'Ode to Nothing', written by a prisoner who signed the book W. Burton:

I trust the execution
Of this little contribution
Makes it worthy of inclusion
In your book of souvenirs
But poetic dissertation
Through a charming recreation
Is devoid of inspiration
When the writer lacks ideas

It is obviously vital
That a poem have a title
Or a moral for recital
But to write without a theme
Or a story for assistance
Is a task that needs persistence
And in future my resistance
To requests will be extreme.

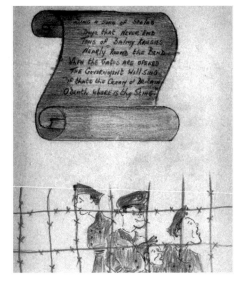

A song from the camp with the men behind the barbed wire.

The casualty mentioned by Nutt was Sergeant T. Stephens USAAF. In company with five other Americans, their escape attempt through the wire ended with the death of Stephens, who was shot while attempting the escape.

The conditions at Thorn quickly induced serious stomach problems for Nutt; dysentery was prevalent amongst most of the men. One primary reason was the water supply, which was pumped up from a well closely situated near a cesspool. At the end of July, Nutt was in a poor state of health. On 4 August news came of a further move, and although weak, the prospect of leaving the horrible camp was reason enough to endure what was about to be imposed upon him.

It was 1 p.m. on 6 August 1944, a very hot summer's day, when Bernard Nutt made his way to the railway station. The contingent of prisoners en route to Stalag 357, Fallingbostel, were crammed into the cattle trucks. The journey was appalling, with the hot weather and the men's body heat creating a stifling environment. When the prisoners arrived at Fallingbostel, conditions immediately improved. They were deloused and given a brief, but hot shower. Bernard makes only brief entries in his log from this point onwards. The reason for this is unknown, but it may well be that his life, and that of the hundreds that were with him, had become seriously difficult. Fallingbostel was a massive camp with fenced compounds. Its roots went back to the pre-war period when Fallingbostel was created as a large training camp for military expansion. The wooden buildings had deteriorated into poorly maintained units, which now held many more people than had ever been anticipated. It had been deployed as a prisoner of war camp by Germany since 1940, housing Polish, French, and Belgium prisoners of war. In 1941, the camp started to expand and house Russians. Typhus, a deadly disease, spread by the human louse, took a strong grip upon the thousands of Russian prisoners in 1942. The Russians in particular were not assisted greatly by their captors in combating these particularly horrid parasites, resulting in typhus taking the lives of many thousands. Living on the human body and in clothing, the lice lay eggs in the seams of underclothing and similarly sheltered places. Lice can live for four days without access to blood, but the best conditions for the spread of these lice are when humans are living close together in primitive conditions, making prisoner of war camps ideal. Body lice helped spread the typhus fever, along with trench fever and louse-borne relapsing fever. It was in the interests of all to carry out regular delousing sessions, with the prisoners consistently endeavouring to disrupt the life cycle of the lice by picking off the eggs that were laid within their clothing. This however, proved to be no more than a token effort in combating the endless problem.

By mid-1944, Fallingbostel camp and its sub-camps were holding 96,000 prisoners of war.[57] With the arrival of the RAF prisoners, 'Dixie' Deans continued with his elected duty as camp leader. Bernard Nutt made an entry in his log: 'Saw American bomber formations going over the camp, bags of alerts.' The daylight USAAF bombing missions had intensified, an example being the consistent raids during August in which the 8th Army Air Force bombed the aircraft factories and synthetic oil plants. These raids were consolidated by the RAF night operations in many instances.

The last few months of 1944 were grim, with food becoming very scarce and the news that filtered into the camp being not particularly good. The Allied invasion appeared to be progressing very slowly from the prisoners of war perspective. Fallingbostel provided little in the way of entertainment; survival became the primary thought for Bernard Nutt and his fellow prisoners. He referred to the time as his 'belting period', which related to his trouser belt requiring new holes to be punched, indicating his weight loss. Nutt had been a prisoner of war for a period rapidly approaching two years. Thoughts of his promotion crossed his mind. He calculated that he should have been a warrant officer by now. Nutt drew a couple of comical pencil references to support these thoughts. Clearly, Nutt's trust in the system was not quite what it should have been; no doubt many men expressed similar concerns during endless conversations about such matters.

'Dixie' Deans had ensured that the camp radio from Heydekrug had been well secured and disguised for the transit across Germany. Aware that a good security search was most likely to be undertaken on arrival at the new camp, it was hidden in a beautifully crafted model of a racing car; not an unusual possession for a prisoner to carry, much like the wartime logs. Feeling strongly about events in early January 1945, Nutt wrote, 'Germans started reprisals, take bedding and tables 14 January.' Morale took a tumble, for in addition to the near starving conditions, the prisoners lost their bedding at the height of winter. The reprisals were the result of apparent injustice to German prisoners of war, the facts of which were never established. Another day worthy of mention during this wretched period was 5 February. Nutt received his first cigarette parcel in over six months. This provided an opportunity to barter for food, but there was none to be had, and malnutrition was fast becoming evident. The conditions were now rife for an outbreak of Typhus. In March 1945, Nutt recorded the words, 'Still belting. Had one twentieth of one food parcel in a month. German rations cut, must think we can live on love.' 'Dixie' Deans was capable of assessing and resolving many situations. His leadership was in itself a most valued ingredient in the life of the men he represented. These were dark days of desperation. And Dean's ability to negotiate with camp commandants was never more tested than at Fallingbostel. He knew that Red Cross supplies would have accumulated in massive quantities at the port of Lubeck. Germany was in turmoil, resulting in the transportation of Red Cross food parcels not being high on anyone's list of priorities. Lubeck was no more than 70

Above left: Drawn by Bernard Nutt in Fallingbostel, 7 September 1944.

Above right: Comical characters drawn by Bernard Nutt.

or 80 miles away from the camp. Deans gained permission to make a journey to Lubeck in a van provided by the commandant. Being driven by a Russian and guarded by a German officer, the enterprise was successful. The Red Cross supplies were located and agreements made to dispatch two railway carriages stacked full of parcels. Deans and the German officer also returned to the camp with the van full of parcels. The two carriages of supplies, when eventually delivered, would equate to roughly half a parcel per man. The supplies in the van were distributed to the sick and most needy men.

These words were penned into Nutt's log:

> Only those who have been prisoners have any concept of the horrors of being a prisoner, or the ineffable joy of release, of the terrible rise and fall of spirit: the fluctuations between the delirium of happiness and madness of despair attendant upon the fluctuating hopes and fears as the possibility of release advances and retreats.

It was not until 29 March that the two goods trucks finally arrived. Nutt made a final pencil entry in his log that same day: 'Good Friday – what a great day, in more ways than one – a break in the belting period.' That final diary entry of Nutt's drew an end to his personal grief. The British had crossed the River Rhine on 24 March. Liberation would be imminent, and his hunger, which had been abated with the delivery of food parcels, would soon cease forever. But although the horrors of Fallingbostel looked as though they were drawing to an end, they were unfortunately to continue. On 5 April, 'Dixie' Deans received official orders from the commandant to abandon Fallingbostel. Nutt drew the events of such bad news in his log, entitled 'The Last Straw'.

Plans were drawn up to organise the withdrawal or evacuation of prisoners from Fallingbostel. Columns of men consisting of up to a thousand, each under the command of an individual leader, were instructed to leave with a separation between each column. 'Dixie' Deans organised one column to hold the radio and other important supplies. On the day prior to the withdrawal, the RAF had undertaken a significantly large bombing raid on Hannover. The smoke continued to rise in the distance, and with nightfall, the glow was clearly visible from the camp. These were terribly worrying times, with aerial activity and shelling from artillery causing routes to swell with German refugees. Deans had sought a way of covering ground between his columns of prisoners by pedal cycling. Always in the company of a German guard, this was a display of his concern and protection that was heart-warming to those thousands of men, with many suffering from various forms of illness, and all suffering from hunger. By design, Deans slowed the pace, knowing that liberation by British or Allied troops might occur at any time. The columns of men were spread out on differing routes, but all heading in the same direction. Deans carried a letter of authority from the commandant, permitting him to commute across the

Light-hearted sketches of the march between camps.

countryside. At night, he slept with whatever unit he was with, and if possible, with the radio operator. Liberation was not to be forthcoming, and offensive military action that was taking place all around the prisoners placed them in a confused and ultimately dangerous position. The guards were also unsure of the situation and well aware of their own vulnerability. Several prisoners died during the march; Captain Pollock RAMC was present when staff Sergeant

13

Shot While Escaping

Within the wartime logbooks, several men made reference to failed escape attempts that resulted in the participants losing their lives. Other incidents occurred that were supposedly interpreted by guards incorrectly, resulting in fatalities. 'Shot while escaping' was the term frequently adopted in official documentation created at the time. The Wehrmacht, as a culpable member of the Geneva Convention, were required to administer such eventualities in a formal process, as indicated within the following prescriptive document.

Supreme Command of the Wehrmacht, Berlin-Schoenberg, 16 June 1941.
Rules and regulations, in the case of a death in a
German prisoner of war camp.

In case of death of a prisoner of war, in addition to the report to the Information Bureau of the Wehrmacht, a special questionnaire must be immediately filled out and submitted to the German Red Cross, Berlin SW 61 Bluecherplatz 2, so that the relatives of the deceased can be notified without delay (Supreme Command of the Wehrmacht OKW file 2 F 24. 62a. Kriegsgef. Vi No. 135/11 dated 7 Jan. 1941). Direct notification of the next of kin of the deceased is not permitted. Double reports are to be avoided. Should the prisoner of war die while in a hospital, the camp is to be informed of the date on which the questionnaire has been forwarded to the German Red Cross. No questionnaires are to be filled out in cases of death of Russian prisoners of war.

23. Re: Cases of death of prisoners of war.

Reports to the Information Bureau of the Wehrmacht on deaths of prisoners of war and the corresponding notices to the German Red Cross through questionnaires are to be drawn up in such a way as to obviate the necessity of further time consuming inquiries.

The following is therefore to be observed:

1. The report of the death of a prisoner of war to the Information Bureau of the Wehrmacht must indicate the cause of death in exact accordance with the facts, and also give the place of death in a way to make the competent registrars office easily identifiable. It is not enough, for instance, to state: 'Shot'. Rather must it be worded: 'Shot while trying to escape', or 'Shot in execution of sentence pronounced by . . . on . . . ' It is likewise not enough to give as place of death merely 'Camp Erlensbusch', but rather 'Camp Erlensbusch near Village X'. The exact location of a work detail in a death report is essential even when such detail is located near a stalag, as it cannot be automatically assumed that the two places belong to the same registrar district.

2. The report on the death of a prisoner of war to the presidency of the German Red Cross constitutes the basis for the notification of the family of the deceased. The death notice is prepared by the German Red Cross and is transmitted to the next of kin through the local Red Cross office of the latter. The questionnaire proper is then forwarded by the German Red Cross to the International Red Cross in Geneva. In preparing the 'death-notice questionnaire', the following is to be observed:

   a. The questionnaire must be speedily & fully filled out and promptly forwarded to the Presidency of the German Red Cross, Berlin S W 61 Bluecherplatz 2. Only this agency is competent to receive such questionnaires. Sending same to any other agency is not permitted, even though the questionnaire was made up by the International Red Cross in Geneva.

   b. Careful formulation of the cause of death in case of unnatural death, as the questionnaire is to be sent abroad (International Red Cross).

   c. The nationality of the deceased must be given right after the name, and the name of the country after the address of his next of kin.

   d. The last question must be answered in the greatest detail, in so far as there are no objections to the answer becoming known abroad.

3. For the time being no questionnaire is to be filled out for deceased Soviet prisoners of war.

4. Deaths of prisoners of war are not to be reported to the protecting powers either by camp commandants, or by the spokesmen.

223. Re: Shooting & severe wounding of prisoners of war & civilian internees (except Poles, Serbs, and Soviet Russians).

An inquiry by a court officer or any other qualified officer is to be initiated in each case of fatal shooting or wounding of a British, French, Belgian, or American prisoner of war or civilian internee. If comrades of the prisoner of war or civilian internee were witnesses of the incident, they, too, will be heard. The result of the inquiry and a copy of the examination proceedings are to be submitted immediately to the OKW Kriegsgef. Aug. (Ia), reference being made to the file number below. This report is to be designated as 'Report on the use of arms by soldier X'. A detailed report against soldier X will be necessary only when there is a suspicion of the latter having committed a legally punishable act and when an immediate court decision appears desirable.

278. Re: Internment of fallen or deceased members of the enemy armed forces.

To remove any doubt as to whether prisoners of war shot during flight or in acts of insubordination are entitled to burial with military honours, the following is ordered:

1. As a matter of principle, every honourably fallen enemy is to be buried with military honours.
2. Flight is not dishonourable, unless dishonourable acts were committed during such flight.
3. Cases of insubordination must be individually examined as to whether acts reflecting on the soldier's honour have been committed. Where such violations of the soldiers code of honour have been established without question, military honours during burial are to be excluded.

840. Re: Killings and serious injuries of prisoners of war and civilian internees (except Poles, Serbs, and Russians).

The reference order has often not been observed, with the result that the OKW has had again and again to learn of cases of violent deaths of prisoners of war through the Ministry of Foreign Affairs or the protecting powers. This situation is unbearable in view of the reciprocity agreements with the enemy governments. The following additional orders are therefore announced herewith:

1. Every case of violent death or serious injury is to be promptly reported through channels to the OKW/Kriegsgef. Alig. (lib) (for exception see 2). In cases involving the use of arms, written depositions of the participants and witnesses, including prisoners of war, are to be attached; action is to be taken by the camp commandant and the prisoner of war Commander (Kommandeur).

    The name, camp, identification number, and home address of the prisoner of war involved must be given. Should a long search for these be necessary: a preliminary report is to be submitted at once, and the result of the search reported later.

    Reports are also necessary, in addition to cases involving the use of arms, in cases of accidents of all kinds, of suicides, etc.; written depositions of witnesses will be mostly unnecessary here.
2. Losses due to enemy action are to be reported immediately to the OKW/ Kriegsgef. Allg. (V) in the form prescribed by reference order to 2.

This official translation was issued after the war by the Liaison and Research branch of the American Prisoners of War Information Bureau. The original document encompasses a wealth of material in addition to the particular subject being addressed here. Clearly the term 'shot whilst escaping' has proven to be deployed in instances of calculated murder; none more blatant example than the Great Escape needs evidencing. However, there are a significantly high proportion of instances where circumstances indicate that the term has been used inappropriately, in effect clouding events where many options existed to guards within the prisoner of war camps. Unfortunately in many cases, the documentation files upon such incidences appear to have been destroyed, lost, or are otherwise unavailable to postwar research.

The RAF prisoner of war Bernard Nutt appeared to have had a friendship with fellow NCO Sergeant John Cecil Shaw. No direct link can be established by way of squadron service, or time served together, and both Sergeants were held in Stalag Luft I at different times. Shaw had been shot down on 7 December 1940. He was piloting a Hampden aircraft of 49 Squadron, engaged on a bombing mission upon Luftwaffe aerodromes in France. His aircraft had been badly damaged by anti-aircraft fire, resulting in a crash landing fifty miles south of Paris. The crew of four survived the crash, but medical assistance was obviously required. Heavy snow covered the ground. The twenty-one year old pilot assessed the situation, and the only option was to seek assistance for himself and his crew. Eventually, the Germans secured the crew, and after medical attention they joined the ranks within the camps. Within Shaw's crew was air gunner Sergeant O'Leary, and his wireless operator Sergeant David Young. It was Young who set off in the snow to seek help after the crash landing. Young became an avid escape artist and was involved in a tunnel escape from Stalag Luft I in which he and four others got away. Discovered by a German forester, they were detained and returned to the camp. Young was involved in two further attempts before moving to Stalag Luft III, where he once again managed to escape and become recaptured. Having been moved to Stalag Luft IV, he planned an escape underneath a food cart in 1944. Despite reaching a port in the hope of boarding a ship, he was once again recaptured. Finally, during a forced march away from his last camp, he made his fifth and final escape. During that final escape he came across an RAF sergeant who had been left by the Germans. He was suffering from a seriously poisoned leg. Young cared for him and remained with him in hospital for a week until he died. David Young's remarkable exploits as a prisoner of war were recognised by the award of the Military Cross in 1946.

Another member of this remarkable crew was the navigator, Pilot Officer Brian Evans. Evans had also been an avid escaper, and was later employed as a 'penguin' involved in the soil distribution of the Great Escape tunnel at Stalag Luft III. As an active member of the escape plot, Evans was allocated an early position in the line of escapees, and consequently managed to escape before the tunnel was discovered. He was recaptured at Halbau, and later selected as one of the fifty prisoners to be executed. Evans was last seen alive on 31 March 1944. He was murdered by 'Lux' and Scharpwinkel; the same men responsible for the murder of Flight Lieutenant Denys Street on 6 April 1944.

Returning to the last member of this amazing crew, Sergeant John Shaw was most probably involved with David Young's tunnel escapades, as well as going to the camp escape committee with his own plan. Stalag Luft I had been enveloped in snow in the new year of 1942. Shaw's simple plan was to take advantage of the snow and conceal himself within the white out. Using a white sheet, he proposed to crawl under the sheet to reach the wire, cut the wire and escape. In essence a most simple strategy, which was agreed as worthy of attempting by the escape committee. On the night of 4 January, Shaw commenced his plan. Progressing well, Shaw reached the wire with ease, but during the cutting, one of the guards operating a search light caught sight of what was taking place. One of the foot patrolling guards responded and challenged Shaw, who realised that his attempt had been foiled. Within the sequence of events, which probably occurred swiftly, Shaw responded by raising his hands and turning towards the guard. As he did so, he was fatally shot. Once again the reference 'shot whilst escaping' was to be documented.

Bernard wrote these words in his log:

They could not die a better death, or fight a finer cause.
Those who died for England's sake, died without a pause.
And in their death they wrote in trails across the sky.
A glorious name for England that will never age, nor die, that every Nation,
    friend or foe, will look to, and revere.
They died in glory, without fear.
So dry your eyes, cease those tears, they died with laughter in their wake.
And all they died for, they die again, ten times for England's sake.

In accordance with the Wehrmacht rules and regulations at the time, Sergeant John Shaw was provided with an honourable military funeral. Within his wartime log, Nutt pasted a series of photographs depicting the funeral of Sergeant Shaw. The funeral arrangement involved Shaw's elaborate coffin pulled by two ponies on a carriage, and exceptionally large floral tributes, complete with the wide ribbon that clearly displays the German Iron Cross and Swastika. These images are evidence of a most respectful process, which was known to exist between the RAF and the Luftwaffe. Shaw's crew mate David Young is identified at the funeral. It may prove difficult for the reader to correlate the apparent murder of Sergeant Shaw against what appears to be a lavish funeral provided by the Luftwaffe.

Above and below: Sergeant John Shaw's funeral, 1942. The three saluting officers: Commandant of Stalag Luft I, Major Burkhardt; Pilot Officer Brian Evans (crew member); and Wing Commander Day (Senior British Officer). Standing with the wreaths are Sergeant O'Leary and Sergeant Young (crew members).

Above and below: The scene at Sergeant Shaw's funeral.

Above and below: The Luftwaffe guard of honour 'firing party' at Sergeant Shaw's funeral.

Another photograph of the funeral with what appear to be unusually lavish arrangements by the Luftwaffe.

This contingent of men present at the funeral represented the entire crew that had crashed together, and were now standing at the graveside of their pilot. Just two years, later Brian Evans would be denied any such respect after his execution on the orders of Adolf Hitler. The Commonwealth War Graves Commission duly erected a headstone on Shaw's grave. At the request of his parents, the inscription on the footstone read: 'Just one of the few who were there in our hour of need.' The RAF forwarded Shaw's name to the King for the award of a Mention in Despatches. This was published as awarded on 2 June 1943. A mention in Despatches was the only form of award apart from the Victoria Cross that could be bestowed posthumously.

14

Mentioned in Despatches

The award of mentioned in Despatches (MID) arose in the eighteenth century after a detached commander in the British Army sent a report to London in a written despatch regarding the service of a deserving officer. The mention of the officer's name in the report could be published in the *London Gazette* to inform the public of the officer's bravery or merit. Other ranks were then included in the award from 1843. In 1902, the MID was formally recognised as an award when it was decreed that the mention must be published in the *London Gazette*. In 1919, the award was certified by the King, and in 1920 the emblem of a stylised oak leaf was presented to the person as an acknowledgement of the award. The MID was given for gallantry or valuable service and could be awarded posthumously.

Medals for service in the Second World War were accordingly determined by the Monarch on the advice of the British Government. In June 1946, following the end of the War, a United Kingdom committee known as the Committee on the Grant of Honours, Decorations and Medals produced a document setting out the conditions for the award of war medals and campaign stars. This document, known as Command Paper 6833, determined the Committee on the Grant of Honours, Decorations and Medals in time of War 1939-1944. It suggested the Battle of Britain clasp to the 1939-43 Star in the Air Ministry memorandum submitted by Sir Arthur Street and Air Vice-Marshal Harries on 11 July 1944.[68]

The command paper also referred to the MID, and provided that, 'The single bronze oak leaf emblem signifying in the Forces and the Merchant Navy, either Mention in Despatches [...] will, if granted for service in the war of 1939-45, be worn on the ribbon of the War Medal.'

The paper did not set out the conditions for the award of the MID. A quota system existed for the award of the MID, which determined that there could be 1 award for every 250 persons in a six month period. This restriction did not apply in the case of Prisoner of war.

The MID and Prisoners of War

In a British Army order published on 5 May 1919, the Army council decided that prisoners of war:

> May be considered appropriate [for the award of the MID] provided that no blame has been attached to the individual in respect of original capture – Exceptional service rendered by officers and soldiers, whilst prisoner of war or interned. Exceptionally gallant conduct and/or determination displayed by officers and soldiers in escaping or attempting to escape captivity.

In October 1942, the British War Office policy was to reward those prisoners of war who showed 'outstanding performance.' The policy quoted the 1919 Army order, noting that prisoners of war would be 'eligible for the same gallantry distinctions as are normally reserved for service under fire', and that the leader of a party that escaped should receive a higher award.

In November 1943, the Imperial Prisoners of War Committee decided that, 'prisoners of war belonging to the Royal Navy, Army and Royal Air Force who were killed while trying to escape shall be regarded as eligible for consideration for the award of a posthumous Mention in Despatches.' The committee suggested that the following procedure be adopted to determine eligibility: 'The Directorate of Prisoners of War [were] to collect information from all sources concerning all prisoners of war killed while attempting to escape.' The immediate MI9 IS9 prisoner of war debriefing reports exposed significant evidence for such award recognition as well as war crime investigations. The procedure continued:

> This information would be passed on in the case of Dominion [...] personnel to the Dominion representative concerned [...] for confirmation or for further information.
>
> The Directorate of Prisoners of War would then decide in the light of all the evidence available whether the escape should be considered as genuine, and if it is considered genuine should submit the facts to the Honours and Awards Branch of the Service concerned or to the Dominions [...] representative for consideration for an award. The decision whether or not a recommendation for an award should be made will be the sole discretion of the Honours and Awards Branch of the service concerned, or to the dominions.

On 16 February 1944, the defence committee noted the decision made by the Imperial Prisoners of War Committee and expressed the opinion that 'the same consideration should be given to prisoners of war belonging to the Commonwealth Forces who are killed while trying to escape'.

Prisoners of War in Europe

For the most part, Germany complied with the Geneva Convention, and escaped prisoners were not shot as a matter of course upon being recaptured. The exception to this was the escape from Stalag Luft III. The award of the MID was applied en masse to the Stalag Luft III escapees because of the extraordinary circumstances of that case.

Individual cases are additionally evidenced. Sergeant Alan Ronald Cook, a wireless operator serving in 101 Squadron, scrambled clear of his crashed Wellington Bomber near Mannheim on the night of 28 August 1942. Cook was captured almost immediately, and later held in the prisoner of war camp at Lamsdorf. On 19 June 1943, he and other prisoners were employed in a work detail nearby Lobden. In company with Sapper Douglas Arthur of the Royal Engineers and Private Albert Parker from the Gloucestershire Regiment, the three men attempted an escape. All three men were subsequently shot and killed; they were each posthumously awarded a Mention in Dispatches on 8 June 1944. The camp newspaper *The Clarion* reported their deaths to the main camp contingent.

The Mention in Dispatches bronze oak leaf was awarded with a small dedication certificate signed by the Secretary of State for the air. A total of 37,508 MIDs were awarded to members of the Royal Air Force during the Second World War: 2,200 to the Royal Canadian Air Force; 1,797 the Royal Australian Air Force; 548 to the Royal New Zealand Air Force; 719 South African air Force; 63 awards to the Royal Indian Air Force.[69]

An example of the award of a Mention in Despatches relative to actions within a prisoner of war camp would be the award to Warrant Officer John William Brodie Snowdon. This pilot had been in the custody of the Luftwaffe from 1941 to 1945, during which he was moved between several different camps. As an active participant in escape activity and member of various escape committees, Snowdon achieved complete escapes on two occasions. The first escape was on Christmas Eve 1941, when Snowdon cut the wire at Lamsdorf and remained at large until being recaptured in mid-January 1942. The other escape was from Stalag Luft VII on the last day of the month in June 1943. He was recaptured this time by the Gestapo during the following month. John Snowdon's prisoner of war activities were recognised by the award of an MID, published in the *London Gazette* on 31 January 1947. The infamous Douglas Bader was similarly recognised in that same gazette entry for his activity as a prisoner of the Luftwaffe. John Snowdon had been an RAF apprentice at Halton, and was an exceptionally well respected warrant officer within the prison camps. He was with Roger Bushell in Stalag Luft III and no doubt took part in the planning of the Great Escape. His historic escaping activity saw him listed as a suspect by the Germans, and he was duly selected alongside several hundred prisoners for removal into the newly constructed camp of Belaria.

15

Squadron Leader Roger Bushell and Flight Lieutenant Peter Cazenove

Roger Bushell's name frequently appears, synonymously connected to his inspirational leadership and ingenuity, which culminated in the Great Escape in 1944. There is another connection to this infamous man that the author has undertaken to explore. Namely, Bushell's connection to the medals awarded to Peter Cazenove; a humble group of medals consisting of the 1939-1945 Star, Aircrew Europe Star, British War Medal, and the Air Efficiency Award. This particular group of medals has no wartime log to accompany them, but they provide a reason to tell the story of Bushell and Cazenove, two 92 Squadron Spitfire pilots who became bound together by fate after both men were incarcerated in the German Stalag Luft camps in 1940.

Born into an illustrious city stockbroking dynasty, Peter Cazenove provided the period portrayal of a wartime fighter pilot. Cazenove had been educated at Eaton College between 1921 and 1925. After leaving school, he experienced life in Argentina, working for the Fray Bentos Company. On returning to his home country, Cazenove joined his father in a new stockbroking venture, which provided a most comfortable lifestyle. Cazenove joined the Royal Air Force Volunteer Reserve as one of the weekend fliers of 615 Squadron. The book *Twenty-One Squadrons* by Leslie Hunt holds a photograph of Peter Cazenove dated 1 September 1938. Many of the student pilots of that time came from privileged lifestyles. Unfortunately, financial difficulties presented themselves to the Cazenove's venture. Eventually, these difficulties proved insurmountable, and on 18 August 1939, the *London Gazette* published that he had been made bankrupt. His address was 442 Nell Gwynne House, Sloane Avenue, Chelsea.[70] Having been declared bankrupt, Peter obligingly resigned from the Royal Air Force Reserve as a matter of expectancy and personal pride.

The outbreak of war that same year provided an opportunity to reapply to the Royal Air Force. At the age of thirty-two, the vast majority of applicants would have been at least ten years younger than Cazenove. His previous qualifications provided the key to his rapid acceptance into the RAF, who were in desperate need of qualified pilots. Cazenove was promoted to Flying Officer,

The medals awarded to Peter Cazenove.

initially serving as a flying instructor before quickly receiving a posting with 92 Squadron. Roger Bushell had also been an academic and was educated at Pembroke College, Cambridge, where he studied law. Similar to Cazenove, Bushell had joined the Auxiliary Air Force. He served in 601 Squadron, known as The Millionaires due to the number of wealthy young men within its group. Bushell was a flight lieutenant with 601 Squadron when the war began. He was soon promoted to Squadron Leader, and on 10 October 1939 was selected for the task of formulating 92 Squadron. Peter Cazenove was to be one of his officer pilots.

The squadron existed only in number or name; in effect, Bushell was tasked with creating a new squadron built around himself. Bushell set to work making the squadron effective and ready for operational deployment. Training was carried out in the crew's allocated Blenheims, and the squadron was relocated to Gatwick, and then onto Croydon. On 5 March 1940, 92 Squadron traded in their Blenheims for new Mark I Spitfires. This was a welcome decision for pilots like Cazenove and Bushell, but the air gunners and observers, who had little time to settle in, were once again posted. The squadron operational records inform that eight Spitfires were received from No. 9 Maintenance Unit, RAF Cosford, and thirteen Spitfires from No. 27 Maintenance Unit, RAF Shawbury.

On 9 May, the squadron moved to Northolt. Seven Spitfires departed in the morning, with Bushell leading another nine to Northolt in the afternoon. The following day, the Germans invaded Holland and Belgium. Peter Cazenove flew twice that day; a sector reconnaissance in the morning and formation flying in the afternoon. Sector reconnaissance sorties were important to pilots, allowing them to plot landmarks and aerodromes; invaluable information when returning from operations with little fuel or bad battle damage. 92 Squadron remained at readiness from that time onwards, and in the following week they flew numerous training sorties. On 14 May, the squadron continued training, with Cazenove embarking on practice attacks in the morning and in the evening, practice dusk landings followed by a night sector reconnaissance, from which he safely landed his aircraft at 11.35 p.m.

During the afternoon of May 15, Peter Cazenove took up Spitfire P9374, the aircraft in which he always chose to fly if possible. Cazenove wanted to push himself and achieve the best possible standard in the air, knowing that engagements with the Luftwaffe fighters were imminent. He performed aerobatics in a thirty-five minute period of intense activity. These training sessions allowed pilots to hone their combat skills, for chasing or evading a fighter in the sky was not an easily gained skill.

On 16 May, three Spitfires from 92 Squadron escorted a Flamingo aircraft carrying the Prime Minister Winston Churchill to Le Bourget airport, near Paris. The DH95 Flamingo aircraft were part of No. 24 Squadron, operating from RAF Northolt on communication and air transport duties. De Havilland built very few of these particular aircraft. Churchill and Eden independently used a Flamingo from this squadron during May and June, and General de Gaulle escaped from France in a Flamingo on 18 June 1940.

The De Havilland 'Flamingo' aircraft, as used by Winston Churchill.

On 19 May, Peter Cazenove took Spitfire P9373 on a lone sector reconnaissance, which proved to be uneventful for him. The following day he was once again engaged in further operational practice, flying simulated aerial attacks. On the morning of 23 May 1940, 92 Squadron received orders for a combat operation, briefed to fly sorties aimed at intercepting German bombing raids against the British and French forces trapped by the German advance into Northern France. The squadron took off early and flew to Hornchurch, where they refuelled and given a full operational briefing. 92 Squadron were deployed for a patrol over the French coast, with Roger Bushell leading the twelve Spitfires who flew down the coast on offensive patrol. They flew over Calais, Boulogne, and Dunkirk but there was no sign of the hundreds of JU 87 Stukas that were supposed to be dive bombing the British troops. Flying closely together, the formation flew up and down the coast for what seemed like hours. Suddenly and without warning, the German fighters struck, with Cazenove's best friend and confidant Pat Learmond becoming the first casualty. Learmond's Spitfire suffered serious damage during that initial hail of fire from the Luftwaffe fighters, and flames were seen streaming from it as he tried to control the stricken aircraft. Immediately, the whole formation split up. Bushell was yelling orders but he couldn't be heard above the many reports shouted by his pilots. The sky appeared to be full of ME109 Luftwaffe fighters. The manic aerial fight was a brutal introduction to the war that had cost 92 Squadron dearly. The pilots Green, Bryson, Bartley, and Tuck had each attacked and assumedly destroyed an ME 109. The total score for the squadron was reported to the intelligence officer as six ME 109s, with the loss of Pat Learmond, whose burning wreck had been seen to crash on the French coast beach line.

During the attack, Bushell had engaged in an individual fight with a ME109, turning, chasing, and fighting to get in a position to shoot it down. But cloud prevented him from doing so. He was immensely disappointed on his return to the aerodrome, but it would not be long before Bushell would return to France; the squadron's Spitfires were being made ready for another operation. 92 Squadron took off again that same day from Hornchurch. Roger Bushell led a patrol that had been briefed to provide aerial cover for the evacuation of the British Expeditionary Force from France. They crossed the channel low and then climbed to about 12,000 feet for the patrol and reconnaissance some twenty miles inland of Calais and Dunkirk. The Squadron records indicate that forty Messerschmitt's had been engaged, and once more, the intensity of the battle had reduced the radio communication to no more than a melee of shouts. Bushell was thrust into a fight for his life with a number of Messerschmitt's surrounding him. He succeeded in bringing one German aircraft into his sights and shooting it down, but his Spitfire had sustained fatal damage in the action; it was trailing smoke and rapidly losing height. Fortunately, Bushell made a safe landing, planting his Spitfire onto a grassy field.

Bushell's Czech accomplice Jack Zafouk was immediately dispatched to Colditz, while Bushell he was taken to Berlin, suspected of being involved in the Heydrich affair. Bushell's identity was later formally established, and fortunate for him, the decision was taken to transport him direct to Stalag Luft III. This appears to be a strange decision, as one would have presumed he would have followed Jack Zafouk to Colditz. At Stalag Luft III, Bushell was quickly brought onto the escape committee, which was headed at that time by Lieutenant Commander James 'Jimmy' Brian Buckley DSC, a Royal Navy Fleet Air Arm pilot who won the Distinguished Service Cross in July 1940.[74] Bushell had known Buckley at Dulag Luft, and they joined forces to create a most productive team. It was around this time that another colleague and friend, Peter Cazenove, joined Roger Bushell in Stalag Luft III, after not having seen each other for three years. Cazenove spoke of his own escape attempts. In Stalag Luft I, he had planned an escape using forged papers and had walked out of the main gate in disguise with flight lieutenants Leeson and Plant. Leeson had been a fellow Auxiliary Air Force pilot in 605 Squadron, and like Bushell and Cazenove, was shot down in the same conflict on 23 May 1940. Leeson was later moved into Stalag Luft III where they once again joined forces.

Cazenove immediately joined the escape committee having been sponsored by Bushell, and in the spring of 1943, Bushell announced the most ambitious escape plan of the war. It was the conception of the Great Escape. He planned that three very long and deep tunnels would be simultaneously dug, codenamed 'Tom', 'Dick', and 'Harry'. The most radical aspect of the plan was not merely the scale of the construction, but the sheer number of men that Bushell intended to pass through these tunnels. Previous attempts had involved the escape of anything up to a dozen or twenty men, but Bushell was proposing to get in excess of 200 out, all of whom would be wearing civilian clothes and possessing a complete range of forged papers and escape equipment. It was an unprecedented undertaking that would require unparalleled planning and execution. As the mastermind of the Great Escape, Roger Bushell inherited the codename of 'Big X'.

During the summer of 1943, all of the tunnels had commenced. However, it was at this time the sight of Russian prisoners cutting down trees outside the camp outlined the intention to build a separate area for the American prisoners. This would prevent the Americans the chance to escape through the tunnel on which they had worked. Bushell decided that the escape committee must do all they could to help the American prisoners. He decided to abandon 'Dick' and 'Harry' in order to put the entire tunnelling effort into 'Tom'. This was a risky proposal, as increased activity could give 'Tom' away, and it was by no means certain that the tunnel would be completed before the new compound had been built.

It appeared that, in spite of the tunnel being dug far below the surface, the microphone detection equipment deployed around the perimeter of the camp had picked up some activity. In the normal and predictable fashion, the 'ferrets' carried out several raids on various barracks, including a most extensive search of barrack 123. However, it was searched again and due to a most unfortunate and completely freak accident on the part of a 'ferret', the entrance to 'Tom' was discovered. Bushell immediately gave the order that 'Harry' should be reopened and pushed on into the woods. The Germans destroyed tunnel Tom and relished in the fact they had prevented such an elaborate escape tunnel.

Work continued on 'Harry', and by February 1944 the tunnel was nearing completion. On 24 March 1944, 'Harry' was declared ready for use, but unfortunately, the weather could not have been worse. The ground was covered with six inches of snow. The general rule was that winter was not the time to make an escape, especially for those who would have to travel cross-country, leaving a trail of their footsteps and suffering from frozen feet. The onerous decision to go would rest entirely upon Bushell's shoulders. If he delayed, it would expose the tunnel to possible discovery by the ever inquisitive 'ferrets'. In his favour, the moon was right and the train timetable was known.

Bushell may well have had representations from his escape committee with recommendations suggesting to delay the attempt for another month, but the tunnel diggers knew that the probable April downpours would put additional pressure on the tunnel. The decision was finally made; Bushell wanted to let the planned escape run. Instructions were given to the team of forgers who only needed to stamp Friday's date on all of the papers, after which everything was ready. Peter Cazenove was excited about the prospect of such a strong plan coming together, but despite his involvement, he was not going to take part. Once again, his height and physique acted against him in an escape; the tunnel was not built for a frame such as his. Another significant individual who worked tirelessly in the escape plan, Pilot Officer Alex Cassie, suffered a similar fate. After a visit to inspect tunnel 'Harry', he experienced claustrophobia and voluntarily stepped aside for fear of impeding the escape. Cassie was engaged in the forgery department and the majority of his fellow forgers were incorporated in the numbers of potential escapees. Their friendship bond is evidenced by the fact that Cassie retained personal letters from them to be sent to their families in the event of tragic circumstances.

On the night of the escape, Bushell and a free French pilot called Bernard Scheidhauer[75] were to escape together in positions towards the front of the tunnel. The first positions were reserved for those who were considered most likely to succeed. It was whilst they were waiting in the tunnel that news came back that the tunnel exit was next to the first line of the fir trees and that they were twenty feet short of any kind of cover. A rope was sought; this would serve as an improvised signalling device between the tunnel and the woods. Once the rope had been produced, the first man climbed out of the tunnel and signalled to Harry Marshall, who was number one at the head of the tunnel, that it was safe to come out and set up the rope around a tree. Marshall did this, and when he saw that the sentry was moving away from him he tugged the rope to signal his escape partner Ernst Valenta to come out, quickly followed by Roger Bushell and Bernard Scheidhauer.

As Marshall and Valenta disappeared into the woods together, Bushell took his turn on the rope and when it was safe he signalled for the next man to come out. Content in the knowledge that the improvised procedure of escape was being passed to each man, Bushell and Scheidhauer then headed into the woods.

Bushell always favoured the use of trains as the best means of getting away from an escape as quickly as possible, so as planned they made for the railway station where they awaited the 3.30 a.m. service to Breslau. Amongst the second class carriages on which they travelled were a further six escapees. The train arrived at Breslau at 5.00 a.m. The tunnel was eventually discovered by a guard, but only seventy-six men had escaped. Unfortunately, Bushell and Scheidhauer were the first escapees to be recaptured. Early on 26 March they had reached Saarbrücken without incident, but they were arrested when police inspected their papers and spotted a minor fault. On 29 March 1944, Roger Bushell and Bernard Scheidhauer were murdered in cold blood; a tragic end for the very brave men who sought to be free and eventually return to the sky in order to continue the fight against the Third Reich.

Bushell's friend Peter Cazenove remained as a prisoner of war and heard the news of the murder of Bushell and forty-nine other escapees. It must have crossed his mind that, but for his size, he might have been able to take part in the escape and been murdered also. His entire service had some association with Roger Bushell, who he regarded in the highest esteem possible. For Alex Cassie, the reality of ensuring the safety of the personal letters and other items handed to him by his forging colleagues who had lost their lives in the escape sat heavily on his shoulders.[76] After his liberation, it immediately became a priority for him to ensure the material was delivered as promised.

Peter Cazenove made no reference in his MI9 report of having taken part in the forced march from Stalag Luft III. He was repatriated to England where he later married his wife in November 1945. They subsequently moved to Nairobi, the capital of Kenya, where he became a representative for a British company, alongside setting up a smallholding that made use of the diploma he had gained in the prisoner of war camp. His marriage unfortunately ended, but upon returning to England, he married Edna Hollis in 1956, and they moved to Ghana. When they eventually returned to England, Cazenove settled on the South Coast, Sussex. He died on 7 December 1980. Had he lived just six weeks longer, he would have seen the media reports exposing the facts that his Spitfire P9374 had risen from the shifting sands exactly where he had left it forty years previously. His wife recalls that he posed the question, 'I wonder what happened to my Spitfire,' shortly before he died.

Peter Cazenove's Spitfire was recovered from its sandy grave and painstakingly restored to flying condition. In 2011, Spitfire P9374 gained its certification to take to the skies once more. When it did so, it was still carrying the exact identification serials and squadron lettering that had been displayed when Peter Cazenove had engaged the Luftwaffe in the sky over Calais on 24 May 1940.

16

Flight Sergeant Frank Wells

Frank Wells was born in 1923 and raised in Middlesex. He volunteered to join the RAF immediately after his nineteenth birthday. Wells was destined to become a fully qualified flight engineer within Bomber Command, and fly in the impressive Avro Lancaster. Passing through the conversion unit at RAF Winthorpe, and then number five Lancaster Flying School, he was finally posted onto 106 Squadron, based at RAF Metheringham, Lincolnshire.

In order to not provide any intelligence to the Germans, Wells purposely avoided illustrating the squadron code lettering in his PoW log sketch. He has however identified his aircraft which carried the identification letter 'L'. The manufacture serial number of the aircraft was ME668, a relatively new aircraft, having only completed two operations with 106 Squadron. Frank progressed well with his tour of duty, completing nineteen successful missions between 22 April 1944 and July 1944. It is at this point in time that we examine his final departure from RAF Metheringham where he was to attack the flying bomb storage facility located at St Leu d'Esserent, France. Winston Churchill described the facility in the following way:

> The main storage depots for the Flying Bombs (VI or doodlebugs) in France now lay in a few natural caverns around Paris, long exploited by the French mushroom growers. One of these caverns at Saint Leu d'Esserent in the Oise Valley, was rated by the Germans to store 2,000 bombs, and it had supplied 7 per cent of all bombs fired to us in June. In July, it was largely destroyed by Bomber Command.

It had taken several return trips to achieve this success, and Wells had been on the last operation. 106 Squadron suffered badly that night. Five Lancasters failed to return, and thirty-six men had been lost. Germany's ability to predict the target led towards mass night fighters being held in the ideal positions to intercept the Lancasters. Wells' aircraft was a true Commonwealth contingent. Two crew members were from Canada, two from Australia, and the remaining three from the United Kingdom. Only the mid-upper gunner

Sergeant Frank Wells 106 Squadron Lancaster, as drawn by him in his wartime log.

Sergeant Gladstone joined Frank in the other ranks; the remainder of the crew consisted of officers. The pilot was Flight Lieutenant Marchant RAAF. The Lancaster crew lifted off the runway at 10.35 p.m., gaining height and being navigated according to instructions towards the turning point and France.

The story of events is described in the words of Sergeant Wells:

When I awoke, the sun was streaming into the billet. I dressed, went to the flights, and learned that a raid had been planned for that night. The raid schedule was up and we were detailed to fly on the operation.

In the afternoon I was told by a colleague that it would be a tough target, because a few people had mentioned the target to him, although he was not flying. After briefing, the crew drove out to the aircraft in the private cars we had, and made arrangements to go into Nottingham the next evening in them. Little did I realise that within three hours I would be suspended over France by parachute.

The take-off was the same as on previous operations. The only difference to me was the fact that my pal Eric was not flying, so he visited us at the air-craft, then waved us off at the end of the runway, we flew on our way to the south coast in the normal way. When we came to the French coast, we could clearly see the gun fire from the beaches around Caen.

Just as we crossed over the mouth of the River Sein, a lot of fighter activity came into being. Fighter flares shot out all around our aircraft so we corkscrewed for a short while. When we resumed straight and level, one of the engines, the starboard inner, caught fire. I feathered it and put out the fire. Everybody, especially me, was very pleased we had been able to put it out, so we all settled down ready to bomb.

When we were about a quarter of an hour away from the target, we saw the flares go down. At that moment a line of red tracer shells shot over our port mainplane. We took evasive action, but it was too late. The aircraft was on fire all along the bomb doors. The skipper ordered us to bale out, so I went back through the smoke, got his chute, fixed it on his harness and helped him hold back the control column. The rear gunner shouted he could not get out but I don't know why.

Postwar enquiries established that captain Flight Lieutenant Marchant RAAF reported that the wireless operator Warrant Officer Bell, rear gunner Flying Officer Paterson, and mid-upper gunner Sergeant Gladstone lost their lives while still in the air. Flight engineer Sergeant Wells and air bomber Flying Officer Kinnis both baled out around 12,000 feet. Lancaster ME668 went into a shallow spin. It had been governable, but with no lateral control, Wells' cockpit was blown away, allowing him to bale out at an estimated 500 feet.[77] His story continues:

The floor was burning around my feet, so I fixed my chute on, pulled the rip cord and dived through the hatch that the bomb aimer had opened. The next thing I knew, I was falling through space with my chute trailing above me. The trouble was that it had not opened correctly, and I was getting too near the earth, so I pulled down the canopy and managed to untangle it. The silk blossomed out and I hit the earth in a small wood. After snapping off my harness I ran into a ploughed field and saw the aircraft burning about a quarter of a mile away. I could see the very cartridges popping out so I considered it useless for me to try and get out anyone left inside.

The remains of Flying Officer Hardcastle, Sergeant Gladstone, and Flying Officer Paterson were later buried together in the cemetery at Oulines, France. Sadly, the body of Warrant Officer Bell was never located.

The next thing that flashed across my mind was escape. I took out my escape kit, found a compass and set off on a cross-country heading south-west. After crossing several fields I came to a small lane, the hedge on the far side was too steep for me to climb, so I walked down to an opening which was a suitable place for me to get through.

Just as I was going through the gate I heard someone shouting for me. I turned around and walked towards them. I found it to be two German soldiers but they were more surprised than I was, for they were shouting for some other comrades. They gave me a quick search, then put me in a lorry

identifiable uniform. Flying battledress jackets that displayed no flying brevets tended to indicate it was a replacement uniform from resources like these. In addition, the Red Cross provided significant and consistent food supplies to this particular camp. The YMCA had also constructed a library, which ended up holding 1,500 books, as well as other recreational supplies.

Ernst Leitz was a large factory complex in Wetzlar. It began in 1849 as an optical institute under the direction of Carl Kellner. During the Second World War, it was producing optical scopes for a multitude of military equipment. Ernst Leitz was responsible for bringing to the world a high quality compact camera that changed the face of 35 mm photography. Incredibly, after dogged research by a British rabbi, it has since emerged that Ernest Leitz, 'the second', had a secret and possibly greater claim to fame, that of saving Jews from Nazi persecution in pre-war Germany.

Days after Hitler's rise to power, Leitz began taking on a string of young Jewish apprentices from the town of Wetzlar. His optics factory began producing Leica cameras in 1925. He purposely trained the young Jewish apprentices so that he could transfer them to New York to work in the Leica showroom on Fifth Avenue, or at distributors across the United States, thus rescuing them from the fate that was to befall many other Jews. The numbers he saved were below 100 in total, but the risks he took were worthy of recognition.[81] The hidden cameras secreted in prisoner of war camps across Germany provided the essential means to produce fake identity documentation. Ironically, many of those cameras had been produced at Ernst Leitz's factory.

At 12 p.m. on 17 July, Frank Wells was removed from the transit camp at Wetzlar, exactly five days after his arrival. In company with other prisoners who were to be transferred to permanent camps, he was advised that the journey would take a few days. Wells was en route to Stalag Luft VII, Poland. Frank had left what was arguably the best Stalag Luft camp. Soon he was going to experience the complete opposite at the most basic Bankau camp within what was now regarded as Germany.

At 7 a.m. on 20 July, Frank marched through the gates into Stalag Luft VII. Subjected to the obligatory search, Frank was once more photographed and his identity allocated to the card index system that was adopted at every camp. Generally, the first prison camp identity number allocated would remain with an individual during their time in captivity. Wells was allocated number 357.

Wells created a personal tribute to his crew which remained incomplete, with the lower panel empty, as the fate of his wireless operator from Australia was unknown to him. Sadly, it continues to remain unknown to this day. His sacrifice is commemorated on the The Runnymede Memorial, where airmen and women lost in operations from bases in the United Kingdom and north-west Europe without known graves can be remembered. Hilton Craig Bell RAAF is amongst the 1,393 Australian names commemorated amongst the 20,389 who were denied a grave.

Despite the lack of writing and drawing material, the completion of Wells' wartime log became a favoured past time for him. Several sketches were completed with a significantly reduced range of crayon colours.

Frank was allocated to hut 111. Fortunately, it was also the hut allocated to three of the men that had travelled with him from the jail in Paris. This small group of aviators were to develop a close, long-standing friendship. Wells recorded their home details in his log:

Flight Sergeant Bill Turner, 84 Chewton Road, Walthamstow, London E17
Flight Sergeant John Brook, 132 Duke Street, Southport, Lancs.
Sergeant Cyril Van-De-Velde, 1 Palmer Avenue, Loughborough, Leics.
Sergeant Henry Garratt, 'Westfield', Branston Heath, Lincoln.

It was a very small barrack hut measuring only 16 feet long and less than 8 feet wide. There was certainly no room to have more than single bunks, as the height to roof was only 5 feet 6 inches, and the roof pitch allowed the men to stand upright only when positioned in the middle of the room. This intimate

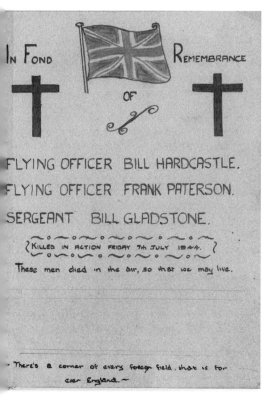
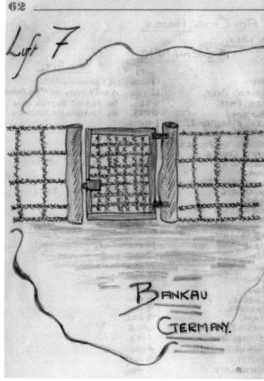

Above left: Frank Wells' personal tribute composed in his wartime log.

Above right: A crayon drawing by Frank of the Stalag Luft 7 Bankau gates.

hut was identified by the sign 'Clueless Cabin', which hung upon the entrance door. Immediately behind the hut ran the no man's land area, and then the twin barbed wire fence lines. Around the hut were two areas of cultivation where Frank grew what he could in the rather barren soil. This unusually small accommodation provided the most basic requirements for the group of friends who did their best to personalise it, choosing to endure their time in captivity in the best way possible. Due to the small dimensions of the huts in Bankau, the men called them the 'dog kennels'.

On 17 August 1944, a stunning watercolour of a venue most likely to have been a public house was created in Wells' logbook. In all probability it had been drawn in that particular hut.

The 'dog kennels' had no electricity, and just one water pump providing for upwards of 800 men. New construction was taking place for expansion into what was referred to as 'the new camp'. It is safe to say that Frank Wells would have been eager to leave as soon as possible. He was aware that the new barracks were massive in comparison to the old huts. Living in such close proximity to the other occupants of Hut 111 brought periods of high tension. Yet the men were relieved that the summer brought longer daylight hours, as with no electricity supply, the 'dog kennels' would have been soul destroying in the winter. Fitted with extremely small windows, very little daylight would get into the room regardless of the time of the year. Every basic need, such as washing, feeding, and toilet functions involved a high level of patience from the inmates at Bankau. Retiring to the bunk was not a great option for any comfort. In keeping with the majority of German prisoner of war camps, mattresses were initially filled with wood bark chip. These rapidly broke down into dust and required topping up or refilling on a regular basis. Regardless of the age of the filling they provided little comfort, but were regarded as better than nothing.

On Monday 18 September 1944, Wells decided to write up a full record of events in diary form, which he maintained until Saturday 5 May 1945. This valuable addition to his logbook evidences his life in great detail, including the period between 19 January and 5 February 1945, the period in which Wells was to endure his own enforced march. These entries provide a personal and factual account of events that produced extreme hardship and loss of life to Allied prisoners of war during the Second World War.

During September, Wells was troubled by a boil over his right eye, and the lack of proper medical treatment saw it cut open on 23 September with a pair of scissors. Towards the end of the month, the weather turned and the prospect of winter dawned as the first three days of October were engulfed in continuous rain. Being confined to the chicken coop of a hut did not help, but news came through that the new camp was ready, and this provided hope of better conditions for the prisoners. The move arrived at 9 a.m. on 13 October. The non-commissioned officers were allocated their respective barrack, each of which was 144 feet long and 40 feet wide; absolutely huge when compared

'The Horse and Groom', painted on 17 August 1944.

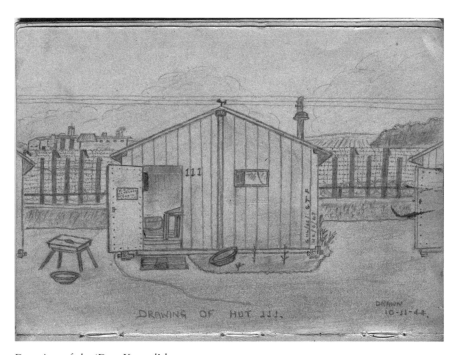

Drawing of the 'Dog Kennel' hut 111.

to the inadequate accommodation they had left in the old camp. Each barrack consisted of fourteen rooms, with a central corridor. Each of the rooms were designed to accommodate as many prisoners as possible, with sufficient space for six or eight double bunks. The barrack occupied by Wells was number 46, which held 117 men. He was allocated room 10, which housed eight double bunks. The room was 24 feet long and 16 feet wide. The inwardly opening door was roughly central to the room's length, and directly opposite the door were two inwardly opening windows, with the bunks fitted around the four walls. The rooms each had a small and rather ineffective fuel stove.

The barracks were wooden and elevated off the ground by blocks. This exposed a gap of some 3 feet between the soil and the floor of the barrack. The ground under each barrack was raked clear, enabling the 'ferrets' to see any ground disturbance that would then always be investigated. The 'ferrets' were known to place stones or other moveable items as markers, which acted as quick reference points for soil disturbance.

There were eight of these newly constructed barracks. The camp was also supported by a new kitchen, store room, toilet blocks, electricity, and an adequate water supply. It was a significantly improved environment that was very much appreciated by the men who now lived amongst the barbed wire boundaries and watchtowers whose night time searchlights systematically swept the grounds; elements that never changed. Wells had become attached to the small, personal garden he had in the old camp. Before he left, he pulled a few reminders of the flowers that he successfully grew and stuck them into the card pages within his wartime logbook.

The YMCA book was conceived and delivered to the camps for just this type of use. These dried flowers provided Frank Wells with irreplaceable memories from the time they were introduced into the book in late 1944. Wells also spent considerable time on an incredibly detailed scale drawing of his barrack block, his room, and the general layout of the camp.

The rooms situated at the far end of the barrack were of differing dimensions. Room 7 was fitted with a basic night toilet, and room 8 served as a common room. Bedrooms 1 and 14 were only capable of accommodating four sets of double bunks. The remaining ten bedrooms accommodated eight sets of double bunks, and differed in configuration. As in normal life, some men were fastidious in keeping their rooms clean and tidy, while others were not interested in making such effort. Despite the military stance on matters of presentation, the unique structure of prison camp life created tensions. Every man had his own private area immediately surrounding his bunk. The walls frequently held photographs, news cuttings, or artwork fixed by various ingenious means. A fellow prisoner's bunk was always regarded as private, and was only to be sat upon by invitation. Social groups between the respective rooms naturally developed, but where relationships were problematic, it was possible to gain permission to exchange bunks. Wells also drew scale

Right: Flowers picked from the garden plot in front of Hut III.

FLOWERS FROM OLD CAMP. (GROWING ROUND HUT III.)

Below: Detailed plan drawn to scale by Frank Wells illustrating Barrack 46.

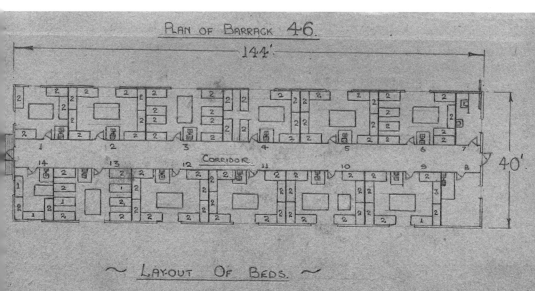

PLAN OF BARRACK 46.

~ LAYOUT OF BEDS. ~

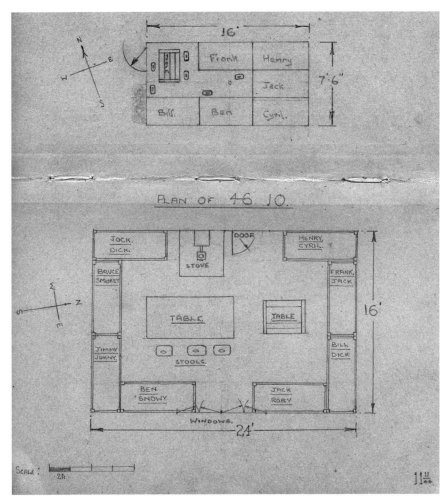

The plan drawings of the 'Dog Kennel' and the upgraded room with bunk allocations.

plans of his old and new rooms, and clearly identified which bunk belonged to which man. All six men from the small 'dog kennel' hut 111, moved into the larger room, where they were joined by a further ten prisoners.

Day-to-day life involved sharing and trusting to a great extent. Where food was involved, this was extremely important. Bread, or any product that was required to be cut and distributed equally, was shared out with utmost scrutiny. It became normal practice for the person cutting to be the last person to receive his portion. This guaranteed that the process produced incredibly accurate distribution, with the responsible person making sure he was not to be left with an unequal portion. Camp life ensured everything was measured, cut, or otherwise distributed with utmost fairness. The daily distribution of coal was treated in the same way, but with coal lumps differing in size, it was first come first served. Each room clearly benefitted from each man trying to obtain the largest lumps possible.

On 21 October, orders were issued by the Germans banning the singing of 'God Save the King'. Clearly it was a practice that had intensely annoyed them. Wells declared in his log that they sang 'Land of Hope and Glory' instead. During the first week of November, a piano and stage were delivered to the camp. The camp celebrated their arrival with a dance, in which fifty men participated as females. The following Monday, Wells recorded the arrival of a new inmate known as 'Smokey', who had come from Lamsdorf. This was Sergeant J. V. Fogg, a flight engineer who had been shot down in a Short Stirling Bomber over Saarbrucken with 218 Squadron on 1 September 1942. From the manner of his entry, it was clear to see that 'Smokey' was known to Wells. He was brought into room 10, and occupied one of the bunks directly opposite Frank.

On 11 November at 11 a.m., the camp conducted a remembrance service in the snow. The weather deteriorated with more snow falling, and from 15 November, Red Cross food parcels were issued daily. The snow caused morning appell to be conducted in the barracks rather than in the open. Room 12 in Wells' barrack appears to have held a rather high spirited group of men. Wells records flame throwing and a séance, adding that he, Bill Turner, and 'Snowy' were in the roof at the time. Morale improved with the delivery of a drum kit, saxophones, another piano, and the much appreciated contingent of books sent from the YMCA for the library. The conditions in Bankau were now a shadow of the past, and the continuing cold weather saw the creation of an ice rink on the camp fire tank where the water had frozen rock solid.

Red Cross parcel rosta, made on 15 November 1944.

Wells wrote up a roster between the men within room 10. Based upon the issue of Red Cross food parcels, the distribution roster allowed for the men to gain the best cross section of food possible. It worked effectively, and was adopted from 15 November. In essence, the quality items from any parcel were always equally distributed amongst all of the men.

The Germans slammed nine men into the cooler after turning up late on the morning parade on 1 December. Despite this, the first week in December was a very good one for the camp. Allied aircraft were seen passing overhead, creating quite a buzz around the camp, and the previously delivered YMCA film projector, which had sat useless without films, burst into life when the prisoners received three films. Dennis Dedman had a cigarette parcel arrive, resulting in 1,000 players being equally split between those that smoked in the room. They were highly prized, as very few cigarette parcels had been arriving. The sharing roster process continued with all deliveries, as no one could guarantee when additional supplies were to be received. Another room mate, called Cyril, caused reason to celebrate when he reached his twenty-first birthday on 12 December. Sergeant Cyril Van-de-Veld had been shot down on 3 May 1944 during the 576 Squadron attack on Mailly le Camp, France. Van-de-Veld evaded capture until his luck ran out on 19 June. He was one of only two survivors from the crew of his Lancaster. That particular raid saw forty-two Lancasters lost, and Van de Veld must have seen several aircraft fall from the sky; no doubt he recounted his own story to his colleagues during the long evenings of conversation. This might well have prompted Frank Wells to make a note reminding him to write to Irvin Chute Company to enroll into the Caterpillar Club, having saved his own life by the use of an Irvin parachute. Wells' notes clearly indicate that at Bankau there was no known communication route to Irvin Air Chutes. In several other camps, the address was passed around, and in some cases, the barrack leaders took up the responsibility to coordinate applications. Many examples exist where the standard camp postcards were sent direct to Irvin Air Chutes and rubber stamped by the censorship process.

In 1945, Irvin Air Chutes published details of the enrolled membership statistics. Between 1939 and 23 February 1945 they had accepted 17,262 members into the European division of the Caterpillar Club. From that figure, 8,570 were direct applicants from prisoner of war camps.[82]

Another room mate, Dick Haggett, received a clothing parcel on 14 December. It was perfect timing, as the knitted garments inside the parcel were very much appreciated in the very cold weather that month. The previous day, discontent had set in, and after a fair bit of discussion the camp leader resigned from his post. The delivery of letters to the camp was not very consistent, and sometimes weeks and weeks passed without anything. On Saturday 16 December, Dennis Dedman received thirty-eight letters in one delivery. Wells maintained a meticulous register of his letters and postcards, and without exception he recorded having dispatched four letters to his family every week.

Any air raid warnings at the camp required an immediate return to the barracks; a rule that was strictly enforced by the Germans. On 17 December, Wells recorded an air raid between 12.10 to 1.30 p.m. Bombs actually dropped into the woods close by, and propaganda leaflets fell into the actual camp. The prisoners were held in the barracks until the Germans had searched the camp. At 11.45 a.m. the following day, another air raid warning occurred. This time, only rumblings were heard from in the barracks. On the third consecutive day, a further raid took place between 12.10 to 1.30 p.m. Bombs were heard, but not as close as had previously been experienced. This caused serious speculation as to the state of the war. The situation of having had no camp leader or 'man of confidence' was resolved by a vote on 21 December. Warrant Officer Ron Mead was duly elected, and his first task was to ensure the camp obtained a functioning radio as soon as possible. That same day an Argentine bulk food supply arrived, sent by the British Committee Council in the Argentine. It was a huge delivery, which once more enabled Wells to create a roster, itemising to the smallest percentages the correct entitlement for each man. This delivery was urgently needed, as the camp stores, and in particular the food parcels, were nearly reduced to emergency rationing status. Cigarettes continued to be in very short supply, which led to severe irritability breaking out amongst the men.

The men's constant company and close proximity to each other remained

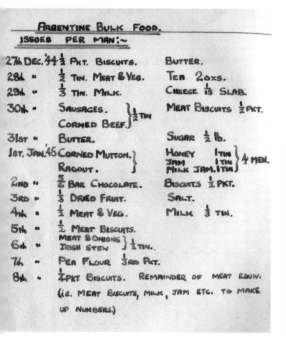

Above left: The Argentine bulk food issue list of content.

Above right: Another crayon drawing, 'Walking the wire in the rain'.

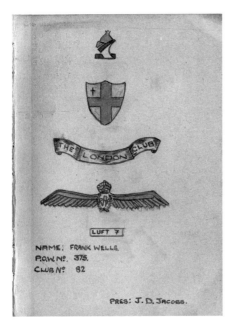

Stalag Luft 7's 'The London Club'.

a continual source of possible tension, and tempers occasionally became easily frayed. Wells chose to take a walk of the wire every day, regardless of the weather. Whenever anything took place at a regular time within camp life, a pattern of predictability was created. Walking the wire with men other than your roommates provided a different conversation, and varying the time of daily events created different mixes of men. Wells drew the picture of daily life walking along the perimeter line.

Christmas was a few days away, and the Argentine food delivery assisted to provide for a full festive day. Christmas Eve was spent creating decorations with crepe paper. On Christmas day, appell was called at 8 a.m., and the prisoners were informed that it would be the only check carried out that day. The news was most warmly received, as standing on parade for upwards of an hour in the freezing cold was never pleasant. Wells described the day's menu: 'Breakfast: porridge, bacon and egg, spam and fried bread. Lunch: Corned beef hash. Tea: Salmon on toast, jam and Christmas cake. Supper: Spam sandwiches.' It had been worth the wait, and a feeling of contentment spread amongst the entire camp. The war abruptly returned to Stalag Luft VII on Boxing Day, with the air raid alarm sounding at midday. The all clear was not called until 1.15 p.m. Fortunately, sufficient time was available for the planned arts and crafts exhibition to go ahead. The camp had developed a wide variety of clubs, but central to many was the library, where books touching on a whole wealth of subjects were distributed. Frank Wells was a member of The London Club, and allocated a membership number of 82. He makes no reference to the club in his log, but he did draw a representation of his membership within it.

Wednesday 27 December 1944 produced another air raid alarm at exactly the same time as the previous day. This air raid was to create a set of circumstances that were to lead to tragedy. At midday, the alarm was correctly responded to by the camp contingent and the required shutdown of camp activity was achieved effortlessly. Once again, the air raid had disrupted the midday meal. Flight Sergeant Stevenson RCAF was eager for the all clear to sound so he could get to the mess. Immediately upon hearing the all clear he dashed out of the barrack, but in his haste he was shot by a guard. Wells wrote, 'Shot after the all clear had sounded, died after forty minutes.' The guard had shot Stevenson because he had dashed out of the barrack upon hearing an all clear signal that had not originated from the camp. Warrant Officer Leslie Howard Stevenson, from British Columbia, died aged twenty. He was an air gunner who had been shot down on operations in August 1944 when his crew been forced to ditch in the sea off the Hook of Holland. The survivors were rescued and made prisoners of war.[83] Shooting incidents at Bankau were not as prevalent as some other camps, but other incidents had occurred. By way of endorsement, yet another air raid warning occurred the following day at exactly the same time. Understandably, no similar mistake occurred this time.

On Saturday 30 December, the funeral of Leslie Stevenson took place, followed by a remembrance service held after the next roll call parade. Leslie Stevenson was laid to rest in the cemetery at Kreuzberg. The camp leader Flying Officer Peter Thompson RAAF was able to secure a photograph of the grave, which was later handed into official channels for transit to the Canadian casualty liaison officers.

As the New Year approached, the Commandant allowed the electricity to remain on in the barracks on New Year's Eve. The hopes of the war concluding swiftly must have been on everyone's mind as lights went out at 1 a.m. The following day, Cyril Van-de-Veld received six letters, which he was seen reading all day; time and time again the pages were turned. That set the ball rolling, as Dick Haggett received a cigarette parcel of 200 players the following day, and the day after that 500 English food parcels arrived.

Friday 5 January 1945 was to be a bad day, as the early appell was badly responded to by several prisoners. The Germans always regarded these parades as very integral to the camp discipline. Several men appeared to arrive late in what may have been an attempt to confuse the head count. Frustrated by the situation, a further four parades were called during the day, most probably ordered as a punishment for the lateness. The additional appells resulted in several hours being spent on parade in very cold weather. It is possible that the Germans thought an escape attempt was being undertaken, or that one had been achieved and efforts were being taken to disguise those who had taken part. Whatever the cause, it made for a seriously unpleasant day for everyone. Wells makes no mention of the 'ferrets' activity, although it was taken for granted that anti-escape measures were being consistently undertaken throughout the day.

The camp leaders' prayer.

Sunday 7 January saw the camp return to normal, with just one appell parade at 10 a.m. The following day, the Germans stepped up the activity again. Wells' barrack block was subjected to a complete search, although nothing was found. However the following day, after a further search, an escape tunnel was located. Wells makes very little comment about the tunnel because he clearly knew nothing of it. The day following the discovery, all barrack stools were taken to the appell. Each stool was examined and all the lose legs were removed. It became obvious that the Germans were in possession of some information related to escape items hidden in a stool. It appeared nothing was found, but at midday a larger search took place, where it was made known they were searching for string and nails. This continued for four days. Wells makes no comment upon the value of string and nails, or any indication that the term related to anything other than the commodities named. The author suspects these terms indicated radio equipment, as nails were used to create aerials for radio reception. The camp commandant insisted that the orders regarding tin cans in the camp were enforced, and the regulations were posted for all prisoners. Wells made a comical representation of the 'Empty Tin Fuhrer' in his log. The posted regulations were as follows:

DISPOSAL OF TIN CANS SENT TO PRISONERS OF WAR.
1. Tin cans of all kinds, with or without their contents may be left in the hands of individual prisoners of war in strictly limited quantities and under strict supervision.
   Purpose of this regulation:

a. To prevent the accumulation of larger amounts of food stuffs to facilitate escape.

b. To eliminate empty tin cans as means of escape, such as in the construction of tunnels, the preparation of imitation buckles, etc.

c. To prevent the smuggling of forbidden messages, and of objects usful in escape, espionage, and sabotage.

2. The individual prisoner of war may be allowed a maximum of six tin cans for the storage of his food supplies (meat, spread on bread, sugar, tea, etc.), provided no other means of storage are available in sufficient quantities and provided there is no danger of the wrong use of these cans. Before a filled tin can is issued, it must be examined before and after opening; such examination may be limited to random sampling in the case of tin cans (and tubes) sent by the British and American Red Cross in standard packages.

3. When new tin cans are issued, the old ones must be withdrawn. Used tin cans must be emptied, cleaned, and stored in a place out of reach of the prisoners of war. They must be sent every 3three months to the scrap metal recovery place, together with tin cans used by the German troops.

4. Compliance with regulations 1, 2, and 3 is to be enforced by orders of the camp commandants.

Sunday 14 January was Frank Wells' twenty-first birthday. This was clearly a rather miserable way to celebrate such an important day, and he had walked the wire several times. The thoughts of home overtook him, but his roommates made a birthday card in their efforts to cheer him up. It was also the day that heralded the commencement of rumour and speculation that there would be an evacuation of the camp. Such a rumour spread through the camp at a great pace, and great speculation upon the state of the war and possible freedom took place. What better twenty-first birthday present could there be. The intensity of camp gossip increased on Tuesday 16, when the camp awoke to an aerodrome having sprung up overnight somewhere just south-east of the camp. Prolific air activity took place all day, but within 24 hours it had completely disappeared. That same day he entered into his log: 'Rumours we are leaving 1 hours notice. To be ready at 12 p.m., panic for food and kit – bags of looting.'

Wells decided to retain two samples of the tea and coffee issued to him that day as a keepsake. He placed them into the cellophane envelopes provided at the rear of his logbook. He made the comment that the tea was mostly used for smoking; when you see the quantity of apparent wood chip and other components it certainly looks far removed from tea. The ersatz coffee was made from barley kernels or acorns, and by all accounts became an acquired taste.

The weather at this time was very cold. Any prospect of securing additional clothing, or more importantly, better footwear was explored by the prisoners. The limited stores were quickly purged, purloined, or simply stolen. In all probability,

Left: Accounting for the camp's tin cans.

Below: The YMCA log cellophane packets used by Frank Wells to hold tea and coffee issued on 16 January 1945.

Wells' comments on looting after the announcement of departure saw the end of acquiring anything of note. The Russian advance upon Warsaw was gathering pace; the German resistance had been resilient but unable to hold. The Russian forces were creating fronts that were most likely to result in Bankau being surrounded. Direct orders were issued from Berlin, stating that the prisoners of war must not be captured. This order forced the camp commandant into undertaking an organised evacuation of the camp. With good will and foresight by the commandant, immediate action was taken to facilitate the removal of the sick. All those prisoners capable of walking were expected to do so as and when ordered.

Wells' log holds the following entry: 'Thursday 18 January 1945: No English allowed in our barrack while some wire was connected. Paraded at 7 p.m., ready to march but postponed until 3.30 a.m.' The entry relates to tuning into the BBC radio news. The prisoners were in a fearful position; the reference to 'no English' is understood to mean that the news was not to be spoken for fear of being detected. The instructions to be ready at 3.30 a.m. resulted in the prisoners of war sleeping with everything immediately available to them. At exactly 5 a.m. on Friday 19 January, the Allied airmen were marched out of Bankau.

Quite extraordinarily, Frank Wells chose to make detailed entries in his wartime log during the march, which took place from 19 January to 5 February, as well as a the subsequent train journey from 5 to 8 February. Writing in the most precise fashion with his ink pen, Frank recorded times, distances, and comments. This information provides a unique record of the march. Without personal works such as these, the true hardship and endurance imposed upon these prisoners of war would not be known. This was the very first forced march undertaken by any of the RAF and Allied prisoners of war in the Second World War. It was a situation created purely by geographical location balanced against the unpredictable Russian advance from the east.

This was also one of the smallest numbers of men to take part in a forced march. 1,565 prisoners left the camp under guard, each carrying as much food as possible. The men had each been issued with a minimum of two days Red Cross Food supplies.[84] In many cases, the men carried more than this. The prisoners were under instruction that any effort to escape would be met with the use of force. It was absolutely clear that the guards were under orders to shoot to kill. It is difficult to comprehend the trepidation and fear that these men were exposed to. Frank Wells recorded a fascinating account. Here, his words are reproduced accordingly:

Friday 19 January. 06.30-16.00
   Bankau–Kreusburg–Konstadt–Winterfield. 28 km.
   Left the camp in raging wind and snow.
   Kit thrown away all along the road.
   Dead horses by the roadside.

still move us on to nowhere and the roads will be worse now with the snow. No definite gen as to where we are going.

Saturday 27 January. 11.00-17.30
   Heidersdorf–Pfaffendorf. 18 km.
   Walked all day up over a steep hill. Slept under a ladder to a loft of a barn.
   Beds frozen over on awakening. Half a cup of soup issued (tasted of paraffin)

Sunday 28 January. 05.00-12.30
   Pfaffendorf–Scweidnitz—Standorf. 25 km.
   Worst days march yet snowing like a hurricane. Strong winds and roads
   in a treacherous state. Half a cup of soup, seven biscuits, one tenth of a tin
   of meat. Slept on tiles in loft of barn, very cold, boots frozen.

Monday 29 January. 17.00-04.00
   Standorf–Steiloy–Jaue– Lauer–Petterswitz. 24 km.
   Worst night march issued with eight biscuits. When setting off snow very
   deep we often walked in single file vehicles of German Army buried in the
   snow all along the route. Saw two cars collide one dead German lying
   frozen by the roadside. Everybody thirsty and eating snow even though it
   was very cold, we were parched. But we kept going at the thought of the
   transport we were promised.

Tuesday 30 and Wednesday 31 January. Resting day.
   Petterswitz woke up at 9 a.m. and heard some of the boys talking about
   the porridge that was spilled so went out with my tin and got stuck into a
   couple of tins. Polish people giving out buckets of soup and coffee. Several
   pails tipped over by our lads fighting for a cupful. Told by the Germans
   that they don't know where to take us.

Thursday 1 February. 08.00-13.30
   Petterswitz–Seicho–Ober–Prausnitz. 14 km.
   Very hilly country and slow travelling sledges won't pull because of the
   thaw. A short march but we were all dog tired boots soaking wet. Issued
   with two fifths of a loaf, one twenty-fourth of margarine, half a cup of
   soup. Lost gold ring.

Friday 2, Saturday 3 and Sunday 4 February.
   Still at the same place told we will wait here until transport arrives at
   Goldberg. Too weak to stand for long time. Boys selling anything for a
   few potatoes. Ordeal by hunger issue of four spuds for two days, one cup
   of porridge and quarter of a loaf. Boys are starving. Gold watches are
   being sold for one or two loaves of bread. Heard we are catching trans-

31

DATE	TIME	FROM ~ TO	KLMS	REMARKS
26th		HEIDERSDORF.		RESTED UP. HAD ISSUE OF 1/2 CUP SOUP AND 1/2 CUP COFFEE AND RAW SPUDS. HEAVY FALL OF SNOW DURING THE NIGHT. HAD TO PUT OUR BOOTS ON A FIRE IN THE MORNING TO THAW THEM OUT. WE ARE ALL IN A BAD STATE BUT THEY STILL MOVE US ON TO NOWHERE AND THE ROADS WILL BE WORSE NOW WITH THE SNOW. NO DEFINATE GEN AS TO WHERE WE ARE GOING.
27th	11.00 ~ 17.30	HEIDERSDORF PFAFFENDORF.	18 / 167	WALKED ALL DAY OVER A STEEP HILL. SLEPT UNDER A LADDER TO THE LOFT OF A BARN. BEDS FROZEN OVER ON AWAKENING. 1/2 CUP SOUP ISSUED. (TASTED OF PARAFFIN.)
28th	08.00 ~ 12.30	PFAFFENDORF SCHWEIDNITZ. STANDORF.	25 / 192	WORST DAYS MARCH YET. SNOWING LIKE A HURRICANE. STRONG WIND AND ROADS IN A TREACHEROUS STATE. 1/2 CUP SOUP, 7 BISCUITS 1/10 TIN MEAT ISSUED. SLEPT ON TILES IN LOFT OF BARN. VERY COLD. BOOTS FROZEN.
29th 30th	17.00 ~ 04.00	STANDORF STREILOV JAUER LAUER PETTERSWITZ.	24 / 216	WORST NIGHT MARCH. ISSUED WITH 8 BIS. WHEN SETTING OFF, SNOW VERY DEEP. WE OFTEN WALKED IN SINGLE FILE. VEHICLES OF GERMAN ARMY BURIED IN THE SNOW ALL ALONG THE ROUTE. SAW 2 CARS COLLIDE. ONE DEAD GERMAN LYING FROZEN BY THE ROADSIDE. EVERYBODY THIRSTY AND EATING SNOW.
				EVEN THOUGH IT WAS VERY COLD WE WERE PARCHED. BUT WE KEPT GOING AT THE THOUGHT OF THE TRANSPORT WE WERE PROMISED.
30th 31st		PETTERSWITZ.		WOKE UP AT 9AM AND HEARD SOME OF THE BOYS TALKING ABOUT THE PORRIDGE THAT WAS SPILLED. SO WENT OUT WITH MY TIN AND GOT STUCK INTO A COUPLE OF TINS. POLISH PEOPLE GIVING OUT BUCKETS OF SOUP AND COFFEE. SEVERAL PAILS TIPPED OVER BY OUR LADS FIGHTING FOR A CUPFULL. TOLD BY THE GERMANS THAT THEY DON'T KNOW WHERE TO TAKE US.
FEB 1st.	08.00 ~ 13.30	PETTERWITZ, SEICHOY OBER-PRAUSNITZ.	14 / 230	VERY HILLY COUNTRY AND SLOW TRAVELLING. SLEDGES WON'T PULL BECAUSE OF THE THAW. A SHORT MARCH BUT WE WERE ALL DOG TIRED. BOOTS SOAKING WET. ISSUED WITH 2/5 LOAF 1/4LB MARG. 1/3 CUP OF SOUP. LOST GOLD RING.
2nd.				STILL AT SAME PLACE. TOLD WE WILL WAIT HERE UNTIL TRANSPORT ARRIVES AT GOLDBERG, TO WEAK TO STAND FOR LONG TIME. BOYS SELLING ANYTHING FOR A FEW POTATOES.
3rd.				ORDEAL BY HUNGER. ISSUE OF 4 SPUDS FOR 2 DAYS. 1 CUP OF PORRIDGE. 1/4 LOAF.

Detailed events written on the march.

port in the morning. Lads in terrible condition and keep passing out half a cup of soup issued. Then travelling ration for next four days issued one third of a loaf, one third tin of meat.

Before we left the camp orders were issued to the effect that for every one man that attempted to escape, five would be shot. At one village several of us attempted to get water from a pump, as I was leaving the ranks one of the guards fired at the pump, so I stayed with the column. On several occasions the guards fired shots into the lofts of our sleeping rack, which resulted in the entire contingent of men in the barrack being advised by the medical officer to gargle as much as possible, and restrict their movements within the camp. The significant problem with such advice was the lack of water; limited stand pipes always caused queues. Diphtheria is highly contagious, as it spreads through respiratory droplets, such as those produced by a cough or sneeze of an infected person. Diphtheria can also be spread by contaminated objects, or foods infecting the nose and throat. The throat infection can then block the airways. In some cases, diphtheria may infect the skin and produce skin lesions. With the general health of the prisoners being poor, there was serious concern that efforts should be made to treat and restrict the spread of the disease. Many men also had skin lesions thought to have been induced by the poor diet and bad conditions. Confining the men to the barrack was not a practical option, as the rooms were damp and dank all the time. The men adhered to the gargling, with efforts made to assist in the supply of water, and a potion supplied by the camp medical officer.

The following day, Wells noted that an aircraft in distress came down close to the camp. It was not close enough to identify, but was thought to have been an RAF bomber type. On the last day of March, 4 oz of quality German cheese was issued to Wells. It was one of the best unexpected surprises to be written in his diary. Wells preserved the labels from the cheese packets and pasted them into the central card section of his YMCA logbook. The doctor later lifted the restrictions in respect of the diphtheria threat, and Wells immediately spent more time at the wire with his old crew mates.

There appeared to have been another influx of food parcels and cigarettes, and

Label of cheese from the German Red
Cross, issued on 31 March 1945.

additional foods were issued to those in greatest need. All timepieces were put forward an hour on 2 April, but many of the men no longer had their watches, as they were traded for food during the dire days en route to the camp.

Rather strangely, the Germans presented Frank Wells with a capture postcard, which he was asked to fill out on 4 April. He chose not to question the reason as to why he had been given this particular postcard in the hope of sending additional news to his family, so therefore he returned it forthwith, duly filled out in accordance to the instructions. The state of the war and the movements between camps had reduced the prisoner's mail flow to almost nothing. Camp appells continued to be called, but little interest or recording of detail appeared to be taken by the guards. However on Friday 6 April, they called a surprised afternoon inspection with full photographic identity checks. This led to speculation among the men that something was happening. There had been no known escapes from the British compound. The state of the war was dictating a situation where it was thought best by all to sit still and wait for the Russian liberation.

The men's greatest fear was that the full identity check was being held prior to being ordered to evacuate the camp. The frequent aerial activity in the area had caused some concern to many of the British and American prisoners. Unaware that the Geneva Convention required prisoner of war camps to have no identification for aerial purposes, the prisoners' suggested that the barrack roofs should be marked in such a way as to avoid any accidental attacks on the camp. It is possible that this concern was due to the great many large tents that were erected in the camp. They held hundreds of men who had been squeezed in, sleeping head to toe. Tents would not be something that the average ground attack pilot would associate with a PoW camp. The camp had become a warren with separate compounds for British, American, French, Italian, and Belgian prisoners of war. Luckenwald had developed into an enormous complex of wire cages, compounds, and tented accommodation.

One of the larger compounds housed the Russian prisoners, who numbered many thousands. As previously mentioned, due the Soviet Union not being a signatory to the Geneva Convention, Russian prisoners were subjected to especially harsh and brutal treatment, and they accounted for the vast majority of deaths in the camp. They were also required to undertake the worse details in the other camps. Latrines were emptied with less than adequate means by these men. The Russians were treated by the Germans in the most barbaric manner, and the total death rate in captivity for Russians prisoners during the war has been estimated to be over 3 million, representing a mortality rate of just over 50 per cent. The German Reich labelled all of the Russians as 'Untermenschens'.[86] Regulations had been issued to all commandants during 1941 regarding the treatment of Soviet prisoners of war, with the order signed by General Reinecke,[87] Chief of the division of German High Command. General Reinecke was responsible for, amongst other duties, the supervision of prisoner of war matters. The orders for Soviet prisoners stated:

The Bolshevist soldier has therefore lost all claims to treatment as an honourable opponent, in accordance with the Geneva Convention [...] The order for ruthless and energetic action must be given at the slightest indication of insubordination, especially in the case of Bolshevist fanatics. Insubordination, active, or passive resistance must be broken immediately by force of arms (bayonets, butts, and firearms) [...] Anyone carrying out the order who does not use his weapons, or does so with insufficient energy, is punishable [...] Prisoners of war attempting escape are to be fired on without previous challenge. No warning shot must ever be fired [...] The use of arms against prisoners of war is, as a rule, legal.

Allied prisoners of war found providing food or scraps to these men were likewise harshly treated. The system caused the Russian soldiers to be pariahs within all of the camps.

Wells' general health improved steadily, as did the supply of food to all the men in the camp. The general morale rose, and even the musical instruments supplied by the YMCA received an airing. The band started to play in the compound, providing a level of entertainment that had been sorely missed. Luckenwalde was never going to be a happy place, but it did become a better place than it had been. Wells frequently met with Geoff Marchant and Arthur 'Art' Kinnis at the wire, showing that the special bond between crew mates had not been lost. On Sunday 8 April, Wells' barrack block pooled as much food as possible and organised a tea party. This took place as a result of lost parcels being distributed from the camp stores. From the same store, Wells was issued with one sixth of a pound of coffee for distribution between four men. Another party was organised when further parcels were issued, and Wells sat with Tom Reeves, Russ, and Les Wolff to soak up the moment. On Wednesday 11 April, Wells received a vaccination injection for TB from the medical officer, and an open air concert was held. It was a fine day, only spoilt by the news that the officers in barrack 3 were to be moved. Wells immediately sought to find Geoff Marchant and 'Art' Kinnis, who confirmed that the orders were for an 8 a.m. departure. Anticipating that it was the last time in captivity that they were likely to see each other, they bid farewell, exchanging personal details with a vow to contact each other once the war was over.

Thursday morning saw the officers and 400 men marched away from the camp. Wells made a simple entry in his log, devoid of any sentiment. It read, 'Officers and boys depart.' On Friday 13, he made another entry in exactly the same way: 'Officers and boys returned.' The men had been loaded into cattle trucks, but the train never left the station. The Allied aerial offensive had destroyed the railway lines to such an extent that the entire network could not function. The men were removed from the cattle trucks and marched back into the camp. Unfortunately for them, their barracks had been reoccupied as soon as they departed, so most of them ended up under canvas in the large tents. That same day, Wells had his clothing deloused in a scheduled barrack purge that sought to clear the almost unsolvable lice problem. The transfer of body lice occurred all the time; it really was a most unpleasant burden to bear for all the prisoners. Fear struck the prisoners at 11 p.m. that night when four rifle shots were heard. Wells' log report states, 'Sergeant Johnston killed after escaping from the lager, Sergeant Crosswell seriously wounded.' Sergeant Geoff Johnson RAF and Sergeant Percy Crosswell RCAF had both been attempting to break out of the camp. The term 'lager' relates to nothing more than an area in the camp itself. It transpired that they boldly tried to climb or cut through the barbed wire fence in an effort to escape. It must be said that little hope existed for such a plan. It has been impossible through research to establish if these two men had been part of the contingent of men taken to the railway earlier that same day. Percy Bruce Crosswell came from Saskatchewan, Canada. He was an air gunner, and had been shot down during an attack on Dusseldorf, on 23 April 1944. Crosswell had escaped by parachute from his stricken Lancaster, and after his safe landing, later made contact with the Dutch underground movement.

The Germans were utilising various means to both infiltrate and frustrate the underground movements, and they had achieved some success during late 1944 and early 1945. Crosswell became a casualty to those efforts; he was arrested by the German police while in hiding. As a prisoner of war, he was incarcerated in Luckenwalde with other non-commissioned officers. Here he met with Flight Sergeant Geoffrey Johnson, a fellow air gunner who had spent a lot of time as a Halifax tail gunner in 158 Squadron. Johnson was just nineteen years old and volunteered to serve direct from the Air Training Corp. He had been engaged on a raid to Essen on the night of 25 October 1944 when disaster struck. Fortunately, his entire bomber crew of seven men escaped death that night over Essen. They were quickly captured and made prisoners of war.

Geoffrey Johnson had been killed instantly at the camp wire, shot by a bullet fired from a guard's rifle. Percy Crosswell had been struck by the rifle fire, but he clung to life for 14 hours before he died at 1 p.m. the following day. Crosswell and Johnson were both buried in the prison camp cemetery at 10.30 a.m. on Monday 16 April 1945. Geoffrey was later re-buried at the Berlin War Cemetery where the Commonwealth War Graves Commission continues to tend his grave in perpetuity. Crosswell's body was never located at the end of the war. His life is commemorated on panel 279 on the Runnymede War Memorial. It should be noted that the Royal Canadian Air Force engaged in exhumations at Luckenwald's prisoner of war camp cemetery during May 1947. There were no official records in existence to assist with the recovery of those victims, and a great many grave markers had been removed or destroyed. The authorities made further concerted efforts to locate the grave of Percy Crosswell, but those efforts failed to locate any trace of his body.[88]

Lukenwalde camp residents witnessed a spectacular aerial attack on

Potsdan on Saturday 14 April. Frank wrote in his log, 'Air raid on Potsdan, best show I have seen.' The Royal Air Force engaged 500 Lancasters and 12 Mosquitos.[89] The targets were the German guard's regiment barracks and the railway infrastructure. It was to be Bombers Command's last raid of the war upon a large German City. Luckenwalde camp was close enough for the men to see and hear the full might and noise of 500 Lancasters engaged on that operation. The robost United States Thunderbolt aircrafts were seen during the next day, engaged in strafing ground targets in the surrounding area. The fighting was intensifying, and once again worries existed in case the camp should be attacked. On 18 April, two waves of RAF Mitchell Light Bombers passed low over the camp. Wells noted that each wave had twenty-seven air-craft, and they were tightly boxed. They passed over during an appell when all of the men were on the parade ground, creating a fantastic display. The Mitchell Light Bombers, part of the RAF Second Tactical Air Force, were at that time providing intense support to the Allied army from 14 to 22 April.[90] No doubt their presence provided the prisoners with a point of speculative conversation for several hours.

Unsurprisingly, Frank Wells returned to the ever present subject of food in his log. All prisoners except the Russians were receiving one full food parcel every fourteen days. Wells exchanged his margarine and forty cigarettes for a loaf of bread, and then a 'klim' can of flour for a 'D' ration bar. His best deal was forty cigarettes for two eggs. The arrival of a seriously bedraggled and weak column of men on 19 April saw an immediate collection of cigarettes and food. The news was that these men had been marching since January. The next morning, air raid warnings constantly sounded. The men could see Pathfinder sky markers being dropped and then the bombs going in. Berlin was being attacked by the RAF for the last time during the Second World War as the Russians were converging on the capital of Germany. After the excite-ment of seeing the daylight bombing, approximately 160 men from Lamsdorf arrived in the camp. The great march exodus from prison camps in the east had created many scattered groups of men, and it was as if Luckenwalde was the only place for them to gain refuge. The sky was full of flashes, and to the prisoners, the intensity of the war appeared to be centered on the prison camp. The welfare of the newly arrived men was given priority, as many were suffer-ing from various physical conditions, with some needing medical care to their feet. It would have been a complete disaster if the Red Cross had not trans-ported food to the camp when it did; without doubt, many hundreds of lives were saved at Luckenwalde. Sadly that was not the case for the poor Russians, despite the Allies' attempts to help wherever possible.

On Saturday 21 April, Wells was able to write in bold capitals, 'RED LETTER DAY.' No morning appell was called, and the Germans had pulled out of the camp. The boys went and looted the offices; many found their own record cards and stuffed them into a pocket as a keepsake. The officers in the camp allowed the men time to roam the camp and then took control, advising that Russian tanks were in Luckenwalde, where Russian and French flags were flying on the buildings.

Somehow, threats had been delivered to the camp by the SS, claiming, 'If any arms are taken up in the camp, 100 men would be shot.' Wells made very specific mention of this message in his log. The SS had previously visited the camp, but nobody had seen any of those dreaded uniforms for several months. The remaining Germans that chose to be left behind were placed in the prison cells or cooler, leaving the guard towers empty. As darkness fell, the barracks were not locked and the windows left un-shuttered. The men awaited the morning that would herald the arrival of an Allied army. To ensure security, the officers posted guards all night, which passed without event.

At 6 a.m., Wells was woken to the boys in the barrack saying that the Russians had arrived and were with the officers. One scout car had entered the camp, followed by lorries brimming full of guns and firepower, which caused the men to gather around and engage in the excitement of the moment. Wells was surprised that most of the equipment was American. He made a note indicating that three Russians had been found wearing German uniforms; they were held and shot in the morning. Wells presumed they were Russians who worked for the Germans. Small arms firing and artillery was going on all day, but it was impossible to find out what was happening. Wells went to forage around areas that he had never entered before, and was most surprised when he found a superb pencil drawing of himself amongst the general rubbish in the Russian quarter. He had no idea that he had ever been drawn. The sketch had been created with great skill, but only dated 1944, with no signature applied. Wells also found and kept a green coloured Russian arm band with the letters SU (Soviet Union).

That evening, Wells was allocated a guard duty between 9 p.m. and 10 p.m.; a bizarre change that necessitated keeping people from entering the camp, as opposed to years of the opposite. The following morning was a little more subdued, even more so when approximately eight Russian bodies were taken through the camp, having died of starvation during the night. A Russian newsreel arrived and started taking pictures of the camp and the dead. One straffing run was made through the camp by a single Luftwaffe aircraft, but fortunately, no one in the British compound was killed.

The initial euphoria of the long-awaited Russian liberation quickly led towards frustration. It was expected that the men would be released from the camp and efforts made to organise their repatriation. The reference to a 'link up' by Wells indicates that they were hoping for the Allied forces to link up around the area of Luckenwalde. The camp continued to function as it had done since 1939, minus the appells and German guards. News filtered through in the camp that the Russians had entered Berlin, but the resistance was, as expected, very resolute. In fact, this news was incorrect. They were in the outer reaches of Berlin, and the priority of the Russian army was to encircle Berlin;

a feat achieved on 25 April. The Russians understandably prioritised their own prisoners, and these men were gradually removed from their squalid and inhumane conditions. The reality however was that the Allied prisoners of war were now under control of the Russians. Their status as prisoners had not changed, other than the fact that they were able to leave the camp as individuals or in small groups should they wish. Fighting was still taking place, with pockets of sporadic resistance all around the Luckenwalde area.

On Tuesday 24 April, Wells worked in the food store and was issued with one quarter of a Canadian food parcel for his labour. He also received thirty-nine Canadian cigarettes; a great commodity, which he hoped to exchange for some chocolate. The night of 26 April saw instructions from the senior British officer requiring all watches to be put forward another hour. This was to conform to the Russian time. The 9,000 Russian prisoners had been removed, but the remaining Allied contingents numbering some 17,000 men waited anxiously while politics and practicalities dictated their lives.

On Thursday 26 April, Wells wrote, '1,200 Germans broke out of Berlin and threatened our safety, nearly evacuated.' That day, American and Russian forces met at Torgau on the River Elbe, approximately sixty-five miles south of Berlin. The Russians also captured Stettin, and the RAF Second TAF attacked German troop concentrations and communication targets across the north-west areas of the German-held territory. The link up between Russia and the Americans was announced in the camp the following day. That news naturally raised expectations of leaving the camp soon.

On Saturday 28 April, Wells joined a party of foragers who left the camp in search of fresh food. He noted, 'Bags of Fun.' They returned with a sack of spuds, chicken, liver, and steaks. He made no mention of where this produce was sourced from, but little imagination is required, as they obviously rummaged and pillaged the local farms. Within that same log entry, Wells noted, 'SS and Panzer Grenadiers fighting within a quarter of a mile from the camp.' At 10 p.m. that night, a Russian food convoy arrived and parked in the central roadway leading into the camp. Wells was amongst the men detailed to unload the goods vehicles, with more vehicles arriving during the night. In total, fifty trucks were unloaded, and the food was stored ready for distribution. Other prisoners of war were being deposited at the camp as the days passed.

Wells noted that 18,000 Germans had surrendered in the area of Luckenwalde, but plenty of gunfire was still being heard. Three Germans were shot by the camp wire on the afternoon of Monday 30 April, the same day that Hitler and Eva Braun committed suicide in the Chancellery in Berlin. Hitler's elite guard were fiercely defending the Chancellery against the Russians, who were pushing forward with relentless power, taking district by district. The British Army had also crossed the River Elbe and established a bridgehead at Lauenburg, south-east of Hamburg.

The German news communique on 1 May broadcast that the Berlin garrison was, 'herded together in a very narrow space but [was] defending itself heroically against the enemy's mass onslaught'. Frank wrote, 'Hundreds of lads leaving to go to meet the Yanks at Wittenberg. Everyone cheesed off with waiting around. No news of our going home yet.' Wittenberg was situated close to the River Elbe, and any movement towards that area would have met up with forces from the Allied army. Wells chose to remain in the camp. The following day he wrote; 'Still waiting. Runner for SBO [senior British officer] between 6 p.m. and 10 p.m. American reported came into the camp said he would see Eisenhower tomorrow.' On 4 May, Admiral Donitz envoys signed unconditional surrender terms for the German forces in north-west Germany, Denmark and Holland. German High Command announced that the battle for Berlin had ended. It was also the day that Frank Wells', prisoner of war number 375, penned his last written entry into the YMCA wartime log: 'Day out. Drunk on Vodka told 83rd Yank Division will take us home tomorrow commencing at 9 a.m.'

On Saturday 5 May 1945, Frank Wells waited for the promised transport, which never arrived. On Sunday 6, further promises of transportation were given. Many men felt that their plight had been forgotten, making the situation extremely frustrating and demoralising. Moods were lifted by the arrival of several American trucks that turned up as a small convoy. It looked like the process of evacuation was about to commence, and it was a rush to see who could secure a place. It caused a bit of a commotion, only to be settled by the Russians. The Allied prisoners of war were their responsibility, and any movements of men would need to be authorised within their own com-

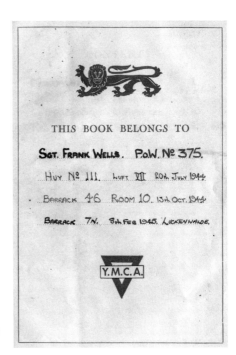

Details of the prisoner of war camps in which Frank Wells has been detained.

mand structure. A rather inflamed situation occurred, which was only settled by the threat of force from the Russians. Shots were fired; not at any particular target, but purely as a means to prevent the departure of the prisoners. The trucks left without any men on board, but it was made known that they would hold up on the road several miles from the camp. Wells made no further entries in his log, and his prisoner of war debriefing document, which he signed on 15 May, declared him as a prisoner of war up to 7 May 1945. These facts draw the author to the conclusion that Frank Wells left the camp on 6 may, seeking to secure a position on the waiting convoy. He was back in the United Kingdom, and interviewed about his service as a PoW eight days later. This time frame would accommodate the transfer to Belgium, where the vast majority of British prisoners were being repatriated from Brussels aerodrome.

7 May 1945 had seen the agreement for the total and unconditional surrender of the German forces, which was accepted and signed by General Dwight D. Eisenhower at 1.41 a.m. The United States withdrew its forces from areas east of the Elbe in accordance with the complicated demarcation agreement with the Russians. Luckenwalde camp continued to be under Russian control. The remaining mass of Allied prisoners became part of a complicated, and no doubt political, negotiation process. It was not until 20 May that the remaining Allied prisoners of war were transported to the American line and granted true freedom.

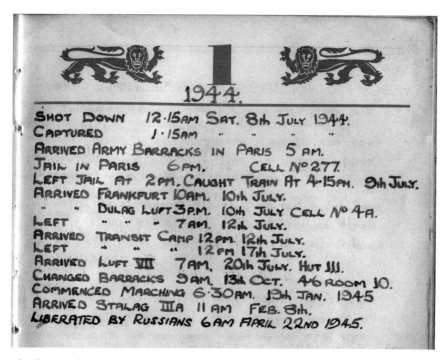

The dates and times recorded in detail during movements 1944-45.

17

Warrant Officer
William Langley Williams

Williams volunteered for service in the Royal Air Force at the outbreak of war. He was just nineteen years old, and had been employed as a buyer with Lever brothers, Port Sunlight Limited. Williams' life changed dramatically following a successful application to become a pilot. He qualified in every aspect of his training, which resulted in him being awarded his wings in July 1941.

With glowing assessments and almost 200 hours flying time recorded within his personal pilot's flying logbook, Williams was selected for duty in light bombers. He was posted to the newly reformed 18 Squadron, flying the Bristol Blenheim for operations over occupied Europe. These light bombers were engaged in attacking specific targets in France and Holland. Unfortunately they were suffering high losses, for the missions were frequently low level, and the bombers had become the target of the Luftwaffe's fighter operations that were deployed against such intruder missions.

Williams' first bombing operation was to attack the dry dock at Dunkirk. Eleven Blenheim Bombers were engaged on the raid, all carrying four 250-lb general purpose bombs. Taking off just before 11 p.m. on 26 April 1942, Williams successfully reached the target and dropped the bomb load at around 7,000 feet. Searchlights and anti-aircraft fire were present, but no casualties were sustained by any aircraft. Williams and his crew members Sergeant Clarke and Sergeant Brown returned to base at 1.15 a.m. the following morning.

Two nights later, Williams crew boarded Blenheim V5683, having been detailed for the bombing of an electric power station at Langerbrugge, north of Ghent. Six aircraft participated. An enemy ME109 fighter engaged the force, but was driven away. One crew was lost in unknown circumstances, but the remainder, including Williams, returned safely, having completed the task successfully and undamaged.

18 Squadron were also engaged in night intruder operations against the Luftwaffe aerodromes across France, Holland, and Belgium. In many instances, these raids involved just a single aircraft, or a pair of bombers. They were in support of the main bomber force offensive intended to disrupt the Luftwaffe's night fighter capabilities. Williams' first raid was on the aero-

Portrait of Flight Sergeant William Williams.

drome at Leeuwarden on 8 May 1942, with a much larger intruder operation taking place on 1 June. On that day, four aerodromes were targeted at St Trond, Venlo, Rheine, and Juvincourt. These particular raids were in support of Bomber Commands anticipated second '1,000 Plan' attack upon the target of Essen.

Three similar raids took place that month, the last of which was on 25 May, which was an attack on the aerodrome at Twente. Alone in the night sky, they located the target and achieved the best possible result. Williams' bomb load was seen to straddle the intersection of runways, and a small fire also ensued after their bomb run. Enemy searchlights and flak was slight. The crew returned home with great elation; it had been most satisfying to see the results achieved on that particular mission.

Events took a bad turn for Williams and his crew during their next intruder sortie. Two crews were sent to bomb the aerodrome at Vechte. Taking off with no more than a minute between them on the evening of 26 July, the two Blenheims made for the target. The first bomber recorded his operation with the following account: 'Located and bombed primary in face of intense opposition. Hit obtained on hangar which was left burning.' Williams' account read: 'Located and bombed primary without incident, but on homeward journey had running fight with ME110 night fighter whose attacks were eventually driven off. Aircraft slightly damaged by fire from enemy aircraft.'[91]

July 1942 proved to be a sobering month for 18 Squadron; they lost six Blenheims on intruder operations. Eighteen men failed to return, including the commanding officer of the Squadron, Wing Commander Chris Jones DFC, who was shot down by an ME110 night fighter during a raid upon Venlo aerodrome. In all probability, it was a night fighter from the unit I/NJG based at that same aerodrome.

During August, Williams and his crew completed two further raids upon the airfield at Twente. They then received instructions that 18 Squadron were going to convert and train in the new Blenheim MkV aircraft known as the Bisley. Further to that, the squadron was to leave Europe and participate in operations over North Africa. Several fuel consumption tests were flown by Williams; rather worryingly, he was recording a number of engine failures in his flying logbook, not quite the events to inspire confidence for the long flight out to North Africa. Williams' old navigator bomb aimer Pilot officer Clarke was replaced by Flight Sergeant McCombie after an incident on 27 September. Flying the Bisley BA805, it suffered an engine failure during formation practice. During the forced landing, Pilot Officer Clarke was injured and unable to continue flying. It had not been a good start for Williams on this new mark of aircraft, but he still had his old wireless operator air gunner with him. The entire crew now held the rank of flight sergeant; their time served having brought this additional rank. With the loss of Clarke, the whole crew reverted back to an NCO rank status. Another engine failure in November saw an entire crew killed, with the Bisley continuing to impress its fickle ways upon the unimpressed crews. With some trepidation, 18 Squadron departed from Portreath. Williams had been allocated Bisley BA870, and the flying logbook entry written by him on 11 November 1942 tells of a most unpleasant experience for the crew: 'Portreath to Blida, North Africa. Fin rudder and petrol tank damaged by Fleet Air Arm Martlets.' It appears the Fleet Air Arm misidentified the Bisley and engaged it as an enemy aircraft.

The eventful sortie took 4 hours 20 minutes daylight flying, and 4 hours night flying, 1 hour of which was flown in thick cloud. The Bisley aircraft BA870 service record indicates that the aircraft was damaged beyond repair on 11 November. Clearly, they were most fortunate to have survived that transit flight. The squadron operational record book fails to identify Williams' aircraft with any specific reference, most probably due to the circumstances involved. However, the records do evidence that eighteen aircraft departed for North Africa, but only eleven arrived without any mishap. Fuel shortages, crash landings, and other incidents created these rather unsavory statistics. Incredibly, of those aircraft that arrived safely, six were immediately dispatched on a raid within just 17 hours of arrival. Jack Brown, Williams' air gunner, provided the author with his personal account:[92]

We lost an engine on trials, lost height at about 300 feet per minute, giving Bill about 4 minutes to find a field in which, expertly as ever, to put her down. Wheels up near Ely, it was farewell to 870, and within a few days we had another engine failure, but managed to land undamaged but unhappy.

We flew out to North Africa on the night of November 10/11 only to be intercepted after dawn by a Fleet Air Arm fighter who took us for a JU88 and shot us up rather severely before recognising their error. We managed to reach Blida, but got another Bisley as ours was no good. At first we had no ground crew on the drome (aerodrome or airfield) so we had to check which of the 11 Bisleys that made it were serviceable, and then refuel by hand from 4 gallon drums, 468 gallons per aircraft. I seem to recall that some armorers turned up, just as well as we were not relishing the prospect of having to bomb up ourselves.

Williams was allocated Bisley BA873, just four days before he was scheduled for an operation. The transit from the United Kingdom to North Africa had been eventful, but more traumas were to be forthcoming. The first operation on Tunis, a night raid on 14 November was straight forward, but on 17 November Williams was amongst twelve crews selected for a daylight attack on the Sidi Ahmed aerodrome. The dashing and competent Wing Commander Hugh Malcolm was to lead the low level attack without any fighter escort. The target was considered to be of utmost importance, a fact that he impressed upon his pilots during the briefing.

The squadron records for that day read:

Twelve Bisleys were detailed to attack Bizerte-Sidi Ahmed aerodrome. The raid was pressed home in formation at heights of 15 to 150 feet, the aircraft having made the approach to the target just above sea level. There was active anti-aircraft and fighter resistance, but eight aircraft attacked successfully, bomb bursts being observed on hangars and airship sheds. Many hundreds of rounds of machine gun fire was seen to enter aircraft parked on the drome. Two aircraft were seen to collide approaching the target and crash at Cap Serrat, one was shot down by ME109F and crashed near the target, as was another, which came down in the sea off Cap Ben Sekka. Four Bisleys were therefore lost. It is believed that two ME109F were shot down by the Bisleys. One aircraft was hit by very accurate light tracer on the run into the target, and the rudder was shot away, but the aircraft went on and bombed, it eventually forced landed at Djidelli after being chased by fighters.

Bisley BA828 flown by Flight Sergeant Williams had been shot down at two minutes past two. His heroic fight in the sky had been witnessed by his Commanding Officer, who was tasked with writing personal letters to the fifteen families affected by that disastrous raid; a raid that, unknown to Hugh Malcolm, would form part of an accumulative recommendation for the ultimate gallantry award, to be given to him in the next few weeks of his life.

Jack Brown's account reads:

Malcolm was always keen to have Bill flying as number two, tucked in tight on his port side. Flying close formation with the leading 'Vic' of three is the secret of keeping the whole of the twelve near enough together to present a rearward effective firepower from twenty-four turret-mounted guns combined. We were told there would be no German fighter opposition and of course we had no fighter escort. We flew for about 3 hours low over the Med, and then over the coast. There was a lot of air turbulence, and tragically two of the rear box of six collided and crashed straight in, blowing up in one big flash of flame. To sit looking astern as we gunners did, and to watch six lads with whom you had recently had breakfast with blown to glory was a grizzly prelude to what lay about twenty miles ahead.

We were to fan out on the bombing run so that all bombs should be dropped within a few seconds of each other. Bombs in the main had 11 second delay fuses for low level work to avoid blowing ourselves up. It follows that if number twelve is eleven seconds behind number one, he is in a lot of trouble.

We turned in to bomb and all hell broke loose. There was a lot of ground defense fire, but worse of all there were Messerschmitt BF109s either on the ground, in the air, or just landing. As you flew over about 25 feet up, one came straight up behind us and of course opened up with his 30 mm cannon. We had dropped our bombs but were only just clear of the target when I saw the starboard engine well on fire. I also had a fair bit of turret damage. We could not speak to each other as the intercom had failed. It was clear she would either blow up, or the engine would stop and we would drop. Bill did the only thing possible and put her down flat on the only bit of clear level ground ahead.

Bill and I got out safely with only superficial damage, but our navigator was trapped. Fortunately, some French troops managed to get the fire out before the tanks blew up, and he was rescued and recovered after a few weeks.

There followed two and a half years separated as prisoners of war, a dull and oppressive existence.

On 29 November, Hugh Malcolm signed his name upon the letter addressed to Williams' father at his home in Cheshire. The letter brought confirmation of the news previously received by telegram. The personal letter from Williams' commanding officer provided much comfort during a time when the fate of Flight Sergeant Williams was completely unknown to his family. Sadly, Wing Commander Malcolm would lose his life just five days after applying his name to this most valued family document.

The introduction of the Bisley Blenheim had been particularly troublesome for the RAF. The skies over North Africa were as deadly as those over Europe. In fact, many Bisley crews thought they were more so. 18 Squadron suffered terrible casualties. The posthumous award of the Victoria Cross to Wing Commander Malcolm provides a fitting testimony to the gallant actions of his Squadron. Flight Sergeant Williams had flown with him many times, none

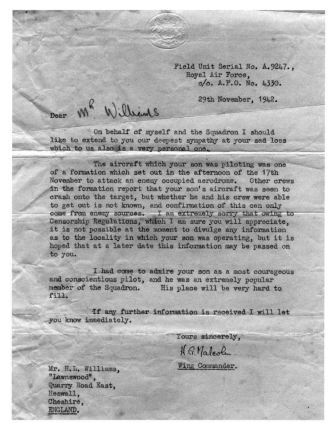

Field Unit Serial No. A.9247.,
Royal Air Force,
c/o. A.P.O. No. 4330.

29th November, 1942.

Dear Mr Williams

On behalf of myself and the Squadron I should
like to extend to you our deepest sympathy at your sad loss
which to us also is a very personal one.

The aircraft which your son was piloting was one
of a formation which set out in the afternoon of the 17th
November to attack an enemy occupied aerodrome. Other crews
in the formation report that your son's aircraft was seen to
crash onto the target, but whether he and his crew were able
to get out is not known, and confirmation of this can only
come from enemy sources. I am extremely sorry that owing to
Censorship Regulations, which I am sure you will appreciate,
it is not possible at the moment to divulge any information
as to the locality in which your son was operating, but it is
hoped that at a later date this information may be passed on
to you.

I had come to admire your son as a most courageous
and conscientious pilot, and he was an extremely popular
member of the Squadron. His place will be very hard to
fill.

If any further information is received I will let
you know immediately.

Yours sincerely,

H.G.Malcolm.

Wing Commander.

Mr. H.L. Williams,
"Lawnswood",
Quarry Road East,
Heswall,
Cheshire,
ENGLAND.

The letter sent by
Wing Commander
Hugh Malcolm.

more telling than that of 17 November. The citation for Wing Commander
Malcolm read:

This officer commanded a squadron of light bombers in North Africa.
Throughout his service in that theatre, his leadership, skill, and daring were of
the highest order. On 17 November 1942, he was detailed to carry out a low
level formation attack on Bizerta airfield, taking advantage of cloud cover.
Twenty miles from the target the sky became clear, but Wing Commander
Malcolm carried on, knowing well the danger of proceeding without a fighter
escort. Despite fierce opposition, all bombs were dropped within the airfield
perimeter. A Junkers 52 and a Messerschmitt 109 were shot down: many
dispersed enemy aircraft were raked by machine gun fire. Weather conditions
became extremely unfavourable and as a result, two of his aircraft were lost
by collision: another was forced down by enemy fighters.[93]

It was due to this officer's skilful and resolute leadership that the remaining aircraft returned safely to base.

On 28 November 1942, he again led his squadron against Bizerta airfield, which was bombed from a low altitude. The airfield on this occasion

was heavily defended, and intense and accurate anti-aircraft fire was met. Nevertheless, after his squadron had released their bombs, Wing Commander Malcolm led them back again and again to attack the airfield with machine gun fire.

These were typical of every sortie undertaken by this gallant officer: each attack was pressed to an effective conclusion however difficult the task and however formidable the opposition.

Finally on 4 December 1942, Wing Commander Malcolm, having been detailed to give close support to the First Army, received an urgent request to attack an enemy fighter airfield near Chouigui. Wing Commander Malcolm knew that to attack such an objective without a fighter escort – which could not be arranged in the time available – would be to court almost certain disaster: but believing the attack to be necessary for the success of the Army's operations, his duty was clear. He decided to attack.

He took off with his squadron and reached the target unmolested, but when he had successfully attacked it, his squadron was intercepted by an overwhelming force of enemy fighters. Wing Commander Malcolm fought back, controlling his hard-pressed squadron and attempting to maintain formation. One by one his aircraft were shot down until only his own aircraft remained. In the end he, too, was shot down in flames.

Wing Commander Malcolm's last exploit was the finest example of the valour and unswerving devotion to duty which he constantly displayed.

London Gazette, 27 April 1943.

The news of Wing Commander Malcolm's death was another blow to the Williams family in Cheshire. They would have hoped for a further letter, knowing that he was most likely to have taken an active interest in securing any news of their son. Unexpectedly, an airmail letter did arrive towards the end of December. The letter was from a friend of Williams, Pilot Officer Eckersley, who had served alongside Williams. Extracts from his letter provided details that promoted hope within the family:

Being one of Bills most closest friends while on the Squadron, I felt that it was my duty to write you, as matter of fact, Jack Brown his air gunner and myself were always together, and when I saw him go down it shocked me as much as I expect it shocked you when you received the telegram. I think I can explain the whole episode, seeing that it happened three weeks ago now and I know you are very anxious to know the details.

Bill was flying number three in the first 'Vic', with the wing commander leading, and after bombing the target was seen to be in difficulties, having apparently been hit by flak over the target, and the next thing known was that he was seen to be going down apparently under control, and [he] apparently did a perfect controlled pancake landing on a smooth field. He was on fire at the time, and without being unduly optimistic, I personally think that he should have got away and escaped from the plane, now I thoroughly hope and think being a prisoner of war.

I would be most obliged to know if you hear any news of Bill from enemy quarters, as would the rest of our squadron with whom Bill was a favourite, from wing commander down. I can also divulge to you that we are stationed in North Africa, a fact that was secret until later.

Pilot Officer Eckersley was a member of Pilot Officer Knickerbocker's crew. They had served alongside Williams during his entire 18 Squadron posting. Eckersley was temporarily parted from his Canadian pilot after Knickerbocker accidently discharged his side arm revolver. It wounded him in the foot, resulting in him being admitted into the Ain Beida Civilian Hospital. The injury resulted in his repatriation to Canada, where he served as an instructor for the duration of the war.

Norman Eckersley himself had been engaged in the V.C. action on 4 December. Flying with his new pilot, he was shot out of the sky and crash landed at Beja. Eckersley was awarded the Distinguished Flying Cross in February 1943. The recommendation stated:

In December 1942 he was the rear gunner of an aircraft detailed to attack an enemy airfield. During the fight, the formation was attacked by fifty enemy fighters. P/O Eckersley destroyed one and damaged three enemy aircraft. He received severe injuries.

The Williams family had been most fortunate to have received the letter from Eckersley. It had obviously been posted just prior to his action with Wing Commander Malcolm. The news received from Eckersley was more than his family could have hoped for.[94] Despite the encouraging news, the Williams family received no further communication until the arrival of a letter from the Base Personnel Office, RAF Eastern Air Command, in early January. The letter advised that as Flight Sergeant Williams was reported missing, believed killed, his personal effects were to be sent to the Central Depository, RAF Colnbrook, Buckinghamshire. It was not the information so keenly sought by the family, and once again it brought forward anxiety regarding their son's fate.

Thoughtfully, the family forwarded the letter received from Norman Eckersley to the Air Ministry. They suggested that the letter should be forwarded to the families of the two crew members from Williams' aircraft. This was carried out by the Air Ministry, who also responded by reply with a letter dated 25 January 1943. They advised that no further information was available, and no information had been received concerning their son.

The parents of Flight Sergeant McCombie and Jack Brown's wife both responded with letters to Mr and Mrs Williams, eternally grateful for the copy of Norman Eckersley's letter. Three families anguish had now been alleviated. The letters endorsed the fact that Williams had been extremely well thought of by his crew, something that they were most grateful of.

On 2 February 1943 at Port Sunlight Limited, Williams' father's place of work, a young post office telegram delivery boy handed a teleprinter message to him. Originating from Gloucester, Williams' father realised that it was going to hold information sent by the RAF about his son. Filled with fear that it would be bad news, Mr Williams found that the telegram provided the opposite:

ACCORDING TO TELEGRAM FROM INTERNATIONAL RED CROSS QUOTING ROME INFORMATION YOUR SON 1067554 FLIGHT SERGEANT WILLIAMS PREVIOUSLY REPORTED MISSING AND BELIEVED KILLED IS NOW A PRISONER OF WAR LETTER FOLLOWES FROM RECORDS TELEX GLOUCESTER

At last after such a long wait, it was confirmed that Bill Williams was safe and well, and being held as a prisoner of war as confirmed by the International Red Cross in Rome. Two days later, an official letter from the RAF records office in Gloucester advised that efforts were under way to establish where the actual place of internment was for Williams.

Returning to the events on 17 November, Bill Williams had been faced with a serious situation. The Bisley was on fire, and the crew would need to get out quickly in order to escape a grizzly death. An immediate crash landing, almost onto the actual target being attacked, was the only option available. Any crash landing would be dangerous, but in these circumstances there was the added danger of being continually shot at. When the aircraft crashed, despite having his Sutton harness as tight as possible, Williams was thrown forward, causing injuries to his face and mouth, and resulting in a number of teeth being displaced. Luckily, all three men escaped the burning aircraft with their lives. All had sustained injuries of some description due to the huge impact upon landing. The crew were immediately captured, interrogated in the Naval Station at Bizerte, and held in custody at that location. They remained there from 17 November to 15 December, when all three men were transported to the Caserta Hospital, Italy.

British prisoners taken in North Africa were normally handed over to the Italians for custody. Most of the injured were taken across the Mediterranean by hospital ship, some going into a hospital at Caserta and some to a hospital at Bari. Williams and his crew were transported to Italy in a Luftwaffe JU52 aircraft. At Caserta, conditions were reasonably good as regards accommodation, and the Italian staff did their best with what they had. Some captured British medical officers and orderlies were allowed to work in the hospital. There were the normal shortages of instruments and drugs. Red Cross capture parcels were of great assistance, as they supplied all the soap and supplemented shortages of toothbrushes, paste, and toilet paper. Food in the hospital was better than in the prison camps, but was still far from adequate. The Red Cross food parcels provided supplements of tea, sugar, margarine, chocolate, and condensed or powdered milk, which would otherwise have been completely absent. Williams belatedly received treatment to his injuries, and on 20 December he was provided with the first opportunity to make contact with his family.

While conditions were reasonably good, Caserta Hospital was overcrowded. In November 1942, in order to ease the situation, 400 prisoners were removed to mainstream Italian prisoner of war camps. Despite this, the hospital numbers remained high at around 1,300 men. At the end of December, Williams was moved into the Italian prisoner of war camp Fara Sabina.

Camp PG 54 at Fara Sabina, forty miles north-east of Rome, was constructed in July 1942. Initially, the camp comprised of two compounds, each containing 2,000 men. Each compound contained four rows of tents accommodating sixty-eight men in each tent. The camp held a high proportion of South African and British men. The issue of two slices of bread and one ladle of soup a day was all any man could expect. As always, the Red Cross parcels sustained the men's balance of nutrients. Prisoners at PG54 often traded with the local Italians. Throwing a bundle of soap or pack of tea over the barbed wire fences would result in a couple of loaves coming the other way. Such

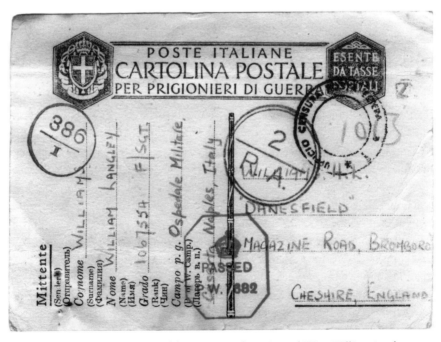

Italian prisoner of war post card bringing confirmation of F/Sgt Williams' safety.

open trading would never have been allowed in Germany, but the Italians sold these luxuries on the black market in Rome.

Williams retained a newspaper cuttings from the *Daily Mail* printed in 1943. The article described life within Italian camps, and the practice of drinking the Red Cross tea and then drying the leaves in the sun. The prisoners would then repack the leaves and trade them for wine with the guards. Once when they ran out of dried tea leaves, they gave the guard a fresh packet of unused tea. The guard immediately returned the next day in a temper, handed back the fresh tea demanding some proper tea. The same article also made a plea for more English text books on handicraft and trades to be sent to the camps in Italy.

Williams was held in PG54 from 31 December 1942 to 5 September 1943. In September, the Allied forces landed on the Italian mainland, the Italian Government surrendered, and the guards simply abandoned the responsibility of guarding the camp. The vast majority of men tore off the large coloured patches sewn onto their uniforms to identify them as prisoners of war, gathered what provisions were available, and dispersed into the hills before any German guards arrived to take control of the camp. Splitting up into small groups, the hillsides ended up holding hundreds of escaped prisoners of war. Living off grape vines and foraging, Williams made his way to Frosinone, a location that was to feature significantly in the Allied campaign in Italy during the coming months. It was the location where he was recaptured by the Germans on 23 October 1943. Williams' Italian tour was over. He was once more a prisoner, and detained in Frosinone for seven days before being transported with other prisoners by train from Italy to Austria.

The men were detained in Munich, Mooseburg, on 9 November, but moved again just thirteen days later. Williams was eventually placed in the permanent camp of Heydekrug on 5 of December 1943. He joined the large, recently moved contingent of men from various other camps across Germany. He was now a very long way from North Africa, but still supporting his original prisoner of war number 460. Once more, his finger prints were taken and another photograph processed for his records at Heydekruk. After delousing and a thorough search, he was allocated a barrack and bunk. The statutory cautiousness of those around him soon lifted once they knew who he was. Amongst a significantly high number of fellow aviators, Williams went through the 'what, where, when' routine, which satisfied the prisoners' thirst for news, regardless of where you came from.

Williams had most certainly completed his evolution as a Kriegie. He had just completed his first full year of detention; life was monotonous and predictable in the camp. Heydekruk guards were required to comply with section 475 of the Compilation of Orders, number 30, issued by the Wehrmacht on 16 October 1943. It created a sinister situation whereby guards were required to stand with their rifles loaded and placed as 'safe', and their bayonets fixed, unless the camp commandant, for special reasons, ordered a deviation from

that rule. The order was extended to guards who accompanied prisoners of war on transport or on their way to and from places of work. When this order was initially put in place, the tension within the camp grew considerably.

Another initiative that led to further unsettlement was caused by the Germans who commenced efforts to stretch the supply of fuel issued to prison camps. Using coal, dust, and clay, the Germans had created the uniformed shape of an egg brick to replace proper coal. These new bricks were ineffective in creating any heat. The barrack stoves were not in themselves very effective even with proper fuel, therefore the new coal eggs reduced heat production for the rooms. It was a development that seriously affected the morale of the men.

The uniformly agreed custom of reading books did while away many hours, but in the winter months, with significantly long and dark evenings, even that was denied to the prisoners. Commandants under orders from the Wehrmacht instigated the examination of all camp lighting within prisoner of war quarters. All superfluous lights were to be eliminated; lighting was only to comply with that found within German squad room barracks:

THE EVOLUTION OF A KRIEGIE.... 33

DOING INTERMINABLE CIRCUITS, OUR KRIEGIE

DEVELOPS A PERMINANT LEANING TO THE LEFT (NOT POLITICALLY)

R A WHILE HIS HEAD 'S TO GO ROUND IN CIRCLES'

HE IS THEN SAID TO BE ROUND THE BEND !!

Pen and ink sketches illustrating 'The Evolution of a Kriegie', parts 1, 2 and 3.

Rooms occupied by one to four men, 40 watts
Rooms occupied by five to eight men, 74 watts
For every additional man, an additional 10 watts

With such low wattage bulbs covering large areas, the only place to be able to read a book was directly under an illuminated bulb. That was an unattractive option to any man trying to read, and it would cause other men to claim that the light, for what it was worth, was being shielded from them; a situation guaranteed to create tension and arguments.

To overcome the reduction in lighting, any room with men engaged in creating forged documents frequently created raised tables to bring the forger closer to the light. Electric light bulbs that became defective were frequently not replaced for several weeks at a time, and in some instances, replacements were known to take months. Light bulbs were generally difficult to obtain, and the only options to acquire greater wattage bulbs was by bribing a tame guard. Commandants frequently enforced rule 687 of the camp regulations, reminding their company commanders that it was their responsibility to educate the subordinates upon the importance of maintaining the proper distance between themselves and the prisoners of war. All conversations between German soldiers and prisoners of war that were not justified by the needs of the service or work assignments were forbidden. Rule 687 was sufficiently enforced, which meant that the process of turning a guard was at times lengthy. A form of entrapment, followed by bribery, frequently resulted in success. The quest to obtain high wattage electric light bulbs existed in every prisoner of war camp.

William wrote this in the camp sometime in 1943:

Blue Skies of Exile

Only to the earth am I imprisoned
There is no fixity about the sky
For often, upwards from the barbed fence gazing,
I see a trace of native air go by.

Breathed into, brightened by the heart I left behind me,
And I think the sky has caught sometimes, the very prayer that you are
Speaking in answer to the light winged homing thoughts,
Which I release to Heaven now and then,
In supplication that an errand star may drop them off,
When in his orbit flying past next the garden where you are.

Only to the earth am I imprisoned
And sometimes when the sky is special blue,
I know it is that selfsame patch of Heaven that yesterday sailed slowly over you. PoW number 460.

The original author of these words is not currently known or identified in any way. Many poems or verses were duplicated into their own wartime logs. The words in 'Blue Skies of Exile' are very appropriate for the captured aviators who frequently looked up to the sky from their wire cages. Williams endured his captivity through the spring and early summer of 1944. The secret radio provided the long awaited news of an Allied forces invasion that June, but it was on 17 July when Williams recorded his movement from Heydekrug to Thorn, Poland. He was most fortunate to only be resident in that horrible camp for no more than eighteen days. William was part of the mass evacuation of prisoners of war moved once more to Fallingbostel, Stalag 357 on 10 August 1944. This move brought stability, and Williams was resident in this camp until 7 April 1945. On that day, the entire camp was evacuated, apart from those who were not fit to march, and were therefore left in the care of the camp. All able-bodied prisoners commenced their enforced march westwards towards central Germany. Williams records this period as nothing more than, 'on the hoof'. Unbeknown to him, he was experiencing one of the longest forced marches in history.

William was 'on the hoof' from 7 April 1945 to 2 May 1945. It would appear that he experienced the full hardship of that march. The British Army are recorded as liberating columns of Allied prisoners of war near Lubeck on that day. Within nine days, medical needs had been addressed, and Williams was back in the United Kingdom. Following a debrief by the MI9 Intelligence Department on 12 May 1945, he was released on prisoner of war leave entitlement.

Warrant Officer Williams volunteered for continued operational service within the Royal Air Force. The Far East conflict was still being fought, and he wished to participate. Williams was selected for a conversion course, which prepared him for flying within the Far East theatre of operations. Williams was photographed in late 1945 with his new crew just prior to their operational posting. As a result of the Allied victory over Japan, the operational needs in the Far East were immediately reduced. This gallant group of aviation volunteers never achieved their joint wish to fly in combat against the Japanese Imperial Army.

Bill Williams returned to civilian life as a clerk, but developed diabetes shortly after his demobilisation in May 1946. The illness was considered to have had some bearing upon the time served as a prisoner of war, but regardless of this, he retired happily with his wife Lucille, and died in December 1989.

Warrant Officer Williams with his new crew ready to serve in the Far East.

18

Flight Sergeant
Ellis Stanley Leach

Ellis Leach volunteered for service in the Royal Air Force in May 1940. Leaving his employment with the London Midland and Scottish Railway Company, he attended the Aircrew Reception Centre, London, in August 1941. Fortunately, having been selected for pilot training, Ellis left the United Kingdom bound for Florida. Leach was a pupil at the primary land plane training centre in Pensacola (the American equivalent of the RAF initial training venue), having commenced his training on 18 March 1942. The station was an American Naval base, where he flew in the N3N aircraft; a United States tandem seat, open cockpit, primary training biplane aircraft built by the Naval Aircraft Factory. The aerodrome in Pensacola was at Grossie ILE, and this was an entirely different arena for pilot training when compared to the United Kingdom, due to safe open skies and large, unobstructed runways on which the basic flying skills were mastered.

In August 1942, Leach attended the No. 35 Elementary Flight Training School, Neepawa, Manitoba, Canada. As part of C Flight, he was in the company of several service students from the navy, army, and air force. The British Commonwealth Air Training Plan saw more than 130,000 personnel from Great Britain, Canada, Australia, and New Zealand graduate from 107 training schools across Canada during the Second World War. The safe skies and open landscape represented the ideal aviation training location. Leach flew the Tiger Moth biplane and then the Airspeed Oxford, accumulating over 200 hours experience by December 1942.

Ellis Leach then moved onto Prince Edward Island, Canada, where he flew reconnaissance and navigation training in the New Year.[95] He then moved onto operational training at Patricia Bay, British Columbia, where he flew the Hampden. He was engaged on torpedo dropping exercises, low level sea firing exercises, and air to air firing. Leach was assessed as an average torpedo bombing pilot at the conclusion of his course in July 1943.

Sergeant Ellis Leach successfully completed his initial training in Canada, and having been presented with his pilots wings at an official passing out parade, he took passage back to the United Kingdom. Leach's next stage of pilot instruction commenced at No. 2 Coastal Command Operational Training Unit at RAF

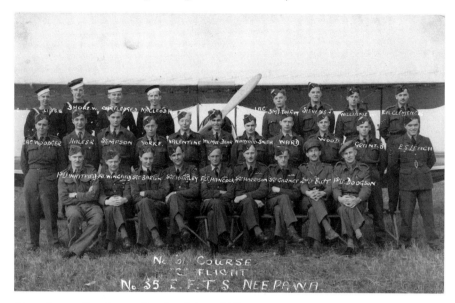

Aircraftsman Leach standing far right, middle row.

Sergeant Leach on 3 June 1943, having dropped two torpedo markers against the towed periscope drogue. The target was designed to create a realistic effect upon the water surface, simulating an enemy U-Boat periscope wake.

Cotfoss, Yorkshire, where he gained experience on the larger Bristol Beaufort aircraft. This training was in preparation for his final operational aircraft, the Bristol Beaufighter. Any pilot posted onto a squadron operating the Beaufighter regarded himself as lucky; it was reported to be an incredible aircraft to fly. The pilot would sit forward, enabling him to experience a superb panoramic view, with the two massive Bristol Hercules engines aligned almost directly alongside the cockpit. The heavily armed Bristol Beaufighter could also be a troublesome aircraft to handle in low speed flight, but nevertheless, it was one of the most lethal warplanes of its era. The aircraft frequently delivered fatal blows against shipping and transport targets with both torpedo and rocket armaments.

Leach teamed up with his navigator Flying Officer Callaghan at the training unit. They were to become a most successful team, which commenced with their initial posting to North Africa where they were required to ferry the Beaufighter NE416 to Cairo West in February 1944. Frustratingly for Leach, on arrival he was required to undertake further flying at the maintenance unit at Heliopolis, and then at Shallufa. This proved to be fortunate, as he was able to qualify with propelled rockets during a short course; the targets having been small caiques or assorted shipping targets. Caigues were small boats that completely disintegrated when struck by a rocket-propelled weapon. The firepower of the Beaufighter was extraordinary in this role of aerial conflict.

In May 1944, Leach and Callaghan left North Africa and were ferried to Calcutta, India. They had been posted to the Far East Beaufighter wing to serve with 211 Squadron against the Japanese in the Burma theatre.[96] The firepower of the rocket equipped Mark X Beaufighter was put to effective use in this strike fighter role. 211 Squadron had been given the task of seeking out and attacking enemy road, rail, and waterborne transport. These operations required them to fly very long distances, frequently at low level and over hostile territory. Additional dangers existed, with little hope of escape in the event of mechanical failure, pilot fatigue, or ultimately being shot down, all of which were distinct possibilities. The Beaufighter had a unique characteristic; it was remarkably silent in its approach at a low level. This enabled the pilots to create surprise attacks on the selected targets, earning the aircraft its macabre nickname 'Whispering Death' from the Japanese forces.

The Far East was a very different conflict to be engaged in compared to the European theatre. Wherever they were in the world, no pilot or member of any aircrew ever wanted to lose their aircraft, which meant they had to parachute onto enemy held territory, regardless of where they served. In the Far East, immense risks were taken, with pilots flying badly damaged aircraft over Japanese held territory; indeed, risks worth taking. Additional time in the air represented the possibility of a crew covering as much distance as possible back towards Allied lines. Allied pilots and aircrew captured by the Japanese during the Second World War were looked upon with contempt, and without exception were regarded as cowards.

Due to the unique circumstances created in the Far East theatre of operations, the RAF designed a specific garment for aircrews, namely the Beadon suit. It was made of a light material suitable for the tropics, and fitted with multiple buttoned pockets that held maps, a compass, a hacksaw, and a machete. These items supported the primary escape kit, which held a supply of anti-malaria tablets and water purification tablets. Every effort was taken to provide the airmen with a means of survival and evasion from the Japanese.

The Japanese military culture saw no place for surrender, and Japanese captors would make it clear to any unfortunate prisoner that his Japanese equivalent would have fought and died rather than be taken by his enemy. Without fail, prisoners would be interrogated by their initial captors. This might be by the senior ranking officer available, or if they were unlucky, by the Kempai Tai, the Japanese equivalent of the Gestapo. English speaking Burmese natives were used as interpreters. Many of these brave individuals later provided vital evidence of Japanese war crimes in the postwar trials. The Japanese placed a high priority in establishing immediate intelligence; in many instances they used undue methods that escalated to the use of lethal force.

The Japanese had struck fear in the minds of aviators; accounts of pilots being beheaded were well evidenced. Japan was not a signatory to the Geneva Convention, and its rules associated with prisoner of war detention were seriously abused. The fate of William Ellis Newton, a pilot serving in the Royal Australian Air Force, provides a graphic example of the Japanese treatment of aviators.

Flight Lieutenant William Newton served in New Guinea from May 1942 to March 1943. He had successfully completed fifty-two operational sorties, but when leading an attack on 16 March 1943, his Boston aircraft was hit repeatedly by anti-aircraft fire. Although it was crippled, he managed to return the aircraft to base, where he made a successful landing. Newton returned to the same target the following day. His aircraft was again hit, and this time it burst into flames. The official account of events recorded by members of his squadron describes:

> Flight Lieutenant Newton maintained control and calmly turned his aircraft away and flew along the shore. He saw it as his duty to keep the aircraft in the air and to take his crew as far away as possible from the enemy's positions. With great skill he brought his blazing aircraft down on the water.

Two members of the crew successfully extricated themselves from the aircraft and were seen by the Japanese to be swimming to shore. One of them was Flight Lieutenant Newton. He was captured and later executed on 29 March, 1943 at Salamaua, New Guinea.

250748 Flight Lieutenant William Ellis Newton RAAF was awarded the posthumous Victoria Cross, published in the *London Gazette* on 19 October 1943:

Without regard to his own safety, he had done all that man could do to prevent his crew falling into enemy hands. Flight Lieutenant Newton's many examples of conspicuous bravery have rarely been equalled and will serve as a shining inspiration to all who follow him.

His body was recovered by Australian troops following the occupation of Salamaua. William Newton was later buried with full military honours in the Lae War Cemetery, New Guinea.[97]

The virtues of operational flying over Japanese territory had been fully understood by Leach and his navigator. In July 1944, they experienced the sight of endless miles of jungle tree tops; a difficult environment to negotiate when seeking out their first target. It was going to be a most challenging tour of duty. On their second operation, six of the squadron Beaufighters were led by Squadron Leader Muller-Rowland DFC for an attack on the Mandalay waterfront. Targets such as barges, steamers, and any trains using the main railway line were sought. The weather conditions created thick cloud, which caused the aircrafts to lose sight of each other. Leach parted with the formation, but found the unmistakable Irrawady River, which cuts through Burma until it reaches the delta of the Indian Ocean. He followed the east bank of the river looking for a shipping target, but as he did so, the Beaufighter unexpectedly received light anti-aircraft fire that caused damage to the aircraft's elevator controls, Leach ordered Callaghan to bale out, for having assessed the damage, he knew it was serious. However, he found that he could hold the Beaufighter by using the trim controls,[98] and immediately counter-ordered the bale out and commenced flying towards Myitkyina. In an attempt to lighten the airframe, Leach let lose all of his rockets and fired all cannon shells. This created further instability, but he was able to keep control, and the reduction in weight enabled the Beaufighter to gently gain further height. With sufficient fuel and height, the crew managed to reach Cox's Bazaar, India. The sortie had taken 5 hours, but they managed to land safely, and both men survived with no injuries. Leach and Callaghan both received transit in order to return to their forward airstrip at Chiringa. Once on station, they explained to the intelligence officer the events that had overtaken them. The anti-aircraft gunfire had appeared out of nowhere; the Japanese became adept at laying formations of three to four anti-aircraft weapons in triangles of fire. These created intensely dangerous fields of fire for any aircraft negotiating that particular sector of air space. In effect they predicted areas of vulnerability and Ellis Leach had unfortunately flown into one such trap.

For the rest of July, Leach flew operations that successfully targeted the railway at Myingyan, the waterfront at Mandalay, and a Japanese army post called Basha, South of Donbaik. In August, he managed to fly low enough on one operation to fire all eight rocket bombs into the railway sheds at Maymyo; a well executed delivery that had been fired off in four pair combinations. The destruction was such that he regarded the target as completely destroyed.

The dangers of these low level, air to ground attacks was brought to bear on Leach on 6 August. Two 211 Squadron Beaufighters were allocated the target of the Thazi railway junction. They located the railway line and navigated eastwards towards the actual junction. Leach reduced his height and fired the rockets, but as he did so his aircraft was immediately struck by light machine gun fire from the ground defences. Leach was wounded in the chest and left shoulder, but managed to control the aircraft and gain some height while leaving the target area. Callaghan tried to assist leach with his injuries, but with the Beaufighter being so tight to manoeuvre, Callaghan could only help Leach by leaning over him, and together they managed to return to base and once again land safely. Leach had sustained some serious wounds and was immediately removed to hospital, leaving the cockpit awash with his blood. A few days later, he was transferred to a larger hospital in India. He did not return to the squadron until mid-November, when he was assessed as being fit to fly once more. Leach flew a further six low level operations upon the Japanese railway network, destroying targets of opportunity.

On 11 December 1944, 211 Squadron published the following in its routine orders, serial number 141:

The following has been mentioned in 'COMMAND MENTIONS'
F/O Callaghan 138079 F/S Leach 990198.

On 6 August 1944, F/S Leach was briefed to attack a well defended enemy railway junction. In spite of intense and accurate ground fire, he pressed home his attack at low level. This NCO was wounded by a machine gun bullet entering his shoulder, which came out through his chest. F/O Callaghan, his navigator, immediately came forward and rendered first aid. Although in great pain and suffering from severe loss of blood, F/Sgt Leach, through sheer courage and determination, flew his aircraft back over 250 miles and made a perfect landing at base before collapsing. F/O Callaghan had rendered every possible assistance in this arduous return trip, and it was largely due to his encouragement that his pilot was able to get back to base. On another occasion, F/S Leach had his elevator shot away when attacking targets in the Mandalay areas. He suggested to F/O Callaghan that he should bale out, but this officer refused and preferred to navigate his pilot back to base, where he again refused to jump out, but stayed with his pilot who made a successful landing by the use of his elevator trim.

MID 211 Squadron Burma.

Ellis Leach continued with his operational tour of duty, flying a further seven missions in December. Interestingly, two night sorties were undertaken, one upon an aerodrome and another upon steam engines running at night. The Japanese took measures to try and camouflage or reduce the identification of steam trains running at night, but the fire box was still likely to provide enough of a target. A similar operation on 1 February saw Leach attack and destroy an eight coach carriage train on the Rangoon to Prome railway. The night operations were taking nearly 5 hours to complete, as flying at night in Burma was not an easy task to perform. Briefed for a further operation the following night, Leach was very pleased to complete it safely and return to daylight operations a few days later.

On 12 February, Leach and Callaghan attended the operational briefing in the accustomed manner. The sortie was similar to many they had already undertaken, flying down to the Gulf of Martaban to seek out any Japanese shipping targets. Flying Beaufighter G NV553, they took off at 4.05 a.m. They never returned, and the squadron records could only record the fact that the aircraft was missing. 'Particulars unknown' had been written by the records compiler.

Unbeknown to the squadron, Leach's aircraft suffered the complete loss of the starboard engine after being in the air a couple of hours. Leach was over the Gulf, but not very far out to sea, therefore an emergency ditching took place. Leach and Callaghan escaped from the aircraft and climbed into the auto-inflated rubber life raft. Unfortunately, they were close to shore and the Japanese had witnessed them ditch into the sea, putting them in a position to quickly capture Leach and Callaghan as they reached the shore. The thought of what was about to take place must have overtaken them completely; intelligence officers had provided full briefings upon such undesirable circumstances. In the knowledge that they would be treated with contempt by all Japanese service personnel, leach and Callaghan knew it was going to be traumatic. They prepared themselves for the initial interrogation.

Leach and Callaghan endured as best as possible the humiliating process imparted upon them. It was not uncommon for the Japanese to march their prisoners long distances before reaching their place of initial internment.

A typical Far East Squadron, briefing for operations.

Rangoon Jail was a primary site used by the Japanese and was in close proximity to their capture; it was to be their final destination. At Rangoon Jail, all prisoners were placed in solitary confinement for a number of days, in effect a similar practice to the Luftwaffe's Dulag Luft interrogation centres. The Japanese system of interrogation and imprisonment was far harsher than any European prisoner of war camp.

Rangoon jail was a most squalid place; food was in short supply and conditions were cramped, dirty, and basic to the extreme. Japanese roll calls were called in the same way as in Germany, but were likely to be horrid experiences. All prisoners had to be present and answer their name and camp number in Japanese. Failure to comply, or answer any question imposed on them was dealt with by swift and brutal beatings by the guards. The beatings often involved the use of rifle butts or hard bamboo poles. Prisoners of the Japanese forces also had to bow and show respect to the guards, particularly whenever a guard entered any room or area. Failure to comply meant another relentless beating. It was common place for prisoners to receive a slap across the head, despite having offered the respect required.

Prisoners were kept in barracks or wings of the jail according to nationality and rank. At Rangoon, the blocks were long, thin buildings, all converging on a central courtyard like spokes of a large wheel. The blocks housed prisoners of war from America, Australia, India, China, and the other British Commonwealth countries. All the men were kept in their separated groups to prevent communication taking place. The numbers of RAF prisoners in the Japanese prison camps were, in comparison to German camps, exceptionally low. The aviators were exclusively detained in block 8. The Australian prisoners in Rangoon were very much aware of the inhumanity of the Japanese towards Allied prisoners of war. The 'death railway' conditions imposed upon thousands of men forced to construct the railway link across Burma were unimaginable. Some of the other camps on the small Pacific islands were provided with almost impossible conditions in which to sustain human life.

Conditions in Rangoon Jail were as unpleasant as anywhere else, but they did not reach the barbaric levels mentioned above. In the small cell rooms, which were all situated off long corridors, there were very few, if any, beds for the men. In many cases, overcrowding created conditions whereby men could not lie down with their legs stretched out. The camp environment was not just uncomfortable, but a disaster when trying to keep disease from spreading through the jail. The European camps created conditions where the body louse spread with ease, but the Far East conditions created hot, humid conditions that assisted in the reproduction of other parasitic beasts, all looking for human hosts to feed upon.

Toilets were holes dug in the ground, with boards to stand upon. In some instances during confinement, a simple empty ammunition box was provided. The exposed matter created a feeding source for the same insects that later sought to bite into the prisoners flesh, becoming horribly infected. Conditions were not helped during the monsoon period, which took place from late March to late May, bringing with it torrid rainfalls that created stifling and oppressive humidity, which allowed disease to thrive in the extreme. The medical officers at the jail were often devastated at the speed at which men would fall ill and quickly die of diseases that could have been dealt with fairly easily had the correct drugs been available. The diagnosis wasn't all that difficult; men lost their appetite, and then their will to live. Medical officers found it difficult to keep the sick alive, with many men simply dying in their sleep. It was as though they could not win over the terrible conditions they had to endure, and gave up on such a miserable and painful existence.

The diseases and ailments rife in Rangoon Jail included dysentery, beriberi, and jungle sores. Food was the main topic of conversation for the inmates of the jail. The Japanese were not worried about prisoners suffering from ailments that could not transfer to them. As an exception, Cholera was a disease that would be acted upon immediately, as it directly put the Japanese themselves at risk. The connection between food and the amount of disease at the jail was an obvious one; with poor rations insufficient to maintain a basic level of nourishment the men grew weaker all the time. There was one main reason why the biggest killer, beriberi, was rampant in the prison. The diet was always that of low grade and polished rice. Polished rice was just the grain and none of the husk or kernel. The husk would have been a natural and vital source of vitamin B for the prisoners; the main weapon against beriberi. Eventually, the medical men realised that they needed to address this problem. The rice was always contained in hessian sacks, which normally resulted in some of the husk material being left within the weave of the sacking. They collected all the chaff and husk, which was made into a paste. The medical men called this substance 'nuka'. It was bitter and foul to the taste, but there was never enough produce to sufficiently provide for the men. Those issued with 'nuka' ate knowing it could be the difference between life and death.

The staple diet was rice. Occasionally, the rice came with small quantities of local vegetable known as 'okra', and infrequently, portions of rank meat and fish would be present. Prisoners of war regarded as fit and capable of work were taken under armed guard into Rangoon or surrounding areas. Regarded as slave labour, the men would dig trenches or unload ships at the docks. All working parties took the opportunities to gather other foodstuffs if at all possible.

Cigarettes were hard to come by, and as in all prison camps, they were valued commodities that facilitated barter and exchange. The Japanese culture towards prisoners of war created significant barriers compared to what had been accustomed in Europe. The Japanese professed to suggest that prisoners were not in need of anything additional to that already provided by to them. Red Cross food parcels were not recognised or facilitated by the Japanese. The Red Cross and neutral powers were thwarted in their efforts to organise any delivery by neutral ships to designated locations. Likewise, the YMCA was anxious to provide assistance to the Far East prisoners of war. Stores were stockpiled, and equipment, including urgently required medication products, was packed and ready for distribution. All these efforts were thwarted by the entire structure of prisoner management in the Japanese army, which was tempered by their belief that suicide was more honourable than surrender.

Death came to many prisoners by this neglectful attitude. Any prisoner who died at Rangoon Jail was provided with a funeral, normally facilitated by the highest ranking officer in that man's cell block. The deceased were placed in rice sacks, stitched together to cover the body. The burials took place in the grounds a little distance away from the jail. The bible was banned under Japanese rule, so any bible in Rangoon Jail became closely guarded and exceptionally well hidden. With no YMCA materials arriving, books also became a most precious possession. Any prisoner found writing would be beaten, and any attempted escape would, without doubt, end with a death sentence. Infringements by prisoners were always met with the wrath of guards, not only to the individual but collectively. Beatings with rifle butts and other offensive weapons would be administered. The Japanese sought to humiliate the captives, and appeared to gain pleasure from doing so. The custom of slapping the prisoners with hands took place on a daily basis with no provocation whatsoever.

As the war drew to its conclusion in Burma, Rangoon was not a safe place to be. The Allied forces rightly expected the Japanese to do what they had always done and fight to the last soldier in the city. However, the Japanese commander General Kimura abandoned the city well before the 14th Army were near to its provinces.

On 25 April 1945, the commandant of Rangoon Jail instructed that all fit and able men from the jail should be selected for movement. Leach and his navigator were naturally selected, having been recent additions to the jail. At around 4 p.m., the selected men, who totalled 437, were forced march out of Rangoon Jail. This was a forced march committed for a far different purpose than that instigated by Adolf Hitler in Germany. The Japanese selected the fit and apparently health prisoners with the intention of marching them to Moulmen. The Japanese Army wanted to ship the prisoners to work camps in South East Asia and mainland Japan. The prisoners were provided with food and whatever additional clothing was available for the march, with hand carts deployed to carry the stores. The Japanese commandant instructed that the men should march at night and rest during the day. The march was well organised, with a mobile vehicle running ahead to facilitate food stops and resting locations. Having walked for three nights, some of the prisoners experienced difficulty in continuing. Many men were in bare feet, and the water store was almost diminished, with food also running out. By the evening of the third day, the prisoners had reached Pegu. The march continued in a north-east direction, but the pace was now very slow. Having walked an estimated total of sixty-five miles, the column of men rested on 29 April. The Japanese realised that the route to Moulmen was no longer possible due to the war front progressing towards Rangoon. The Japanese commandant gave the prisoners their liberty, leaving them to fend for themselves. The prisoners were mainly wearing drab khaki uniforms, which were sighted by a flight of Allied Hurricanes flown by pilots of the Indian Air Force. Thinking that they had sighted a column of Japanese soldiers, the Hurricanes took several runs, strafing the area with their machine guns. This was an identical problem to the one experienced by the marching columns of prisoners trudging towards central Germany. With no visual recognition to aircraft of their status, such large groups of men were always likely to be attacked and sustain casualties in these circumstances. Ellis Leach and his navigator were fortunate to survive the strafing. The march had ceased, and on the afternoon of 29 April 1945, the 14th Army reached their position and immediately tended to the wounded, supporting the prisoners' needs as best possible. It was in fact the 1st Battalion, West Yorkshire Regt of the 17th Division that came across the prisoners of war.[99]

The remaining prisoners in the jail had no means of communication. Aware that Allied aerial activity was increasing, and that the replacement Japanese guards had vacated the jail completely, a decision was taken to place a message on the roof of one of the cell blocks. Finding some white paint, the large white lettering simply read 'Japs Gone'.

The message appeared to bring no results, so it was decided to use the last remaining paint and display 'Extract Digit', a phrase that the RAF would understand, and one that could only have been placed by a captive airman. Insufficient paint was left to complete the job properly, but thankfully, enough was done for the message to be understood. A photograph showing the newly added message was taken by a Beaufighter from 211 Squadron. The remaining prisoners in the jail could think of nothing worse than to be killed by bombs dropped by their own side.

Shortly after the message had been recognised, a Liberator aircraft flew over and dropped Red Cross parcels and army rations into the jail. The army rations, known as K packs, consisted of cigarettes, chocolate, biscuits, and chewing gum. They dropped them right into the compound, with one even going through the cookhouse roof. The first aid packages with fresh clean bandages had not been seen in the jail for several years. Rangoon Jail was finally liberated by the 71st Brigade, 26th Indian Division XV Corp on 3 May 1945.

In the last few days before liberation, the Burma Defence Army and the Indian National Army,[100] two groups that had previously struggled for power, seized upon the fact of the Japanese withdrawal, and assisted the senior officers present within the jail. Ironically, both of these groups had also collaborated with the Japanese in one way or another.

The graves at Rangoon Jail were exhumed by the Allies and the Imperial War Graves Commission in late 1945, and the remains of the men were later interned in the Rangoon War Cemetery. Within that cemetery are a number of men who suffered the fate of beheading by the Japanese. Flight Sergeant Stanley James

Rangoon Jail with 'Japs Gone' painted on the jail roof by the prisoners.

'Extract Digit' painted on the roof of Rangoon Jail, indicating the need to liberate the jail as soon as possible.

Halifax aircraft. The Halifax was taken on numerous circuits and landings over the aerodrome at Riccall, the home of No. 1658 Heavy Conversion Unit. The boundaries of the Halifax were explored by the pilots flying on two and three engines, and preparing for the onset of full operation flying.

Brace and his crew were posted to 76 Squadron, Bomber Command. This was a squadron with a fully committed Halifax unit, which was flown consistently between 1941 and 1945. The crew joined the squadron at RAF Holme-on-Spalding Moor, Yorkshire, during April 1943. The 'A flight' Squadron Leader undertook a short cross-country flight with his new crew, no doubt applying a personal quality check. Sergeant McCann and the crew all passed the competency exercise, resulting in a first operation to bomb Stettin, which took place on 20 April. It was no gentle start for Brace, as the raid upon Stettin was some 600 miles from their aerodrome, and took 9 hours 25 minutes to complete. Bomber Command was pleased to report that the raid was most successful, but it was at a tragic cost. Twenty-one bombers failed to return from this deep penetration raid into Germany.

The crew's next raid was to Duisburg on 26 April; a 5-hour operation for which Brace dropped the bomb load on the Pathfinder indicators that were clearly visible. The very next day a different task presented itself to Brace; releasing aerial mines into the sea. These raids were to some extent regarded as low level, but accuracy was a prerequisite on the part of the navigator and bomb aimer. This particular operation was completed in less than 4 hours. The following month, four raids were engaged upon against Dortmund, Dusseldorf, Essen, and Wuppertal. By sheer coincidence, each operation took a very similar time scale of around 5 hours 30 minutes. Brace submitted his bold red flying logbook for inspection and approval at the end of the month. Lying on the commanding officer's desk, it would have stood apart from all other logs. It was common practice for all crewmembers to pen their names on the closed book pages, thus when in a pile, the owner was immediately identified. Another unique fact concerning the SAAF issue logbooks was that there was less room on the pages, resulting in insufficient space available to follow this long standing RAF tradition. John Brace's flying logbook was returned to him, having been endorsed by his commanding officer for having the correct account of his competed flying hours and operations.

Brace commenced a sequence of bombing operations in June, concentrating efforts on Dusseldorf, Le Creusot, Krefeld, Mulheim, and Cologne. These raids enabled Brace to add a further 23 hours 55 minutes of operational flying over Germany into his flying logbook. With Brace approaching half way through his tour of duty, which had progressed with no major incidents, he was well aware that 76 Squadron had been suffering heavy casualties.

Bomber Command had been engaged in an intense campaign against the German Ruhr, with the industrial targets being top priority. The huge 4,000-lb bombs carried by the Halifax looked unlike any traditional bomb, and they were known as 'cookies'. They were massive cylindrical tubes, with colour coded bands painted around the circumference of the bomb. The coloured bands identified the type of explosive contents within the device. Minol was an explosive mixture of 40 per cent TNT, 40 per cent ammonium nitrate, and 20 per cent powdered aluminium, which was added to increase the blast effect. Various developments led to differing proportions of these basic components. The Amatol/TNT mixture proved to be a relatively insensitive type of explosive, allowing the armourers some level of safety during transit and storage. The fuse, or initiator, designed to set off the 'cookie' was made from a far more sensitive explosive. This was fitted only at the time of loading the bombs into the aircraft's bomb bay. The bomb was designed to create a huge blast effect upon the ground, resulting in damage to buildings, roofs, and other structures. The development of this bomb had originated from the German 'G' parachute mine which had created huge devastation on buildings across London and Coventry. The British 'cookie' continued development during the war, and various types were deployed by Bomber Command. The standard load for a heavy bomber would be a 4,000-lb HC bomb, or 'cookie', and a number of 4-lb incendiary bombs; the large bomb to blast the target apart and the incendiaries to then set fire to the destroyed buildings within the target area. Incendiary bombs were designed to ignite after impacting on the ground, and to be capable of generating a great heat in the immediate target area. The 4-lb bombs contained thermite pellets within a magnesium alloy body. After the pellets had reached a high enough temperature, the magnesium case would ignite and continue to burn for up to 10 minutes.

A Bomber Command Halifax bomber being loaded with a 'Cookie' blast bomb.

In July of that year, Halifax DK 240, with the identification letter 'H', became the regular aircraft used by Brace's crew. The aircraft had been built by the Fairey Aviation Company Limited under contract No. ACFT/891/SAS. 150 aircraft had been requisitioned within the contract, with deliveries to the RAF commencing at the end of 1942. DK240 was from the final production run, and after acceptance, would have arrived at 76 Squadron around mid-1943.

Halifax DK 240 was flown consistently by Brace and his crew, commencing on 3 July to Cologne, then Gelsenkirchen, Aachen, and Montbeliard on 15 of that month. Two consecutive operations on 9 and 10 August took place to Mannheim and Nurnberg, where on the latter operation, the aircraft turned back home after only 2 hours due to technical faults. A well earned rest of two days took place, but on 12 August, the crew were briefed for another operation. This was for a long run to Milan in northern Italy; a new experience for the crew, away from German and French targets. The pilot Bryan McCann had been appointed a commission to pilot officer. However, seniority in rank within the crew remained with Brace, who by this time had been appointed as a flying officer. The remaining men in the crew were all sergeants; the youngest was Harold Martin, aged nineteen, from Ontario Canada, and the oldest was Alec Samuel, aged twenty, from the Isle of Wight. Six young men climbed aboard DK 240 at around 8.15 p.m. on 12 August, all independently checking their communications and oxygen equipment. At 8.45 p.m., the pilot engaged all four engines at full power and lifted the Halifax from the concrete runway. This was to be Brace's nineteenth operation with the crew, which was now to be regarded as an experienced one. 76 Squadron sent twenty-two aircraft on the raid, with only one aircraft fatally lost. DK 240, along with John Brace and his crew, was thought to have been shot down over France.

Only two men escaped from the Halifax with their lives, one of which was Flying Officer John Brace. Five members of his crew were later buried in the Bernay St Croix Cemetery, France; five consecutive Commonwealth war grave headstones side by side, ensuring the crew of DK 240 remained together in perpetuity.

Halifax DK 240 had been attacked by a German night fighter within 10 minutes of crossing the French Coast. Brace, sitting in the front section of the cockpit, was blown out of the aircraft by an explosion. His parachute deployed correctly, providing a safe landing in a field near Melicourt. Hiding his parachute and mae west in a ditch, he found his way to a farmhouse, where the occupants provided him shelter for the night. But with Germans in the area, Brace was moved into the woods, taking some food with him.

A resistance member, Jean Baptiste Celliez, arrived in the woods and provided civilian clothing for John. He was then taken to Argille, where he was housed in another farmhouse and taken under control by the local resistance group. Brace was advised that the resistance would be making arrangements to move him from the farm and pass him along the escape network in order to get him back to England. A few uneventful days passed, after which he was moved to a farmhouse owned by Andre Lavignee in St Laurent du Tersement. Brace remained there for approximately three weeks before he was advised of the next move, which was going to require a long cycle ride through the countryside. He was provided with a pedal cycle and a guide, who accompanied him on the two day ride to Beaumontel.

At Beaumontel, Brace remained in one house, living with the occupant Madam Rina Delaire. He was given a fake identity card in preparation of his planned escape. There was no doubt that Madam Delaire was risking her life by harbouring Brace while engaged in leading the resistance movement in Beaumontel. Three American airmen joined him in the house, 2nd Lieutenant Norman Toft, Technical Sergeant Delbert Klump, and Staff Sergeant Vandegriff. The Americans had been part of the crew from a B17 Flying Fortress of the 524th Bomber Squadron that had crashed at Epinay, Normandy. They had been hit by flak during a daylight raid to Romilly on 3 September 1943. From the crew of ten men, seven escaped with their lives, three of which were located and sheltered by this particular resistance unit. Brace experienced an enjoyable time while in hiding with the American aviators. Plans were underway for their passage into Spain, and presumably thence Gibraltar for passage to England.

The evaders were taken in a group by train to Le Mans, where they should have been handed over for the next stage of the journey. However no contact was established at the prearranged exchange location, and after a rather uncomfortable and dangerous wait at the railway station, the group returned to Beaumontel in the late evening. No explanation was forthcoming, and the group remained in Madam Delaire's house for a few weeks, keeping a low profile. There had been some concern over the lack of contact at Le Mans, and the evaders were moved between several farmhouses until the first week in November. At that time, they were advised that plans were in place to move them across the border into Spain. They embarked on the journey, which entailed taking a train to Paris accompanied by resistance operatives, then moving to the outskirts of the city, where they stayed in a small hotel. New identity cards were provided at that location, and once again they were moved by car to a small village, where they stayed with a family until 15 December. The carrying of identity cards by the French population was made mandatory by the Germans, and the design and type of the identity card changed at irregular intervals. This security measure induced by the Germans put evading airmen at a great disadvantage, as all of the identity cards carried a photograph of the individual. MI9 had instructed all aircrews engaged on operations over occupied Europe to secretly carry portrait photographs for the purpose of deployment upon fake identity cards created by the resistance network, if needed. The type of photographic paper used and the background of the images were all calculated accordingly.

John and the three Americans were later collected and taken to the railway station, where they were put on a train to Toulouse in order to continue their journey onto Limoges. 30 minutes into the journey, the Gestapo made a routine check of identity cards. The train tickets were held by a young French girl who was escorting the men, but with suspicious aroused, the Gestapo searched the men, and found an identity disk upon one of the Americans. The group were detained and transported under arrest to Paris. The four evaders and the young female resistance member were taken directly to Fresnes Prison. Brace was interrogated by the Gestapo and held in the prison for a month, with the threat of being executed as a spy held over him. Brace's interrogation was undertaken in an effort to gain evidence of the resistance operatives who had protected him during his time in France. The young French resistance worker, who was no doubt operating within the comet escape network, was never heard of again. Brace and the Americans were eventually removed from the jail and taken to the Dulag Luft on 16 December 1943. Here another interrogation process was endured, but this time the information sought had no connection to his evasion; he was questioned in relation to his squadron and where he had been flying from. On 8 January 1944, John left the Luftwaffe's interrogation centre, where he was subsequently absorbed into the prisoner of war camp at Stalag Luft III, Belaria, on 10 January.

Stalag Luft III, Belaria, was opened in early 1944. It was built a short distance north-east of Sagan, and various accounts explan that the original Stalag Luft III had grown to its maximum capacity, or that it was adapted to house those prisoners thought to be engaged in consistent escape activity. The author feels that last assumption may well have evolved due to the fact that handpicked men were removed from the original camp just prior to the Great

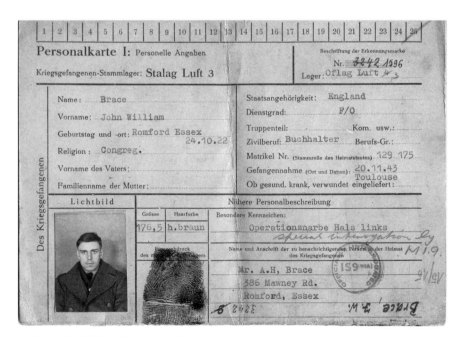

Stalag Luft III identification card.

Escape. 500 officers were transferred from Sagan during the second week of January. John Brace's camp record card indicates that Belaria had been temporarily designated as Stalag Luft IV. However, that title was passed to Gross Tychow, and instead the camp became an annex of Stalag Luft III. Belaria, originally a German military training camp, had additional barracks built on the site, which resulted in six extensive blocks that became fully occupied by mid-1944. Despite the camp being extended, facilities remained poor for the prisoners. Squadron Leader Bryce Cousens was to become an infamous personality in Belaria. He produced the camp news, titled *The Log*, which in July 1944 informed all the readers that the establishment had reached 728 officers and non-commissioned officers; 449 were British, 184 Canadian, 40 Australian, 28 New Zealanders, 27 South African, and 3 rabbits. Interestingly, the German prisoner of war regulations touched upon the cost of raising rabbits, which was to be governed by the charging to the Reich. However, Angora rabbit warrens and rabbit equipment were to be taken over at a fixed price by an agricultural expert of the military district applicable to the camp. Proceeds of any transaction were returned to the prisoner of war canteen once complete. This rather extraordinary inclusion into the regulations might be explained by previous actions taken by the Germans in removing any Irving fur lined flying jackets from the British prisoners. The jackets were apparently required for the German soldiers fighting on the Russian front, but each garment was sabotaged before the Germans could take them, with the seams cut and torn in order to render them useless.

The Belaria rabbits may well have escaped such extraordinary actions, as Squadron Leader Cousens mentioned in his camp news that the rabbits had a large exercise pen and were a constant source of amusement due to their efforts of digging out into the camp!

Flying Officer John Brace was allocated the prisoner of war number 3242. Brace was fortunate to secure a copy of a wartime log from a YMCA delivery to the camp, as there were never enough copies available for everyone. His first entry stated:

Belaria Camp Sagan:
The surrounding countryside appears to be flat and uninteresting. The word 'Belaria' so I am told means Good Air. As yet I have not noticed that this description can be applied to the air in the camp!

John went on to describe his first impressions of domestic life in the camp, written in pencil during July 1944:

The camp houses some 700 officers with 50 NCOs. There are six huts used as living and sleeping quarters, part of one of these is secured for the hospital. This means therefore that the camp is overcrowded; there are ten or twelve

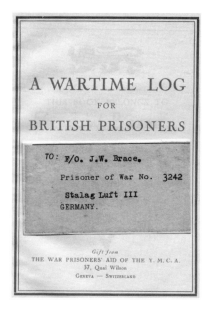

John Brace's wartime log.

men in each room. There is a threat that more prisoners are to be expected, and if they do arrive things will definitely become uncomfortable.

The orderlies are responsible for the cleanliness of the wash house and latrines, but the inmates of each room have to do all their own cleaning and cooking. This is good for me; it certainly provides occupation for some of the time, and helps to relieve the boredom. In my room, the duties are performed according to a roster, and we work in pairs. Thus for three days, one pair would be cooking the evening meal and washing up afterwards, and for the next three days they would be preparing the evening brew and so on.

Most of our food is provided by the Red Cross parcels, which are issued one to each man per week. The chocolate – there is one bar in each parcel, is divided equally amongst the members of the room, but the remainder of the contents is placed in the communal food cupboard.

The German authorities provide a weekly ration of food consisting of potatoes (sometimes), sugar, jam, barley in huge quantities, and cheese. The cheese unfortunately has a peculiar taste and smell, it does not appeal to us!

This highly repugnant product was known as 'fisch kase', or fish cheese, crusty on the outside, but with a soft almost milky interior. It was wrapped in triangular packets, but bore little resemblance to cheese. Despite their need, most Kriegies found it almost impossible to eat; the vile smell and texture induced the natural response to gag when it was swallowed.

There is a communal kitchen with a stove and sink in each hut; this is where all the cooking is done. Each room has a special time for using the stove and as there are thirteen rooms, it will be seen that there is something of a rush to get the meal ready. After a time, one becomes quite expert on the culinary front and many varied dishes are prepared, some very good and tasty, but others alas not so successful. Most meals have a strong taste of barley, if any person on our return to civilisation offers us tinned prunes or barley he is liable to get severely damaged!

Another of our domestic occupations must not escape mention. It is laundering. Every fortnight or so we find that we do a visit to the cookhouse to obtain hot water, proceed to the washhouse and use the soap provided by the Red Cross. It is a valuable commodity here, we use a 'sobie stick', simply made with a piece of wood and several empty tins. After sufficient pounding, you wash the soap out, providing the water is on, the Germans have a nasty habit of turning it off at the slightest provocation. After rinsing, the clothes are normally reasonably clean, since becoming a PoW we have realised the truth in the old saying, 'a woman's work is never done'.

July 1944 J. B.

John Brace was living in room 15, block 15, with nine other men all accommodated in his room. Two of these, J. Stephenson and Frank Collett, had been crew members together. Their Lancaster LM546 had been attacked by a night fighter over Stuttgart in July 1944, and both managed to parachute to safety. However, upon capture they were fortunate to end up together in the same camp, barrack, and room.

The longest serving prisoner of war within room 15 was Kenneth Noel Holland. He had been shot down over Belgium with 51 Squadron on 16 June 1941, only a matter of a few weeks after his marriage. Holland had been the navigator in Whitley Z6479, which suffered a violent and effective attack by night fighters, and later crashed near Limburg, Belgium. He was the only member of the crew to survive. Suffering from a fairly serious head wound, he had made good his escape from the crash scene, but after only a couple of days he was detained by a German soldier, who came upon him suddenly and without warning.

Following his capture, Holland served in several camps, one of which was Oflag XXIB, where he was involved in the construction of a tunnel, which led to a successful escape. With the help of twenty-four fellow prisoners, a total of thirty-three men eventually broke out using the tunnel, which began from an elaborate entrance in an outside lavatory. The manpower was required, as it was necessary not only to excavate the tunnel, but to also construct a holding room for escapees to secret themselves on the day of the escape, as the prisoners would be unable to get from barracks to tunnel entrance after the camp had locked down at night. The tunnel was supplied with air through an elaborate airline made of tins and a pump. Holland managed to escape along with three companions, Flying Officer Kirtland, Flying Officer Williams, and Flying Officer Asselin, who was a Canadian fighter pilot.

Holland was recaptured, and he eventually arrived in Stalag Luft III, where his previous studies at the Oriental School in London were enhanced with further studies on the Japanese language. His escape partner Joseph Asselin joined him in Stalag Luft III, where he became further engaged in working with the escape committee. Asselin subsequently received a Mention in Despatches in 1946 for his escape activities. Kenneth Holland no doubt also continued his activities, but received no recognition. He survived his war and continued to serve in the RAF. He was presented with the Air Efficiency Award medal in May 1946, and performed duties as an interpreter for the RAF in postwar Japan. Tragically, upon his return to the United Kingdom and while still serving in the RAF at Trimley Heath, he was killed in a motor car accident, on 19 September 1951.[102] Kenneth Holland was provided a full military funeral at the military cemetery at Tidworth.

By sheer coincidence, two other roommates had also been shot down on 20 December 1943, while operating on different squadrons; Reginald Evans on 44 Squadron and John Pakeman 76 Squadron. That same day also saw the demise of Flying Officer Leslie Rutherford's flying career. He was a fellow bomb aimer, who struck up a friendship with John Brace. Rutherford had survived a harrowing parachute descent with his chute only clipped on by one of the hook fasteners. He had been in the bomb aimer's position when the Lancaster exploded. He regained consciousness and found himself amongst parts of the aircrafts fuselage, which was tumbling down in the sky. He managed to pull the ripcord, which successfully deployed the parachute, resulting in him being jerked free from the wreckage. Although his leg had been damaged, he had survived an amazing escape. In August 1944, rutherford drew a sketch of the famous Pilot Officer Prune in Brace's wartime log, adding his signature and best wishes. Pilot Officer Prune, a character drawn by David Langdon in the RAF's wartime training memorandum Tee Emm,[103] frequently had an extended finger as a motto. In Rutherford's sketch, the abbreviation beneath the hand equates to 'pull your finger out', clearly making reference to their liberation from the prisoner of war camp.

Amongst all the 'Bomber boys' in Brace's room was a young 41 Squadron Spitfire pilot called Leslie Prickett. He had suffered engine trouble during a bomber escort operation to Watten on 27 August 1943. Forced to take his Spitfire down and commit to a forced landing, he chose the best possible field available and successfully came down near Campagne-les-Boulonnais in France. The resistance network covering Riotte, Renty, and Auxi-le-Chateau protected him until the end of October. The resistance operatives moved prickett by train to Amiens and then into Paris, but unfortunately, while awaiting collection in Paris in Decemeber, he was arrested by the Gestapo. Prickett was interrogated in the infamous Fresnes Prison, Paris. This prison was used by the Gestapo for holding and interrogating resistance, and British SOE suspects. It was a repulsive place where terrible measures were taken to extort information from such brave men and women.

Above: Flight Lieutenant Kenneth Holland in Japan. (*David Satchell*)

Right: Leslie Rutherford's sketch of Pilot Officer Prune.

Fresnes Prison, Paris.

Interrogation consisted of violent beatings and sadistic torture, and the corridors were frequently filled with screams of personal agony and occasional single gun shots. Prickett's identity was eventually established as a British fighter pilot, and he was then fortunately transferred to the custody of the Luftwaffe at the Dulag Luft interrogation centre. Prickett was subjected to the normal interrogation and documented accordingly. He was then included amongst a new intake of prisoners destined for Belaria.

This young pilot was well liked within his barrack block, and given any opportunity, he sketched his beloved Mk XII Spitfire EN236 in several other prisoners' wartime logs. His detailed drawing in Brace's book was completed on 16 August 1944. Such was his passion for the Spitfire, Prickett even drew a miniature representation when adding his signature to any document, particularly when providing his personal details and home address on contact lists that were passed around amongst the men. His skills were also used in the making of utensils, plates pots, and such like from coco cans, earning him the title of 'chief utensil maker' in the camp.[104]

There was another interesting addition to Brace's log on 3 August 1944. He asked another barrack friend, Maurice H. G. Wilson, to sketch his particular aircraft. Wilson created the picture of him flying in his Mk1 Mustang AG545 over the English Channel, leaving the white cliffs of Dover behind. He had depicted his daylight sortie to France on 18 January 1943, when operational with 4 Squadron from his airfield in Kent. He was flying a photographic tactical reconnaissance sortie along the French coast.[105] Wilson failed to return

Leslie Prickett's sketch of the Mk XII Spitfire EN236.

Maurice Wilson's sketch of the Mk1 Mustang AG545 flying over the English Channel.

from that sortie, as his Mustang came down in France, and after a short period of freedom assisted by the resistance movement, he was arrested and issued the PoW identity number 3290. John Brace was no doubt advised of Maurice Wilson's full story, but he made no mention of any additional information in his log. He did however note Maurice's home address in Castle Douglass, Scotland.

There was an important event for the prisoners that took place at Belaria on 12 August. Brace recorded the detail of the event, which occurred on the cricket pitch. It was not just a friendly match to while away the hours and allow another day's imprisonment to be marked on the calendar; it was to be a match of the utmost importance:

English PoWs verses Australian PoWs.
There were no huge crowds, no beautiful green grounds, and the players with one exception were not of first class cricket fame, but still the rivalry was present. The two teams were selected from the best English and Australian cricketers in the camp. The game, which was of 4 hours duration, commenced at 11.30 a.m. on the sports field adjoining the camp.

England won the toss and elected to field first. The two opening Australian batsmen Grimbley and Smith faced Wainwright, who was bowling. Grimbley showed he was on form by opening the scoring in the first over with two boundaries. Smith on the other hand played a very careful game, concentrating on defence. Neither Wainwright nor Kelshaw, the two bowlers, appeared to be troubling the batsmen. It was a surprise when Grimbley was bowled by Wainwright with a total of 47. He had played a delightful innings for 20 minutes and had shown forcibly that there was nothing to fear in the English bowling.

Pilot Officer Grimbley had been the pilot of Lancaster JB 548, of 57 Squadron, when attacking Berlin on the night of 1 January 1944. The entire crew became prisoners of war, with both officers in the crew ending up in Stalag Luft Belaria.

Hogg was the next man in. He and Smith added another 10 runs before the latter was bowled by Kelshaw for 11. Carmody, the Australian war time test captain, came to the wicket and proceeded to give the spectators a fine display of batting. One particular stroke must not escape mention, a hook for 6. It was a prodigious hit and the ball went well into the outside field.

We had given up hope of seeing the Carmody Hogg partnership broken, but one of the surprises that always seem to happen in cricket matches occurred. Hogg mistimed a drive and gave the bowler an easy catch. It was 107 for 3 wickets; Carmody was 59 not out but Magguire the next batsman was unexpectedly run out in the same over and Carmody after hitting another 6 was out LBW on the last ball of the over. It was now 118 with 5 wickets, a truly remarkable change, and the collapse continued as the Australian batsmen seemed to be demoralised, which resulted the innings closing at a surprisingly low 126 runs.

The England innings opened with half an hour to go before lunch. Rice and Strong were the two batsmen, but the former did not last long. With 1 run on the board, Rice was clean bowled by Keen, Australia's first bowler. Kelshaw, England's best batsman, came in to join Strong at the wicket where they settled down to play out the time before lunch. Strong was uncomfortable, especially when playing Pearson, the spin bowler. The lunch interval arrived, play re-opened brilliantly, but when the total had reached 47, Strong mis-timed a ball from Pearman and was caught on the boundary. He had scored a valuable, if rather chancy, 15 runs. Kelshaw continued to bat very confidently. Goddall had joined him and was content to let him keep scoring. At 73 Goddall was out, caught by the wicket keeper off Pearson.

The total had reached 95 runs when Kelshaw, who had seemed perfectly at home with the spin bowling, was clean bowled by Pearson for 58. His innings had shown the spectators the best batting of the day. He left England with 6 wickets in hand and only 32 runs required to win. A victory appeared certain. To everyone's amazement however, England proceeded to follow in Australia's footsteps and wickets fell with awful rapidity. Pearson admittedly was bowling very well, but this was not sufficient excuse for the batting collapse. Seven men were out for 102 runs when Peas came to the rescue and proved that Pearsons bowling was not unplayable, but even he did not stay to see England to victory. When he was out they only needed 4 runs with one wicket in hand.

The excitement was intense; spectators could hardly bring themselves to watch the play. Turner and Wainwright, the last batsmen, had an almost overwhelming responsibility on their shoulders, but they performed a miracle. One by one the total mounted until Turner, with a push to leg for another single, made the winning stroke. The English supporters applauded madly, even the Australians could scarcely forbear a cheer. Turner was out without any further additions to the score, and so the match ended, Australia 126, England 127.

Douglas Carmody was a first class cricketer who had played for New South Wales prior to the war. As a serving member of the Royal Australian Air Force, he had been recruited to play in the Australian Services team; they later toured England and India.

The Australian aviators within Belaria formed The Boomerang Club, which was exclusively for Australians. Camp clubs were formed by groups of men from countries, counties, or any other identifiable reason to bond with small groups. This practice was normal, acceptable, and respected within the prisoner of war camp infrastructure at that time.

In September, the Germans closed the sports field, and it became out of bounds to all prisoners. It was assumed that this was imposed as a form of penalty, but the exact reason for this action was unclear. The Australians were to be denied any opportunity to redeem themselves on the cricket pitch, and this sports facility was sorely missed for a considerable time.

In November, another barrack block was added to the camp, with rumours abound that they were to expect a purge of captive Americans. This was bad news, as the Red Cross food parcels were getting extremely low and a quarter parcel rationing was being seriously considered. The senior British officer made attempts to communicate with the International Red Cross.

The American contingent of prisoners eventually arrived from Sagan in company with British and Commonwealth prisoners. By 4 December, the new arrivals had settled, and the camp resumed what normality it could. However, the food situation remained unresolved. Representatives of the YMCA were able to advise the camp leaders that some 3,000,000 Red Cross food parcels had recently passed through Sweden. These were apparently destined for prisoner of war camps in Eastern Germany, and it was anticipated that some would arrive at Belaria soon. To try and compensate for the lack of food, parts of the camp were used as allotments to grow a few vegetables, but the soil was very poor. Potatoes and tomatoes did grow, and the gardening club grew proficient at coaxing whatever was possible through the sandy soil. The YMCA responded to requests for seed, but frequently they arrived too late for the appropriate seasons.

The comical sketch of an escaping prisoner digging a tunnel under the feet of a Luftwaffe guard.

The common thoughts on escape were with a majority of the men across all the camps. John Brace was no exception; in his personal log he sketched a comical situation of the German guard on patrol in the rain, with a prisoner digging an escape tunnel directly under the guard. The soil at Belaria was not ideal for tunnelling, being very loose and sandy, and as such required excessive shoring with wood. A few opportunistic escapes were attempted, but none achieved any real success. Repatriations were another form of escape, and a small group of prisoners departed from the camp in mid-December. Each man selected had a personal suffering or disability of some description, which had entitled him to such a selection. One exception to that rule would be Eric Foster, shot down on 14 June 1940.[106] He had broken both legs after a malfunction to his parachute created a rather rapid descent. During his eventful imprisonment, which included several escape attempts, he took to studying some medical text books supplies by the YMCA. The subject of mental illness was well absorbed by Foster, and he embarked upon a journey of deception by replicating the symptoms. In Stalag Luft III, his charade caused serious concerns to those who experienced his 'madness'. The medical advice given in December 1943 was to put him in the hospital in Lamsdorf, and on 9 January 1944 he was recommended for repatriation. His charade was played out day and night. The repatriation board convened on 3 May, and Eric appeared in a sorry state, with the addition of enhanced blue circles around his eyes and a completely unkempt appearance. This resulted in Foster being recommended for his return to the UK within the Patronisation Scheme. The YMCA books had provided the key to his escape plan. Arriving in the UK in October 1944, Eric Foster had to convince the authorities that his mental diagnosis was just an act, having to prove his sanity to an RAF medical board.

One of the conventional routes for prisoners of war being repatriated was through the Special Repatriation Centre at Annaburg. At Stalag IVD/Z, the conditions and medical care were excellent. Prisoners were able to receive treatment for mental conditions, which were quickly diagnosed. Amputations were quite prevalent, and the most common stomach conditions were treated. Hospital trains from this and other collecting centers went to Constance on the Swiss frontier, which enabled trainloads of Allied repatriates to pass into Swiss territory, in exchange for similar numbers of Germans repatriations who were returned back into their own country.

Books in Belaria were a scarce commodity. There was a library, but it held very little stock. Men who were transferred from Luft III Sagan experienced the stark reality of finding very little reading material. The camp news sheet published a report advising that very few books were held within the fiction library, and little, if any, prospect existed for a new supply. Therefore, any prisoner of war receiving personal books was requested to hand them into the library once they had been read. Technical books were only available to officers teaching under the camp education scheme or by those studying for a particu-

Breslau some 35 km away, and snow was very thick on the ground and still falling. Brace describes the situation as very confusing, with differing times reported for their departure. This caused difficulties, as some two to three hundred bunks had been torn down to make sledges, so when the move was delayed even further, many men had nowhere to sleep or rest. After a few false alarms and several hours later, a column of about 1,000 men departed from Belaria. A great deal of bartering had taken place between the men, and each carried what they regarded as important and necessary for survival, with the medical team and their cart bringing up the rear as they left the camp. The medical cart contained the majority of medical supplies taken from the camp, and it was situated at the end of the column so that any sick marchers could drop out and be picked up. Guards marched on each side of the column at equal intervals. The word 'march' was not very appropriate, as the weather conditions induced more of a head down and trudge as best possible. The bitter snow was being forced into the prisoners with some ferocity, and the temperature was well into minus figures. The prisoners covered about 20 km the first day, starting early and passing the main Stalag Luft III camp on the way. It appeared to the column that the main camp had left in advance of them, as it looked unusually empty.

The official report of the evacuation of Stalag Luft III indicates that the south compound departed at 9.20 p.m. on 27 January, and the west compound followed at 11.30 p.m. The north compounds commenced at 1.00 a.m. hours on 28 January, with the east compound departing at 6.00 a.m. The compound at Belaria did not leave until 6.00 a.m. on 29 January.[110] Some of these prisoners of war were in their sixth year of captivity, and a high proportion of men had been held captive for three years or more.

The hastily constructed sledges made at Belaria performed well, enabling extra food rations and valuables to be carried reasonably easily in what were terrible conditions. Squadron Leader Bryce Cousens had ensured that *The log* manuscript, from which he envisaged printing a souvenir book for the Kriegies, was packed, with every effort taken to get it home. The prisoners finished walking at around 4 p.m., and they were housed for the night in the barns of a farm. Brace noted in his log that the spam was frozen and difficult to eat from the tin. The next morning, several men were found to be suffering from frostbite. Breakfast consisted of just one slice of bread, and they were expected to march 15 km that day. Many of the prisoners, including Brace, had to thaw out their boots in order to be able to move properly. For the price of a few cigarettes, some hot water was available from the farmhouse. Soap, coffee and cigarettes could buy almost anything. The column arrived at a large farm at Nieder Harlmannsdorf, and it was here that Brace noted the very first issue of Reich rations, including one cup of barley. That night, the column of men slept inside a barn, which was comfortable in comparison to the other stops, with the thick straw keeping them reasonably warm overnight. The Germans decided that they would stay another day, resting on 30 January at Nieder. Potatoes were exchanged for cigarettes, and hot water was allowed for some basic cooking. Blisters and frostbite injuries were prevalent, but the rest of the prisoners served to gather strength despite the continuing severely cold weather. Advice was passed to place their socks near to their own bodies to dry them as best possible.

January 31 became the last day on which Brace pencilled an entry within his wartime log:

> We set off again at 9 a.m. feeling much rested and cheered by fantastic rumours of the Russians being close behind us. A long and weary march in bad weather took us to a huge single barn where we slept well in plenty of straw.

Unknown circumstances appear to have prevented further entries into Brace's log. It is known that the Germans carried on with the route westwards, with the main party progressing to Spremberg railway junction in Germany. The prisoners of war were assembled in two very large sheds, where other Kriegies from the main camp were being held. The inevitable cattle trucks arrived, and the men, including John Brace, were taken to Luckenwalde camp, south-east of Berlin. The whole trip from Belaria had taken eight days over 80 km. Luckenwalde was a miserable experience for these men. The conditions, as evidenced in the account of Frank Wells, deserve no further explanation other than a personal recognition of the hardships endured by all the prisoners at that time.

Squadron Leader Cousens had been successful in his quest of retaining the manuscripts from the camp, but unfortunately, over half of the printed newspapers had been lost on the final march to Luckenwalde. Cousens maintained a distribution list of names and addresses for the prisoners who expressed a desire to obtain his proposed book. John Brace was one of those who provided Cousens with an improvised payment cheque; this was in the form of a piece of paper promising to purchase a copy of *The Log* upon its publication.

Stalag IIIA, Luckenwalde, was eventually liberated by the Russians on 20 May 1945. After the prisoner of war repatriation process had been completed, British banks were inundated with scraps of paper written as payments to others. In effect, 'IOUs' or promises to pay various individuals. Most banks accepted these personal notes as lawful tender, processing the accounts in the same way as a normal written cheque account. The abundance of paper pledges included many debts incurred by gambling, as several camps had run serious bridge and poker clubs.

The paper shortage in postwar Britain presented great problems for Cousens. He eventually sourced a supply of paper and oversaw the publication of the book. Later than expected, he fulfilled his promise to his camp inmates, and in 1947, the souvenir book *The Log: Stalag Luft III, Belaria Sagan, 1939-1945* was printed. The book was finally distributed to the list of recipients, who acknowledged that the book was dedicated to the memory of their fellow officers murdered by the Germans after escaping in 1944.

20

The RAF in Buchenwald

On 3 August 1944, one crew from 514 Squadron took part in what was an almost routine bombing operation to France. In an effort to stem the V1 Flying Rockets being launched from France, Bomber Command sent a heavy force to attack the rocket storage facility in Bois de Cassan. Any operation to France was seen by the crews as a relief from the Ruhr and the long runs deep into German.

Just before midday, John Topham, a pilot, took off in his Lancaster 'G2' LL716. Topham, who had volunteered for service from the Newcastle City Police, was in company with eighteen other aircraft from 514 Squadron, No. 3 Group Bomber Command. Five other Squadrons within the group were involved in the attack, resulting in No. 3 Group supplying 112 aircraft. The time over the target for all these aircraft was between 2.03 p.m. and 2.10 p.m., a total of just 7 minutes. No. 4 Group's Halifax Bombers were also attacking the same site, and their allocated time over the target was between 2.01 p.m. and 2.14 p.m. As the reader will determine, a significant overlap existed; a not an infrequent case. Indeed, on 3 August, a total of three flying bomb sites were attacked, with the strength of aircraft deployed by Bomber Command totalling 1,114.

During the raid on 3 August, Flying Officer Topham was on his bombing run, and in the time slot allocated, he was in company with many other aircraft when his Lancaster suddenly received strikes from bombs being dropped from above. Another bomber flying at a higher altitude had released their bombs, most probably a Halifax bomber from within No. 4 Group. Topham's Lancaster suffered serious damage to its wings. One bomb had passed through each of them, and an additional bomb had torn away an engine, making the aircraft almost impossible for Topham to control. The bomb aimer and one air gunner immediately escaped by parachute, but insufficient time was available for any other crew members to jump as the Lancaster plummeted towards the ground. John Topham managed to perform a crash landing not far from the target area. The Lancaster split into two main sections and eventually slewed across a roadway. On one side of the road there were fields and on the other

Tail section of Lancaster LL716. Mr Danis senior with his son Claude standing far right. (*Claude Danis*)

side, woodland. This proved to be significant to the remaining crew members. Those in the rear section were located quickly by the Germans, while those from the front section were able to escape into the woodland. John Topham had sustained some serious injuries to his legs in the crash landing. In fact, one leg had been broken and the other badly damaged. Despite this, he managed to crawl away into the woods, where he met two members of his crew.

The local French farmers had seen the raid taking place in broad daylight, and the crash landing of Flying Officer Topham's Lancaster had been witnessed. Despite the heightened German activity, the resistance members sought to assist those from the crew who they presumed had escaped. As dusk fell, one of Topham's group left the woods to seek help. He located some of the resistance members, who later sought medical help for the injured Topham. At this point, it was quickly realised how badly the injuries to his legs were. Civilian clothing was brought to the three airmen in the woods, and a doctor attended, later removing John Topham by hiding him on the backseat of his car as best as possible.

The crew of Lancaster LL716[111] consisted of Flying Officer John Topham, Flight Sergeant Harry Gilmore, Warrant Officer William Egri, Warrant Officer John McClenaghan, Flying Officer Stuart Baxter, Sergeant John Reid, Sergeant John Scully, and Flight Sergeant Dennehy. The two remaining crew members, Baxter and Reid, were later collected from the woods and taken to safe accommodation by the resistance.

One of the parachutists who had managed to escape by parachute from the aircraft was Australian air gunner Flight Sergeant Dennehy. He landed safely and sought help in a small village called Parmain. Fortunately, Dennehy was

Wreckage of Lancaster LL716 resting adjacent to the woods. (*Claude Danis*)

handed over to the resistance, who hid him from the Germans and later moved him to Paris. He was to remain there until the French capital was liberated.

Harry Gilmore and the Canadian William Egri DFM, managed to escape from the immediate crash scene, but both men experienced only a short period of freedom, as they were arrested within a few hours. Both men remained in each other's company during questioning at the Luftwaffe centre, and then after a short confinement they were transported to the prisoner of war camp in Bankau. They arrived at the camp on 22 August 1944, and were allocated prisoner of war numbers 584 and 574 respectively. Joining them in Bankau was their crew mate John Scully, who was issued with the number 627.

The resistance movement had managed to gather together John Reid, Stuart Baxter, and John McClenaghan, and moved them to L'Abbeville, where they were requested to hand over their escape identity photographs. False identity papers were created for them using these photographs, and five days later the men were taken to Pontoise, where they were handed over to three resistance guides; a Frenchman, his sister, and another woman, who took them into Paris on a brewer's cart. The three evaders stayed in a flat occupied by a friendly French couple. The following day, a person who identified himself as Jacques interviewed the men. This man was English and stated he was working for the secret service.[112] He advised that the men would be escorted to Spain, and that his secretary would arrive to collect them as soon as possible. An attractive blonde arrived at 3 p.m. the following day and took them to the centre of Paris, where two men collected them in a vehicle. They embarked on a short journey, only to be delivered to the Gestapo HQ in Paris,[113] and then onto Fresnes Jail in Paris. The group's betrayal had been well orchestrated; three days later, the French brother and sister who had transported the men on the brewer's cart, and the resistance operatives from L'Abbeville were also thrown into the same jail. This infamous old building was used as a holding and interrogation centre for captured resistance members, the majority of which were brutally interrogated by the Gestapo and then executed or dispatched in groups to the infamous concentration camps. Within the jail were several captured RAF airmen detained or arrested by the Gestapo wearing civilian clothing. These men were regarded as spies or collaborators.

The pilot John Topham was by this time receiving adequate medical treatment while in the custody of the resistance movement in the tiny town of Beaumont. He was well hidden in the town school, and cared for by the brave school mistress. The school was later occupied by the Germans for their own use, but not before Topham was moved. The Germans had commenced to actively search the town, and the only option available was to hide Topham in a shallow grave dug in the back garden of the house where he was being hidden. A rubber tube had been provided for him to breath, and wooden boards protected him from the weight of the soil. Flowers were placed on the grave for effect. This emergency hideaway was expected to be endured for only a short time. The SS officers and a few soldiers eventually reached the house and searched it as they had all through the town. The householder, a man called Duval, advised that he had buried a shot down British airman and he showed them the grave. Unexpectedly, the two SS officers saluted the grave and then departed. However, they left two sentries who were posted in close proximity to Duval's property. It appeared that further troops were arriving in the locality, but nobody knew what was happening. Duval was prevented from releasing Topham from his grave until the Germans withdrew, and he had no idea when that would be. When Topham was finally dug out he had been in the grave for 36 hours. He was in a poor state, and Duval assisted him into the house in order to recover.

Within a short period of time, another SS officer approached the house, but this time he was unaccompanied. Duval recovered his hidden revolver and handed it to Topham. As the SS officer entered the room, he was shot and killed. Duval and Topham carried his body out and placed it in the empty grave, which was then covered over as it had been previously. That same day, the town of Beaumont was liberated by the American advance and John Topham commenced his journey home.[114]

Just ten days prior to John Topham's final liberation by the American's, his crew members held in the Paris jail had been included in a transportation of inmates to Buchenwald concentration camp. This was not the normal procedure for prisoners detained in that terrible place; it had become common place for most resistance operatives to be taken after interrogation to the abattoir at Mont St Marsin and executed. John Reid, Stuart Baxter, and John McClenaghan had been amongst 2,000 prisoners evacuated from the jail. An

arrested. Undeterred, he continued his enquiries and obtained information that enabled the desperate situation to be rectified. On six occasions he narrowly escaped arrest. He returned to England on 15 November 1943, bringing British intelligence archives that he had secured from a house watched by the Gestapo. This officer was again parachuted into France in February 1944. Despite every security precaution, he was betrayed to the Gestapo in Paris on 21 March. While being taken by car to Headquarters, he was badly beaten up. He then underwent four days continuous interrogation, interspersed with beatings and torture, including immersions, head downwards in icecold water, with legs and arms chained. Interrogations later continued for two months, and Wing Commander Yeo-Thomas was offered his freedom in return for information concerning the Head of a Resistance Secretariat. Owing to his wrist being cut by chains, he contracted blood-poisoning and nearly lost his left arm. He made two daring but unsuccessful attempts to escape. He was then confined in solitude in Fresnes Prison for four months, including three weeks in a darkened cell with very little food. Throughout these months of almost continuous torture, he steadfastly refused to disclose any information. On 17 July, Wing Commander Yeo-Thomas was sent with a party to Compiegne Prison, from which he twice attempted to escape. He and thirty-six others were then transferred to Buchenwald concentration camp. On the way, they stopped for three days at Saarbrucken, where they were beaten and kept in a tiny hut. They arrived at Buchenwald on 16 August, and sixteen of them were executed and cremated on 10 September. Wing Commander Yeo-Thomas had already commenced to organise resistance within the camp, and remained undaunted by the prospect of a similar fate. He accepted an opportunity of changing his identity with that of a dead French prisoner, on condition that other officers would also be enabled to do so. In this way, he was instrumental in saving the lives of two officers. Wing Commander Yeo-Thomas was later transferred to a work kommando for Jews. In attempting to escape, he was picked up by a German patrol and, claiming French nationality, was transferred to a camp near Marienburg for French prisoners of war. On 16 April 1945, he led a party of twenty in a most gallant attempt to escape in broad daylight. ten were killed by fire from the guards. Those who reached cover split up into small groups. Wing Commander Yeo-Thomas became separated from his companions after three days without food. He continued alone for a week and was recaptured when only 500 yards from the American lines. A few days later, he escaped with a party of ten French prisoners of war, whom he led through German patrols to the American lines. Wing Commander Yeo-Thomas thus turned his final mission into a success by his determined opposition to the enemy, his strenuous efforts to maintain the morale of his fellow-prisoners, and his brilliant escape activities. He had endured brutal treatment and torture without flinching, and showed the most amazing fortitude and devotion to duty throughout his service abroad, during which he was under the constant threat of death.

Buchenwald's eventual liberation resulted in an immediate memorial to be constructed by the Allies. The memorial was erected in the main courtyard, acknowledging the initial estimate of 50,000 deaths in the camp. General Eisenhower instructed that members of his delegation should visit the camp. On 28 April 1945, the temporary memorial was viewed by his delegation, present were Lt General Vandenburg and Major Kepner USAAF.

John Topham was lucky to escape imprisonment and the appalling conditions at Buchenwald. He did however experience his own trauma, having being hidden in the temporary grave to avoid capture. After completing his MI9 debriefing, he was immediately awarded a Distinguished Flying Cross, the recommendation making clear reference to his evading capture and great courage.

For Topham's crew, leaving Buchenwald concentration camp was truly a life-saving experience. Once they became integrated into the prisoner of war camp at Sagan, they gained physical strength and experienced the almost euphoric conditions of being able to read books and play cards. Yet it was a respite of only thirteen weeks, as Stalag Luft III was ordered by High Command in Germany to be evacuated. On 28 January, Baxter, Reid, and McClenaghan were forced to endure yet further hardship in The Great March westwards.

Temporary Buchewald memorial.

Having survived incredible hardship together, the greatest upset was not what lay before them, but the fact that they were to be parted. Baxter was amongst the 2,000 men who departed for Luckenwalde, while Reid and McClenaghan were in the contingent to the combined navy camp in Marlag, and the merchant navy camp in Milag Nord.

Arriving on 5 February, the exhausted prisoners were subjected to a most protracted search, before entering the recently evacuated camp. Regarded as most unnecessary, representations were made, which resulted in a quicker admission. Unfortunately, the camp had been practically gutted; most of the twelve wooden barracks had neither electric light nor stoves. Reid and McClenaghan made the best possible use of the damp straw to form a mattress and get some rest. The Germans then required the men to respond to a prolonged roll call, endured over two days in the rain and bitter cold.[117]

Despite the poor physical condition of the three men from Buchenwald, they survived the forced marches. They had little, if any, personal possessions, unlike the fellow prisoners of war alongside them; making their story of survival all the more incredible. Baxter successfully fended for himself and remained at Luckenwalde until it was liberated by the Russian Army on 22 April 1945.

But for his close friends Reid and McClenaghan, their lives as prisoners of war continued to present great challenges. The German guards at the old Navy camp were to once again demonstrate their willingness to shoot prisoners. A Beaufighter pilot, Flight Lieutenant Charles Kenneth Lesbirel Bryson, flying from the island of Malta, had been shot down in the Mediterranean on 21 August 1942.[118] He had been rescued from the sea, and had endured the hardships of being a prisoner of war since that date. He had been held in Stalag Luft III, surviving the long march only to be seen close to the wire in the Marlag camp and shot at by one of the guards. Bryson was seriously wounded, and eventually died on 9 April 1945 as the result of septicemia and pneumonia caused by a bullet wound to his liver and lungs. He had been in the process of trying to barter with a camp guard at the time of being shot. Bryson is buried in the Becklingen War Cemetery, Germany. His grave is tended by the Commonwealth War Graves Commission for perpetuity.[119]

On 10 April 1945, Reid and McClenaghan were engaged in a further evacuation. Leaving the Marlag camp and heading towards Lubeck, this time the Germans were attempting to escape the British Army advance from the west. The huge column of men who realised this made slowed the pace as much as possible, but trigger happy guards demanded greater progress. In addition, the obvious dangers from the Royal Air Force who continued flying in daylight sorties were always present. They were attacking any targets of opportunity, which created great danger for the displaced prisoners of war. Taking advantage of the general disorganization, and delaying the progress of the march as best possible, the men never actually reached another camp. They were finally liberated by the British 11th Armored Division of the 2nd Army just outside Lubeck.

The particular prisoner of war in this account had no opportunity to create splendid drawings in any wartime logs, and had no opportunity to partake in the brave escape attempts. It is in fact a story of great sadness, as it demonstrates the reality of the brave civilians who were betrayed to the Gestapo and made to pay the ultimate price. Rarely can any members of a Lancaster crew within Bomber Command have endured so much. After their repatriation, Baxter, Reid, and McClenaghan each compiled reports to the intelligence services. Neither man received recognition for their hardship, nor the experiences endured in what were unique circumstances. John Topham DFC returned to service as a police constable in the Newcastle Upon Tyne City Police. His incredible story eventually surfaced, and appeared in print after it was released by the censors.[120]

Buried flier used tube to breathe

P.C. John Topham
D.F.C. *for his exploits*

News Chronicle Reporter
NEWCASTLE-ON-TYNE,
Thursday.

CENSOR - STOPPED story of a grave in Normandy which hid a fugitive British flier for 36 hours and finally contained the body of one of his hunters was told for the first time here tonight.

News clipping of John Topham's wartime experience.

21

Prisoner of War
Intelligence Network

The field operational intelligence unit of MI9 was formally abbreviated to IS9 (intelligence School 9), and it had the rather bizarre signals or telegraphic address of 'nineeyes'. IS9 was responsible for the intelligence gathering briefings of all British evaders and ex-prisoners of war incarcerated by the German forces. Their official address was Care of Room 900, The War Office, Whitehall. MI9 itself had commenced operating almost immediately from the declaration of the Second World War, and rapidly grew in capability and effectiveness.

On 6 October 1942, the United States secretary of war Henry L. Stinson established Department MIS-X from within the Military Intelligence Service of the US War department. MIS-X was designed to replicate MI9, and to perform identical functions for US military forces. Both units cooperated and facilitated good relationships in the sharing of intelligence. IS9 working in Room 900 placed a high level of security upon the intelligence received regarding agents and helpers in occupied Europe. The officer commanding MI9 at that time was Major Norman Crockatt DSO, MC.

After the Luftwaffe blitz bombing of London in 1940, Crockatt moved his MI9 to Wilton Park in the Chiltons. This venue was identified as Beaconsfield, and it had responsibilities across all three military services and in all theatres of operation. The department was responsible for the following directives, which were published in the Royal Air Force general and routine orders 26 May 1944:

SECRECY – ESCAPE OR EVASION FROM ENEMY TERRITORY

1. The utmost secrecy is to be maintained concerning escape or evasion from enemy or enemy occupied territory.

2. Except by special permission of the chief of the Air Staff, escaped or repatriated prisoners of war, or those who have evaded capture, are forbidden to write, publish, repeat, or transmit in any form, particulars of any escape

or evasion, effected or attempted, or to publish photographs connected therewith.

3. If permission is given, under terms of para. 2, for an escaped prisoner of war or an evader to lecture on his experiences, a draft script must be submitted through CHQ intelligence channels and Air Force Headquarters for Air Ministry approval. No further preparations are to be made pending such approval.

4. No officers, except those authorised by the War Office, London, or corresponding organizations elsewhere, are to interrogate any escaper or evader on the circumstances of his escape or evasion. In Allied and neutral countries, British Military and Air Attaches are so authorised.

5. In addition to secrecy concerning actual escape or evasion, an escaped or repatriated prisoner of war is to say nothing that might react unfavorably on other prisoners of war or mislead their relatives. He is to confine himself strictly to welfare matters, such as food, clothing, educational, religious or recreational facilities.

6. Commanding officers are to ensure that this order is reproduced in DROs immediately and quarterly thereafter.

Before the Allied invasion of France on D-Day, 6 June 1944, all returning evaders were expertly interviewed in compliance with the directives by MI9. These important reports were given a SPG reference number, and can now be found in the public records under series WO 208/3298-3327. The intelligence gathered was significant, and included the collation of the names and addresses of anyone involved in an escape. This process assisted in building a picture of collaboration, as well as exposing suspects potentially infiltrated by the Germans into the network of Allied operatives. The Royal Air Force contributed the bulk of intelligence for MI9.

After D-Day and the establishment of Allied forces in France, units from IS9 undertook the initial interviews of returning evaders at established locations in Europe. They would either fully debrief the returning escaper/evader, or partially debrief them and send them on for a more detailed interview conducted by MI9 in London upon their return to the UK. This system proved to be most successful, and basically remained in place for the duration of the war. It must be remembered that the routine work of that department continued in relation to its responsibilities to evaders across occupied Europe. The intelligence gleaned from every evader who had passed through an organised escape route or otherwise continued to build up the overall picture. As time pressed on, IS9 became aware of coded messages from the prisoner of war camps that expressed that German reprisals were feared. The prisoners of war felt very vulnerable, and there were rumours of men being used by the Germans as human shields, or purely being shot by the SS. In some instances, the senior British officers had gone as far as planning for such eventualities. The German military disorganisation, and the fears of a Russian advance soon settled the situation, resulting in orders to evacuate the camps being carried out by the vast majority of camp commandants.

The imminent German collapse of late 1944 and early 1945 brought forward a plan identified as En-Dor, conceived to process released ex-prisoners of war as fast and efficiently as possible at the cessation of hostilities. An IS9 department estimate from 5 September 1944 had presupposed that there were approximately 160,000 British Commonwealth prisoners in German hands, a significantly large proportion of which were situated in camps east of the River Elbe. The United States of America had an estimated catchment of 30,000 men, a high proportion of these again being east of the Elbe.

The required administration process to facilitate the debriefing of these brave men was an enormous task. An overriding objective was for the system to be efficient and not to protract the repatriation process for the prisoners of war. In effect, every prisoner was required to complete an initial short form prior to the boarding of any aircraft returning to the UK. All prisoners of war were ideally processed at the dedicated staging posts in France and Belgium.

Prisoners of war were identified within the repatriation documentation as 'PWX', and three different questionnaires were used to facilitate the process: white forms for all prisoners of war; pink forms for all prisoners of war who had served on escape committees and related intelligence or sabotage activities; Q Forms for prisoners of war who had knowledge of atrocities and war crimes.

These questionnaires secured evidence for later in-depth investigation. The concept was extraordinary, and in retrospect, it secured vital evidence on a truly mammoth scale. The MI9 evasion reports were always copied to the deputy director of Military Intelligence, P/W MI6, before being cascaded to other associated departments.

The identity of some suspected collaborators had been secured by the intelligence services throughout the duration of the war. Those suspects were subjected to intensive screening within the mass of prisoners being processed, but it was a daunting task to do so. Operation En-Dor was well planned, and initially executed in mid-1944. Several instances of escaping or evading Allied personnel having ventured into Russian and Baltic territories created greater difficulties in both locating and extracting any individual. The British and American departments of MI9 and MIS-X had no direct working relationship with the Russians. The Yalta Conference had provided for some inter-Allied cooperation, which did result in the recovery of several thousands of men.

The department MI19, a division of the British Directorate of Military Intelligence, was responsible for the intelligence gathering process undertaken by all enemy-held prisoners of war. This department worked closely with MI9, and the sharing of information frequently provided excellent results.

It was intended that the majority of British ex-prisoners should be processed at the Allied Prisoner of War Transit Centre in Brussels. This particular centre received and dispatched some 40,000 men in a three-week period at the end of April and early May 1945. At the centre, each prisoner was provided with showers, new uniforms, and an immediate advance on salary. A hotel run by the Belgian Red Cross Society was also made available, and the ever present YMCA provided additional support wherever possible. Many men took advantage of these facilities, and went to buy presents in Brussels city. At this time, it was inevitable that many of the cherished YMCA wartime logs would finish abruptly, with no further comments needing to be made.

During the immediate postwar years, a club known as the 919 Club thrived with a strong membership. The staff engaged in the repatriation facilitation, and those that helped in the evading societies frequently attended an annual event, which ran for several years.

The Royal Air Force itself sponsored the formation of the RAF Escaping Society. They adopted the Latin motto 'Solvitur ambulando', meaning 'solved by walking'. The society was created to foster continued friendship between escapees, evaders, and their helpers. Air chief marshal Sir Basil Embry was the president of the RAFES from its formation in 1946.

2,847 members[121] of the Royal and Commonwealth Air Forces aircrew who were shot down or crashed into enemy occupied territories during the Second World War managed either to escape from captivity or, in the majority of cases, to evade capture. In many cases, the men's eventual return to Allied territory was by clandestine means. In escaping or evading they forced the enemy to devote scarce resources to do everything they could to stop the escape networks. They also gave hope to the Allied forces operating over enemy territory and aircrews knew that it was actually possible to get back home. With the passing of time, the RAF Escaping Society itself was disbanded on 17 September 1995 with the laying up of its flag standard in Lincoln Cathedral.

The last society president was air chief marshal Sir Lewis Hodges. The Royal Air Force and her Commonwealth Air Forces had honored the bravery of the men who evaded and escaped from prison camps during the Second World War. This recognition is also due to the work within the secret departments that instigated such effective means to support them and the heroic civilians who frequently paid a very high price for freedom.

22

Liberation

The liberation of prisoner of war camps by the advancing Allied forces always brought great expectations, excitement, and joy. Obviously, the circumstances of Allied prisoner's liberation from the camps varied considerably, and a high priority of care was applied to those unfortunate individuals that had suffered physical abuse and medical negligence. Those conditions were frequently prevalent amongst the men exposed to the great forced marches and, who experienced liberation on the rubble strewn roads of a destroyed Germany.

The St John and Red Cross associations of Britain, Australia, Canada, India, South Africa, and New Zealand strove to send every registered prisoner of war a personal greeting card; a concept designed to enforce the message that these men had never been forgotten.

Vastly different conditions of depravity were exposed to the forces that liberated the sordid and vile concentration camps. Unimaginable scenes of human barbarism were witnessed; evidenced for the world to see, but never understand. Some of those conditions had been personally witnessed by those few unfortunate aircrew prisoners of war that had been displaced in Buchenwald. Buchenwald, as previously described, was a Class II concentration camp for political prisoners, mainly Communists, but it was also one of the main camps where French, Polish, and Dutch resistance fighters who had been fighting as partisans in the Second World War were imprisoned. Partisans or insurgents were not entitled to protection under the Geneva Convention because they were fighting illegally, in violation of the convention. Buchenwald was also used to hold Catholic priests who openly preached against the Third Reich.

The liberation of Buchenwald camp came about by Communist prisoners gaining control just before the arrival of the Allied forces. The Communists had killed some of the guards during their offensive actions, which forced the rest of the guards to flee into the nearby woods. Within a few hours of those events on 11 April 1945, the camp was finally liberated by the 6th Armoured Division of the United States Third Army, commanded by General George S. Patton. At that time, there were approximately 21,000 prisoners at Buchenwald, including approximately 4,000 Jewish inmates who were survivors transported from the death camps in Poland, and over 900 children, the vast majority of whom were orphans.

General Patton's 6th Armoured Division also liberated the Mulhausen prisoner of war camps. These were a series of camps that created a number of individual labour camps for non-commissioned men, amongst them soldiers and airmen from the Allied forces.

The Stalag camps were identified with sequential number references, and Stalag IXC appears to have held aircrew prisoners on a regular basis. Many of these camps had absorbed the displaced men who had been engaged in the forced marches. The prisoners in one particular camp provided the fighting front and advancing 6th Armoured Division with large white identification markings labelled 'POW' in order to avoid any casualties inflicted by aerial attack or mobile artillery. The photograph below illustrates the large lettering on the ground. It was taken by the United States forces at an unidentified prisoner of war camp in Mulhausen. Another point of interest within this photograph is the two wooden ventilation boxes fitted to the outside walls. These were the standard design of ventilation or air voids fitted to cell blocks in Buchenwald.

Above left: Red Cross postcard.

Above right: Mulhausen prisoner of war camp 4 May 1945. (*United States Signal Corp*)

23

Stalag XII-A
Prisoner of War Camp

Stalag XII-A was a large prisoner of war camp situated just west of Limburg at a location identified as Diez, Germany. It was a depressing camp estimated to hold 20,000 men, primarily used as a holding and interrogation facility for British and Americans. In addition, it held and retained a large population of Indian soldiers captured in North Africa. Very few, if any, RAF men were held within the facility, but in common with most camps, Stalag XII-A had a large contingent of Russian captives that suffered terrible conditions. No prisoners, regardless of status, had bunks. Instead, all men slept on the floor and tried to use anything possible to create some level of comfort. Some straw was available, but it was insufficient for everyone. Despite being a supposed transit camp, many men remained there on a permanent basis. The railway yards situated in Limburg featured in the vast majority of prisoner movements. In September 1944, the Germans captured many British soldiers during the battle of Arnhem, and the majority of those men were transported to Limburg on the rail network.

On the night of 23 December 1944, the Royal Air Force deployed fifty-two of its wooden-constructed, twin-engine Mosquito Light Bombers to attack the large railway yard complex at Limburg. It was a minor operation when compared to the large, heavy bomber raids that utilized several hundred aircraft. The railway yards were important targets, and these minor operations within the command were important to the strategy of limiting the movement of troops and materials within Germany.[122] It has to be remembered that, in compliance with the Geneva Convention, no PoW transportations were identified; Allied pilots had no means of knowing who or what was within rail rolling stock.

The weather conditions over Limburg on the night of the intended bombing raid created unexpectedly high winds. The pathfinding Mosquitoes identified the target and dropped the marking flares, which were then used by the remaining aircraft as target markers for their bomb loads. Unfortunately, the high winds drew the markers away from the intended target, creating a scattered target pattern. Some flares reached the location of Stalag XII-A and

Stalag XII-A Limburg, April 1945.

resulted in the death of sixty-three prisoners of war.[123] In March 1945, the same railway yard was used to evacuate British and American prisoners from the camp. Further casualties were incurred by the unfortunate men in Stalag XII-A when the goods train was strafed by Allied ground attack aircraft. The remaining men left in the camp were eventually liberated by the American 1st Army in early April 1945.

Ex-prisoners of war returning to normal life frequently endured a difficult journey. Postwar Britain in particular exposed the harsh reality of gaining employment for the men who had endured as many as five years behind barbed wire; it was not a simple task. Postwar rationing created some hardships, but they were nothing in comparison to that endured by the country's prisoners of war. It became a strange environment to experience complaints and selfish attitudes from those that the ex-prisoners regarded as well off and well catered for.

Pay or salary that the prisoners thought or expected to be present in their accounts was subject to question. Officers had suffered significant salary deductions, apparently justified as a result of the hospitality provided to them by their captors. The NCOs and men suffered similarly, with the added insult of being worked as force labour, and having received very little, if any, recompense. As can be seen, the subject of pay to prisoners of war was mentioned in the House of Commons during the war years, and continued to be a point of discussion. See appendix, 'House Of Lords Question 31 October 1980.'

Unlike the American and Commonwealth camp inmates, British ex-prisoners of war received no additional entitlements or allowances, and no medal was struck to indicate the particular hardship they had endured during the Second World War.

Loss of freedom is hard to bear for those who have lived as free men in a free country.

Queen Elizabeth's words published in 1942. [124]

Only those who have been prisoners have any concept of the horrors of being a prisoner, or the ineffable joy of release, of the terrible rise and fall of spirit: The fluctuations between the delirium of happiness and madness of despair attendant upon the fluctuating hopes and fears as the possibility of release advances and retreats.

Wartime Log of Warrant Officer Nutt PoW No. 1031.
Fallingbostel 1945.

Epilogue

In amongst the plethora of redundant prisoner of war camps situated within the postwar Russian and Allied zones of the broken German Reich, there were several camps that served to hold the captured Reich leaders. The tide had turned for Adolf Hitler's military forces, and many of his high ranking Nazi officers became prisoners, incarcerated behind the very barbed wire that served to contain Allied men. In the American zone of control, Bad Hersfeld prison camp held nearly 300 German generals, admirals, and ranking representatives across the entire military forces of Germany.

Bad Hersfeld, November 1945. (*Associated Press*)

Appendices

Geneva Convention 1929: Treatment of Prisoners of War

(1) To all persons referred to in Articles 1, 2, and 3 of the regulations annexed to the Hague Convention (IV) of 18 October 1907, concerning the Laws and Customs of War on Land, who are captured by the enemy.
(2) To all persons belonging to the armed forces of belligerents who are captured by the enemy in the course of operations of maritime or aerial war, subject to such exceptions (derogations) as the conditions of such capture render inevitable. Nevertheless, these exceptions shall not infringe the fundamental principles of the present convention; they shall cease from the moment when the captured persons shall have reached a prisoners of war camp.

Art. 2. Prisoners of war are in the power of the hostile government, but not of the individuals or formation that captured them. They shall at all times be humanely treated and protected, particularly against acts of violence, from insults, and from public curiosity. Measures of reprisal against them are forbidden.

Art. 3. Prisoners of war are entitled to respect for their persons and honour. Women shall be treated with all consideration due to their sex. Prisoners retain their full civil capacity.

Art. 4. The detaining power is required to provide for the maintenance of prisoners of war in its charge. Differences of treatment between prisoners are permissible only if such differences are based on the military rank, the state of physical or mental health, the professional abilities, or the sex of those who benefit from them.

CAPTURE
Art. 5. Every prisoner of war is required to declare, if he is interrogated on the subject, his true names and rank, or his regimental number. If he infringes this rule, he exposes himself to a restriction of the privileges accorded to prisoners

of his category. No pressure shall be exercised on prisoners to obtain information regarding the situation in their armed forces or their country. Prisoners who refuse to reply may not be threatened, insulted, or exposed to unpleasantness or disadvantages of any kind whatsoever. If, by reason of his physical or mental condition, a prisoner is incapable of stating his identity, he shall be handed over to the Medical Service.

Art. 6. All personal effects and articles in personal use – except arms, horses, military equipment and military papers – shall remain in the possession of prisoners of war, as well as their metal helmets and gas masks. Sums of money carried by prisoners may only be taken from them on the order of an officer and after the amount has been recorded. A receipt shall be given for them. Sums thus impounded shall be placed to the account of each prisoner. Their identity tokens, badges of rank, decorations, and articles of value may not be taken from prisoners.

EVACUATION OF PRISONERS OF WAR

Art. 7. As soon as possible after their capture, prisoners of war shall be evacuated to depots sufficiently removed from the fighting zone for them to be out of danger. Only prisoners who, by reason of their wounds or maladies, would run greater risks by being evacuated than by remaining, may be kept temporarily in a dangerous zone. Prisoners shall not be unnecessarily exposed to danger while awaiting evacuation from a fighting zone. The evacuation of prisoners on foot shall in normal circumstances be effected by stages of not more than 20 km per day, unless the necessity for reaching water and food depots requires longer stages.

Art. 8. Belligerents are required to notify each other of all captures of prisoners as soon as possible, through the intermediary of the Information Bureaux organised in accordance with article 77. They are likewise required to inform each other of the official addresses to which letter from the prisoners' families may be addressed to the prisoners of war. As soon as possible, every prisoner shall be enabled to correspond personally with his family, in accordance with the conditions prescribed in article 36 and the following articles. As regards prisoners captured at sea, the provisions of the present article shall be observed as soon as possible after arrival in port.

PRISONERS OF WAR CAMPS

Art. 9. Prisoners of war may be interned in a town, fortress, or other place, and may be required not to go beyond certain fixed limits. They may also be interned in fenced camps; they shall not be confined or imprisoned except as a measure indispensable for safety or health, and only so long as circumstances exist that necessitate such a measure. Prisoners captured in districts that are unhealthy, or whose climate is deleterious to persons coming from temperate climates, shall be removed as soon as possible to a more favourable climate. Belligerents shall as far as possible avoid bringing together in the same camp prisoners of different races or nationalities. No prisoner may at any time be sent to an area where he would be exposed to the fire of the fighting zone, or be employed to render by his presence certain points or areas immune from bombardment.

Art. 10. Prisoners of war shall be lodged in buildings or huts that afford all possible safeguards as regards hygiene and salubrity. The premises must be entirely free from damp, and adequately heated and lighted. All precautions shall be taken against the danger of fire. As regards dormitories, their total area, minimum cubic air space, fittings, and bedding material, the conditions shall be the same as for the depot troops of the detaining power.

FOOD AND CLOTHING OF PRISONERS OF WAR

Art. 11. The food ration of prisoners of war shall be equivalent in quantity and quality to that of the depot troops. Prisoners shall also be afforded the means of preparing for themselves such additional articles of food as they may possess. Sufficient drinking water shall be supplied to them. The use of tobacco shall be authorized. Prisoners may be employed in the kitchens. All collective disciplinary measures affecting food are prohibited.

Art. 12. Clothing, underwear, and footwear shall be supplied to prisoners of war by the detaining power. The regular replacement and repair of such articles shall be assured. Workers shall also receive working kit wherever the nature of the work requires it. In all camps, canteens shall be installed at which prisoners shall be able to procure, at the local market price, food commodities and ordinary articles. The profits accruing to the administrations of the camps from the canteens shall be utilised for the benefit of the prisoners.

HYGIENE IN CAMPS

Art. 13. Belligerents shall be required to take all necessary hygienic measures to ensure the cleanliness and salubrity of camps, and to prevent epidemics.
Prisoners of war shall have for their use, day and night, conveniences that conform to the rules of hygiene and are maintained in a constant state of cleanliness. In addition, and without prejudice to the provision as far as possible of baths and shower-baths in the camps, the prisoners shall be provided with a sufficient quantity of water for their bodily cleanliness.

They shall have facilities for engaging in physical exercises and obtaining the benefit of being out of doors.

Art. 14. Each camp shall possess an infirmary, where prisoners of war shall receive attention of any kind of which they may be in need. If necessary, isolation establishments shall be reserved for patients suffering from infectious and contagious diseases. The expenses of treatment, including those of temporary remedial apparatus, shall be borne by the detaining power. Belligerents shall be required to issue, on demand, to any prisoner treated, and official statement indicating the nature and duration of his illness and of the treatment received. It shall be permissible for belligerents mutually to authorise each other, by means of special agreements, to retain in the camps doctors and medical orderlies for the purpose of caring for their prisoner compatriots. Prisoners who have contracted a serious malady, or whose condition necessitates important surgical treatment, shall be admitted, at the expense of the detaining power, to any military or civil institution qualified to treat them.

Art. 15. Medical inspections of prisoners of war shall be arranged at least once a month. Their object shall be the supervision of the general state of health and cleanliness, and the detection of infectious and contagious diseases, particularly tuberculosis and venereal complaints.

INTELLECTUAL AND MORAL NEEDS OF PRISONERS OF WAR
Art. 16. Prisoners of war shall be permitted complete freedom in the performance of their religious duties, including attendance at the services of their faith, on the sole condition that they comply with the routine and police regulations prescribed by the military authorities. Ministers of religion, who are prisoners of war, whatever may be their denomination, shall be allowed freely to minister to their co-religionists.

Art. 17. Belligerents shall encourage as much as possible the organisation of intellectual and sporting pursuits by the prisoners of war.

INTERNAL DISCIPLINE OF CAMPS
Art. 18. Each prisoners of war camp shall be placed under the authority of a responsible officer. In addition to external marks of respect required by the regulations in force in their own armed forces with regard to their nationals, prisoners of war shall be required to salute all officers of the detaining power. Officer prisoners of war shall be required to salute only officers of that power who are their superiors or equals in rank.

Art. 19. The wearing of badges of rank and decorations shall be permitted.
Art. 20. Regulations, orders, announcements, and publications of any kind shall be communicated to prisoners of war in a language that they understand. The same principle shall be applied to questions.

SPECIAL PROVISIONS CONCERNING OFFICERS AND PERSONS OF EQUIVALENT STATUS
Art. 21. At the commencement of hostilities, belligerents shall be required reciprocally to inform each other of the titles and ranks in use in their respective

armed forces, with the view of ensuring equality of treatment between the corresponding ranks of officers and persons of equivalent status.

Officers and persons of equivalent status who are prisoners of war shall be treated with due regard to their rank and age.

Art. 22. In order to ensure the service of officers' camps, soldier prisoners of war of the same armed forces, and as far as possible speaking the same language, shall be detached for service therein in sufficient number, having regard to the rank of the officers and persons of equivalent status.

Officers and persons of equivalent status shall procure their food and clothing from the pay to be paid to them by the detaining power. The management of a mess by officers themselves shall be facilitated in every way.

PECUNIARY RESOURCES OF PRISONERS OF WAR

Art. 23. Subject to any special arrangements made between the belligerent powers, and particularly those contemplated in article 24, officers and persons of equivalent status who are prisoners of war shall receive from the detaining power the same pay as officers of corresponding rank in the armed forces of that power, provided however, that such pay does not exceed that to which they are entitled in the armed forces of the country in whose service they have been. This pay shall be paid to them in full, once a month if possible, and no deduction therefrom shall be made for expenditure devolving upon the detaining power, even if such expenditure is incurred on their behalf. An agreement between the belligerents shall prescribe the rate of exchange applicable to this payment; in default of such agreement, the rate of exchange adopted shall be that in force at the moment of the commencement of hostilities. All advances made to prisoners of war by way of pay shall be reimbursed, at the end of hostilities, by the power in whose service they were.

Art. 24. At the commencement of hostilities, belligerents shall determine by common accord the maximum amount of cash that prisoners of war of various ranks and categories shall be permitted to retain in their possession. Any excess withdrawn or withheld from a prisoner, and any deposit of money effected by him, shall be carried to his account, and may not be converted into another currency without his consent. The credit balances of their accounts shall be paid to the prisoners of war at the end of their captivity. During the continuance of the latter, facilities shall be accorded to them for the transfer of these amounts, wholly or in part, to banks or private individuals in their country of origin.

TRANSFER OF PRISONERS OF WAR

Art. 25. Unless the course of military operations demands it, sick and wounded prisoners of war shall not be transferred if their recovery might be prejudiced by the journey.

Art. 26. In the event of transfer, prisoners of war shall be officially informed in advance of their new destination; they shall be authorised to take with them their personal effects, their correspondence and parcels that have arrived for them. All necessary arrangements shall be made so that correspondence and parcels addressed to their former camp shall be sent on to them without delay. The sums credited to the account of transferred prisoners shall be transmitted to the competent authority of their new place of residence. Expenses incurred by the transfers shall be borne by the detaining power.

Art. 27. Belligerents may employ as workmen prisoners of war who are physically fit, other than officers and persons of equivalent statue, according to their rink and their ability. Nevertheless, if officers or persons of equivalent status ask for suitable work, this shall be found for them as far as possible.

Non-commissioned officers who are prisoners of war may be compelled to undertake only supervisory work, unless they expressly request remunerative occupation. During the whole period of captivity, belligerents are required to admit prisoners of war who are victims of accidents at work to the benefit of provisions applicable to workmen of the same category under the legislation of the detaining power. As regards prisoners of war to whom these legal provisions could not be applied by reason of the legislation of that power, the latter undertakes to recommend to its legislative body all proper measures for the equitable compensation of the victims.

ORGANISATION OF WORK

Art. 28. The detaining power shall assume entire responsibility for the maintenance, care, treatment, and the payment of the wages of prisoners of war working for private individuals.

Art. 29. No prisoner of war may be employed on work for which he is physically unsuited.

Art. 30. The duration of the daily work of prisoners of war, including the time of the journey to and from work, shall not be excessive, and shall in no case exceed that permitted for civil workers of the locality employed on the same work. Each prisoner shall be allowed a rest of twenty-four consecutive hours each week, preferably on Sunday.

Art. 31. Work done by prisoners of war shall have no direct connection with the operations of the war. In particular, it is forbidden to employ prisoners in the manufacture or transport of arms or munitions of any kind, or on the transport of material destined for combatant units. In the event of violation of the provisions of the preceding paragraph, prisoners are at liberty, after performing or commencing to perform the order, to have their complaints presented through the intermediary of the prisoners' representatives whose functions are described in articles 43 and 44, or, in the absence of a prisoners' representative, through the intermediary of the representatives of the protecting power.

Art. 32. It is forbidden to employ prisoners of war on unhealthy or dangerous work. Conditions of work shall not be rendered more arduous by disciplinary measures.

LABOUR DETACHMENTS

Art. 33. Conditions governing labour detachments shall be similar to those of prisoners of war camps, particularly as concerns hygienic conditions, food, care in case of accidents or sickness, correspondence, and the reception of parcels. Every labour detachment shall be attached to a prisoners' camp. The commander of this camp shall be responsible for the observance in the labour detachment of the provisions of the present convention.

PAY

Art. 34. Prisoners of war shall not receive pay for work in connection with the administration, internal arrangement, and maintenance of camps. Prisoners employed on other work shall be entitled to a rate of pay, to be fixed by agreements between the belligerents. These agreements shall also specify the portion that may be retained by the camp administration, the amount which shall belong to the prisoner of war and the manner in which this amount shall be placed at his disposal during the period of his captivity. Pending the conclusion of the said agreements, remuneration of the work of prisoners shall be fixed according to the following standards:

(a) Work done for the State shall be paid for according to the rates in force for soldiers of the national forces doing the same work, or if no such rates exist, according to a tariff corresponding to the work executed.

(b) When the work is done for other public administrations or for private individuals, the conditions shall be settled in agreement with the military authorities.

The pay which remains to the credit of a prisoner shall be remitted to him on the termination of his captivity. In case of death, it shall be remitted through the diplomatic channel to the heirs of the deceased.

RELATIONS OF PRISONERS OF WAR WITH THE EXTERIOR

Art. 35. On the commencement of hostilities, belligerents shall publish the measures prescribed for the execution of the provisions of the present section.

Art. 36. Each of the belligerents shall fix periodically the number of letters and postcards that prisoners of war of different categories shall be permitted to send per month, and shall notify that number to the other belligerent. These letters and cards shall be sent by post by the shortest route. They may not be delayed or withheld for disciplinary motives. Not later than one week after his arrival in camp, and similarly in case of sickness, each prisoner shall be enabled to send a postcard to his family informing them of his capture and the state of his health. The said postcards shall be forwarded as quickly as possible and shall not be delayed in any manner. As a general rule, the correspondence of prisoners shall be written in their native language. Belligerents may authorise correspondence in other languages.

Art. 37. Prisoners of war shall be authorised to receive individual postal parcels containing foodstuffs and other articles intended for consumption or clothing. The parcels shall be delivered to the addressees and a receipt given.

Art. 38. Letters and remittances of money or valuables, as well as postal parcels addressed to prisoners of war, or despatched by them, either directly or through the intermediary of the information bureaux mentioned in article 77, shall be exempt from all postal charges in the countries of origin and destination and in the countries through which they pass. Presents and relief in kind intended for prisoners of war shall also be exempt from all import or other duties, as well as any charges for carriage on railways operated by the State. Prisoners may, in cases of recognised urgency, be authorised to send telegrams on payment of the usual charges.

Art. 39. Prisoners of war shall be permitted to receive individual consignments of books, which may be subject to censorship. Representatives of the protecting powers and of duly recognized and authorised relief societies may send works and collections of books to the libraries of prisoners' camps. The transmission of such consignments to libraries may not be delayed under pretext of difficulties of censorship.

Art. 40. The censoring of correspondence shall be accomplished as quickly as possible. The examination of postal parcels shall, moreover, be effected under such conditions as will ensure the preservation of any foodstuffs that they may contain, and, if possible, be done in the presence of the addressee or of a representative duly recognised by him. Any prohibition of correspondence ordered by the belligerents, for military or political reasons, shall only be of a temporary character and shall also be for as brief a time as possible.

Art. 41. Belligerents shall accord all facilities for the transmission of documents destined for prisoners of war or signed by them, in particular powers of attorney and wills. They shall take the necessary measures to secure, in case of need, the legalisation of signatures of prisoners.

COMPLAINTS OF PRISONERS OF WAR RESPECTING THE CONDITIONS OF CAPTIVITY

Art. 42. Prisoners of war shall have the right to bring to the notice of the military authorities, in whose hands they are, their petitions concerning the conditions of captivity to which they are subjected. They shall also have the right to communicate with the representatives of the protecting powers in order to draw their attention to the points on which they have complaints to make with regard to the conditions of captivity. Such petitions and complaints shall be transmitted immediately. Even though they are found to be groundless, they shall not give rise to any punishment.

REPRESENTATIVES OF PRISONERS OF WAR

Art. 43. In any locality where there may be prisoners of war, they shall be authorised to appoint representatives to represent them before the military authorities and the protecting powers. Such appointments shall be subject to the approval of the military authorities. The prisoners' representatives shall be charged with the reception and distribution of collective consignments. Similarly, in the event of the prisoners deciding to organise amongst themselves a system of mutual aid, such organization shall be one of the functions of the prisoners' representatives. On the other hand, the latter may offer their services to prisoners to facilitate their relations with the relief societies mentioned in article 78. In camps of officers and persons of equivalent status, the senior officer prisoner of the highest rank shall be recognised as intermediary between the camp authorities and the officers, and similar persons who are prisoners, for this purpose he shall have the power to appoint an officer prisoner to assist him as interpreter in the course of conferences with the authorities of the camp.

Art. 44. When the prisoners' representatives are employed as workmen, their work as representatives of the prisoners of war shall be reckoned in the compulsory period of labour. All facilities shall be accorded to the prisoners' representatives for their correspondence with the military authorities and the protecting power. Such correspondence shall not be subject to any limitation. No prisoners' representative may be transferred without his having been allowed the time necessary to acquaint his successors with the current business.

PENAL SANCTIONS WITH REGARDS TO PRISONERS OF WAR

Art. 45. Prisoners of war shall be subject to the laws, regulations and orders in force in the armed forces of the detaining power. Any act of insubordination shall render them liable to the measures prescribed by such laws, regulations, and orders, except as otherwise provided in this chapter.

Art. 46. Prisoners of war shall not be subjected by the military authorities or the tribunals of the detaining power to penalties other than those which are prescribed for similar acts by members of the national forces. Officers, non-commissioned officers, private soldiers, or prisoners of war undergoing disciplinary punishment shall not be subjected to treatment less favourable than that prescribed, as regards the same punishment, for similar ranks in the armed forces of the detaining power. All forms of corporal punishment, confinement in premises not lighted by daylight and, in general, all forms of cruelty whatsoever are prohibited. Collective penalties for individual acts are also prohibited.

Art. 47. A statement of the facts in cases of acts constituting a breach of discipline, and particularly an attempt to escape, shall be drawn up in writing without delay. The period during which prisoners of war of whatever rank are detained in custody (pending the investigation of such offences) shall be reduced to a strict minimum. The judicial proceedings against a prisoner of war shall be conducted as quickly as circumstances will allow. The period during which prisoners shall be detained in custody shall be as short as possible. In all cases, the period during which a prisoner is under arrest (awaiting punishment or trial) shall be deducted from the sentence, whether disciplinary or judicial, provided such deduction is permitted in the case of members of the national forces.

Art. 48. After undergoing the judicial or disciplinary punishment that has been inflicted on them, prisoners of war shall not be treated differently from other prisoners. Nevertheless, prisoners who have been punished as the result of an attempt to escape may be subjected to a special régime of surveillance, but this shall not involve the suppression of any of the safeguards accorded to prisoners by the present convention.

Art. 49. No prisoner of war may be deprived of his rank by the detaining power. Prisoners on whom disciplinary punishment is inflicted shall not be deprived of the privileges attaching to their rank. In particular, officers and persons of equivalent status who suffer penalties entailing deprivation of liberty shall not be placed in the same premises as non-commissioned officers or private soldiers undergoing punishment.

Art. 50. Escaped prisoners of war who are recaptured before they have been able to re-join their own armed forces or to leave the territory occupied by the armed forces that captured them shall be liable only to disciplinary punishment. Prisoners who, after succeeding in re-joining their armed forces or in leaving the territory occupied by the armed forces which captured them, are again taken prisoner shall not be liable to any punishment for their previous escape.

Art. 51. Attempted escape, even if it is not a first offence, shall not be considered as an aggravation of the offence in the event of the prisoner of war being brought before the courts for crimes or offences against persons or property committed in the course of such attempt. After an attempted or successful escape, the comrades of the escaped person who aided the escape shall incur only disciplinary punishment therefor.

Art. 52. Belligerents shall ensure that the competent authorities exercise the greatest leniency in considering the question whether an offence committed by a prisoner of war should be punished by disciplinary or by judicial measures. This provision shall be observed in particular in appraising facts in connexion with escape or attempted escape. A prisoner shall not be punished more than once for the same act or on the same charge.

Art. 53. No prisoner who has been awarded any disciplinary punishment for an offence, and who fulfils the conditions laid down for repatriation shall be retained on the ground that he has not undergone his punishment. Prisoners qualified for repatriation against whom any prosecution for a criminal offence has been brought may be excluded from repatriation until the termination of the proceedings and until fulfilment of their sentence, if any; prisoners already serving a sentence of imprisonment may be retained until the expiry of the sentence. Belligerents shall communicate to each other lists of those who cannot be repatriated for the reasons indicated in the preceding paragraph.

DISCIPLINARY PUNISHMENTS

Art. 54. Imprisonment is the most severe disciplinary punishment that may be inflicted on a prisoner of war. The duration of any single punishment shall not exceed thirty days. This maximum of thirty days shall, moreover, not be exceeded in the event of there being several acts for which the prisoner is answerable to discipline at the time when his case is disposed of, whether such acts are connected or not. Where, during the course or after the termination of a period of imprisonment, a prisoner is sentenced to a fresh disciplinary penalty, a period of at least three days shall intervene between each of the periods of imprisonment, if one of such periods is of ten days or over.

Art. 55. Subject to the provisions of the last paragraph of article 11, the restrictions in regard to food permitted in the armed forces of the detaining power may be applied, as an additional penalty, to prisoners of war undergoing disciplinary punishment. Such restrictions shall, however, only be ordered if the state of the prisoner's health permits.

Art. 56. In no case shall prisoners of war be transferred to penitentiary establishments (prisoners, penitentiaries, convict establishments, etc.) in order to undergo disciplinary sentence there. Establishments in which disciplinary sentences are undergone shall conform to the requirements of hygiene. Facilities shall be afforded to prisoners undergoing sentence to keep themselves in a state of cleanliness. Every day, such prisoners shall have facilities for taking exercise or for remaining out of doors for at least 2 hours.

Art. 57. Prisoners of war undergoing disciplinary punishment shall be permitted to read and write and to send and receive letters. On the other hand, it shall be permissible not to deliver parcels and remittances of money to the addressees until the expiration of the sentence. If the undelivered parcels contain perishable foodstuffs, these shall be handed over to the infirmary or to the camp kitchen.

Art. 58. Prisoners of war undergoing disciplinary punishment shall be permitted, on their request, to present themselves for daily medical inspection. They shall receive such attention as the medical officers may consider necessary, and if need be, shall be evacuated to the camp infirmary or to hospital.

Art. 59. Without prejudice to the competency of the courts and the superior military authorities, disciplinary sentences may only be awarded by an officer vested with disciplinary powers in his capacity as commander of the camp or detachment, or by the responsible officer acting as his substitute.

JUDICIAL PROCEEDINGS
Art. 60. At the commencement of a judicial hearing against a prisoner of war, the detaining power shall notify the representative of the protecting power as soon as possible and in any case before the date fixed for the opening of the hearing. The said notification shall contain the following particulars:
(a) Civil status and rank of the prisoner.
(b) Place of residence or detention.
(c) Statement of the charge or charges, and of the legal provisions applicable.
If it is not possible in this notification to indicate particulars of the court that will try the case, the date of the opening, of the hearing and the place where it will take place, these particulars shall be furnished to the representative of the protecting power at a later date, but as soon as possible and in any case at least three weeks before the opening of the hearing.

Art. 61. No prisoner of war shall be sentenced without being given the opportunity to defend himself. No prisoner shall be compelled to admit that he is guilty of the offence of which he is accused.

Art. 62. The prisoner of war shall have the right to be assisted by a qualified advocate of his own choice, and if necessary, to have recourse to the offices of a competent interpreter. He shall be informed of his right by the detaining power in good time before the hearing. Failing a choice on the part of the prisoner, the protecting power may procure an advocate for him. The detaining power shall, on the request of the protecting power, furnish to the latter a list of persons qualified to conduct the defence. The representatives of the protecting power shall have the right to attend the hearing of the case.

The only exception to this rule is where the hearing has to be kept secret in the interests of the safety of the State. The detaining power would then notify the protecting power accordingly.

Art. 63. A sentence shall only be pronounced on a prisoner of war by the same tribunals, and in accordance with the same procedure as in the case of persons belonging to the armed forces of the detaining power.

Art. 64. Every prisoner of war shall have the right of appeal against any sentence against him in the same manner as persons belonging to the armed forces of the detaining power.

Art. 65. Sentences pronounced against prisoners of war shall be communicated immediately to the protecting power.

Art. 66. If sentence of death is passed on a prisoner of war, a communication setting forth in detail the nature and the circumstances of the offence shall be addressed as soon as possible to the representative of the protecting power for transmission to the power in whose armed forces the prisoner served.

The sentence shall not be carried out before the expiration of a period of at least three months from the date of the receipt of this communication by the protecting power.

Art. 67. No prisoner of war may be deprived of the benefit of the provisions of article 42 of the present convention as the result of a judgment or otherwise.

END OF CAPTIVITY, DIRECT REPATRIATION, AND ACCOMMODATION IN A NEUTRAL COUNTRY

Art. 68. Belligerents shall be required to send back to their own country, without regard to rank or numbers, after rendering them in a fit condition for transport, prisoners of war who are seriously ill or seriously wounded.

Agreements between the belligerents shall therefore determine, as soon as possible, the forms of disablement or sickness requiring direct repatriation and cases that may necessitate accommodation in a neutral country. Pending the conclusion of such agreements, the belligerents may refer to the model draft agreement annexed to the present convention.

Art. 69. On the opening of hostilities, belligerents shall come to an understanding as to the appointment of mixed medical commissions. These commissions shall consist of three members, two of whom shall belong to a neutral country and one appointed by the detaining power; one of the medical officers of the neutral country shall preside. These mixed medical commissions shall proceed to the examination of sick or wounded prisoners and shall make all appropriate decisions with regard to them. The decisions of these commissions shall be decided by majority and shall be carried into effect as soon as possible.

Art. 70. In addition to those prisoners of war selected by the medical officer of the camp, the following shall be inspected by the mixed medical Commission mentioned in article 69, with a view to their direct repatriation or accommodation in a neutral country:

(a) Prisoners who make a direct request to that effect to the medical officer of the camp.

(b) Prisoners presented by the prisoners' representatives mentioned in article 43, the latter acting on their own initiative or on the request of the prisoners themselves.

(c) Prisoners nominated by the power   in whose armed forces they served or by a relief society duly recognized and authorized by that power.

Art. 71. Prisoners of war who meet with accidents at work, unless the injury is self-inflicted, shall have the benefit of the same provisions as regards repatriation or accommodation in a neutral country.

Art. 72. During the continuance of hostilities, and for humanitarian reasons, belligerents may conclude agreements with a view to the direct repatriation or accommodation in a neutral country of prisoners of war in good health who have been in captivity for a long time.

Art. 73. The expenses of repatriation or transport to a neutral country of prisoners of war shall be borne, as from the frontier of the detaining Power, by the Power in whose armed forces such prisoners served.

Art. 74. No repatriated person shall be employed on active military service.

LIBERATION AND REPATRIATION AT THE END OF HOSTILITIES

Art. 75. When belligerents conclude an armistice convention, they shall normally cause to be included therein provisions concerning the repatriation of prisoners of war. If it has not been possible to insert in that convention such stipulations, the belligerents shall, nevertheless, enter into communication with each other on the question as soon as possible. In any case, the repatriation of prisoners shall be effected as soon as possible after the conclusion of peace. Prisoners of war who are subject to criminal proceedings for a crime or offence at common law may, however, be detained until the end of the proceedings, and if need be, until the expiration of the sentence. The same applies to prisoners convicted for a crime or offence at common law. By agreement between the belligerents, commissions may be instituted for the purpose of searching for scattered prisoners and ensuring their repatriation.

DEATHS OF PRISONERS OF WAR

Art. 76. The wills of prisoners of war shall be received and drawn up under the same conditions as for soldiers of the national armed forces. The same rules shall be followed as regards the documents relative to the certification of the death. The belligerents shall ensure that prisoners of war who have died in captivity are honourably buried, and that the graves bear the necessary indications and are treated with respect and suitably maintained.

BUREAUX OF RELIEF AND INFORMATION CONCERNING PRISONERS OF WAR

Art. 77. At the commencement of hostilities, each of the belligerent powers and the neutral powers who have belligerents in their care shall institute an official bureau to give information about the prisoners of war in their territory.

Each of the belligerent powers shall inform its information bureau as soon as possible of all captures of prisoners affected by its armed forces, furnishing them with all particulars of identity at its disposal to enable the families concerned to be quickly notified, and stating the official addresses to which families may write to the prisoners. The information bureau shall transmit all such information immediately to the powers concerned, on the one hand through the intermediary of the protecting powers, and on the other through the Central Agency contemplated in article 79. The information bureau, being charged with replying to all enquiries relative to prisoners of war, shall receive from the various services concerned all particulars respecting internments and transfers, releases on parole, repatriations, escapes, stays in hospitals, and deaths, together with all other particulars necessary for establishing and keeping up to date an individual record for each prisoner of war. The bureau shall note in this record, as far as possible, and subject to the provisions of article 5, the regimental number, names and surnames, date and place of birth, rank and unit of the prisoner, the surname of the father and name of the mother, the address of the person to be notified in case of accident, wounds, dates and places of capture, of internment, of wounds, of death, together with all other important particulars. Weekly lists containing all additional particulars capable of facilitating the identification of each prisoner shall be transmitted to the interested powers. The individual record of a prisoner of war shall be sent after the conclusion of peace to the power in whose service he was. The information bureau shall also be required to collect all personal effects, valuables, correspondence, pay-books, identity tokens, etc., which have been left by prisoners of war who have been repatriated or released on parole, or who have escaped or died, and to transmit them to the countries concerned.

Art. 78. Societies for the relief of prisoners of war, regularly constituted in accordance with the laws of their country, and having for their object to serve as intermediaries for charitable purposes, shall receive from the belligerents, for themselves and their duly accredited agents, all facilities for the efficacious performance of their humane task within the limits imposed by military exigencies. Representatives of these societies shall be permitted to distribute relief in the camps and at the halting places of repatriated prisoners under a personal permit issued by the military authority, and on giving an undertaking in writing to comply with all routine and police orders which the said authority shall prescribe.

Art. 79. A central agency of information regarding prisoners of war shall be established in a neutral country. The International Red Cross Committee shall, if they consider it necessary, propose to the powers concerned the organisation of such an agency. This agency shall be charged with the duty of collecting all information regarding prisoners which they may be able to obtain through official or private channels, and the agency shall transmit the information as rapidly as possible to the prisoners' own country or the power in whose service they have been. These provisions shall not be interpreted as restricting the humanitarian work of the International Red Cross Committee.

Art. 80. Information bureaux shall enjoy exemption from fees on postal matter as well as all the exemptions prescribed in article 38.

APPLICATION OF THE CONVENTION TO CERTAIN CATEGORIES OF CIVILIANS

Art. 81. Persons who follow the armed forces without directly belonging thereto, such as correspondents, newspaper reporters, sutlers, or contractors, who fall into the hands of the enemy, and whom the latter think fit to detain, shall be entitled to be treated as prisoners of war, provided they are in possession of an authorisation from the military authorities of the armed forces which they were following.

EXECUTION OF THE CONVENTION GENERAL PROVISIONS

Art. 82. The provisions of the present convention shall be respected by the High Contracting Parties in all circumstances. In time of war if one of the belligerents is not a party to the convention, its provisions shall, nevertheless, remain binding as between the belligerents who are parties thereto.

Art. 83. The High Contracting Parties reserve to themselves the right to conclude special conventions on all questions relating to prisoners of war concerning which they may consider it desirable to make special provisions.

Prisoners of war shall continue to enjoy the benefits of these agreements until their repatriation has been effected, subject to any provisions expressly to the contrary contained in the above mentioned agreements or in subsequent agreements, and subject to any more favourable measures by one or the other of the belligerent powers concerning the prisoners detained by that power . In order to ensure the application, on both sides, of the provisions of the present convention, and to facilitate the conclusion of the special conventions mentioned above, the belligerents may, at the commencement of hostilities, authorise meetings of representatives of the respective authorities charged with the administration of prisoners of war.

Art. 84. The text of the present convention and of the special conventions mentioned in the preceding article shall be posted, whenever possible, in the native language of the prisoners of war, in places where it may be consulted by all the prisoners. The text of these conventions shall be communicated, on their request, to prisoners who are unable to inform themselves of the text posted.

Art. 85. The High Contracting Parties shall communicate to each other, through the intermediary of the Swiss Federal Council, the official translations of the present convention, together with such laws and regulations as they may adopt to ensure the application of the present convention.

Art. 86. The High Contracting Parties recognise that a guarantee of the regular application of the present convention will be found in the possibility of collaboration between the protecting powers charged with the protection of the interests of the belligerents; in this connexion, the protecting powers may, apart from their diplomatic personnel, appoint delegates from among their own nationals or the nationals of other neutral powers. The appointment of these delegates shall be subject to the approval of the belligerent with whom they are to carry out their mission. The representatives of the protecting power or their recognised delegates shall be authorised to proceed to any place, without exception, where prisoners of war are interned. They shall have access to all premises occupied by prisoners and may hold conversation with prisoners, as a general rule without witnesses, either personally or through the intermediary of interpreters. Belligerents shall facilitate as much as possible the task of the representatives or recognised delegates of the protecting powe. The military authorities shall be informed of their visits. Belligerents may mutually agree to allow persons of the prisoners own nationality to participate in the tours of inspection.

Art. 87. In the event of dispute between the belligerents regarding the application of the provisions of the present convention, the protecting powers shall, as far as possible, lend their good offices with the object of settling the dispute. To this end, each of the protecting powers may, for instance, propose to the belligerents concerned that a conference of representatives of the latter should be held, on suitably chosen neutral territory. The belligerents shall be required to give effect to proposals made to them with this object. The protecting power may, if necessary, submit for the approval of the powers in dispute the name of a person belonging to a neutral power or nominated by the International Red Cross Committee, who shall be invited to take part in this conference.

Art. 88. The foregoing provisions do not constitute any obstacle to the humanitarian work which the International Red Cross Committee may perform for the protection of prisoners of war with the consent of the belligerents concerned.

The Responsibilities of a Prisoner of War

Instructions and guidance for all ranks in the event of capture
by the enemy

EUROPEAN THEATRE OF OPERATIONS ONLY

Note: during hostilities a copy of this publication is to be issued to every member of aircrew, whether operational or under training; and COs are also to ensure that *all* other personnel have a general knowledge of the principles laid down herein.

Issued for the information and guidance of all concerned.
By Command of the Air Council.

NOT TO BE TAKEN INTO THE AIR

-- I --
The responsibilities of a prisoner of war

1. It is the duty of all ranks to protect the security of the Royal Air Force by every means within their power. Each individual must clearly understand that he is personally responsible for safeguarding service information at all times. This responsibility is greatest after capture.
2. The enemy is known to attach the utmost importance to the interrogation and search of prisoners, but he can learn nothing from a silent and resolute prisoner whose pockets are empty.
3. The Geneva Convention of 1929, which was signed by all the great powers, laid down that a prisoner of war is only required to give his name, bank, and number, and that no pressure may be brought to bear upon him in order to obtain any further information.
4. No further information whatsoever should be given. Remember that a prisoner who systematically refuses to give information is respected by his captors.

Behaviour under interrogation

1. Any member of the Royal Air Force who falls into enemy hands should observe these simple rules when facing interrogation. He should:

    a. Stand correctly to attention.

    b. Give his name, rank and number and nothing else.

    c. Maintain a rigid silence thereafter, avoiding even the answers 'yes' or 'no'. If pressed, he may reply 'I cannot answer that question'.

    d. Avoid all attempts to bluff or tell lies.

    e. Preserve throughout the interrogation a disciplined and strictly formal attitude, addressing any officer senior to himself as 'Sir'.

    f. Avoid all fraternization, and refuse all favours.

    g. Establish from the outset that he is a type from whom nothing can be learnt.

2. After the official interrogation is over, a prisoner must remember that further efforts will be made to extract information from him. Only by constant vigilance and alertness can he avoid the many traps which may be set for him.

--2--

3. He should therefore trust no one until he is absolutely certain of his integrity, and he should view every act on the part of the enemy with suspicion. He should also remember that, although he is a prisoner of war, he is still a member of the Royal Air Force, and that the disclosure of Service information is an offence under the Air Force Act.

Remember that a silent and resolute prisoner without articles or papers of any sort is an interrogator's nightmare

What the enemy will try to find out from you

1. Information about any unit of the Air Force, or of the Navy and Army.

    What is your squadron number?

    Where is it stationed? And what is its strength?

    Where are other squadrons stationed?

    What have been their recent movements? Any rumours as to future movements?

    What do you know about casualties suffered?

2. Types of Aircraft, performances, new designs, and armament. Building and supply.

3. Airfields and landing grounds at home and abroad.

4. Any information about Allied training and tactics, and how much you know of enemy tactics.

5. Information about air raid damage in UK or to British ships.

6. Anything about the weather, recent or forecasts.

7. Air Defence organization and AA Defences.

8. Home conditions, politics, food supply, spirit of the people and serving Forces.

A few careless words about these things and the whole of your operational war effort may be rendered valueless in comparison

How information is obtained by the enemy

Sources

1. Examination of captured aircraft and material.
2. Search of prisoners of war for notebooks, letters, diaries, and any other incriminating articles or papers.
3. Interrogation of prisoners, either by direct questioning or by indirect methods such as the following:

--3--

Methods

1. Fraternization. The commonest trick of all. Prisoners are well treated, entertained, and given plenty to drink. An atmosphere of good fellowship is carefully built up, and service matters are then casually discussed. A skilled interrogator will be present to guide the talk into the right channels.
2. Microphones. These are always extensively used, and are sensitive to the slightest whisper. Some will be so cunningly hidden that not even an expert can find them.
3. Stool-pigeons, speaking perfect English and carefully briefed, will be introduced among prisoners. They will not be easy to recognise, and may even be the first to warn every one of the need for caution when discussing service matters.
4. Agents. The enemy will have agents working among the nurses, doctors, attendants, or guards who look after prisoners. These may either pretend to be sympathetic; or else pretend that they cannot understand English. Like the stool-pigeon, they will be good actors and very difficult to recognise.
5. Know-all approach. 'We know everything already, so there is no point in your keeping silent.' It may be suggested that another prisoner has talked; or an imposing looking file may be produced, which appears to give detailed information about RAF units, aircraft, equipment, and personnel, and may contain a number of photographs, newspaper cuttings, and other such items.
6. Intimidation. A prisoner may be threatened, or attempts may be made to bully or browbeat him. A fake shooting of other prisoners may be staged. Blackmail may be tried.
7. Ill-treatment may occasionally be resorted to by the enemy, even though the Geneva Convention forbids it. Attempts may be made to lower a prisoner's morale and to undermine his resolution by means of unsuitable diet, overheated cells, or solitary confinement.

8. Bribery. A prisoner may be offered preferential treatment, with special liberties and luxuries, if he will cooperate with his captors, either by talking himself or by persuading others to talk. A prisoner who collaborates with the enemy in return for an easy life is a traitor.

--4--

9. Bogus forms may be produced in the hope that the prisoner will answer the questions that they ask. They may appear to be genuine Red Cross forms or official documents. Put your pen through every question except name, rank and number, otherwise the enemy may fill in the answers above your signature in order to bluff other prisoners. (Note: failure to fill in a Red Cross form does not delay notification to relatives, who are informed through official channels.)

10. Propaganda. From the moment a prisoner is captured he is subjected to enemy propaganda. He will continually be told lies about the war situation, and about his country and her Allies, in the hope that his resolution will weaken, and that his courage will fail.

These are only ten of the enemy's tricks. Be on your guard.
He has many others up his sleeve.

Do's and Dont's

1. Do give your name, rank and number, but nothing else.
2. Do convince your interrogator from the very outset that you are the type who will never talk under any circumstances. Therein lies the whole secret of successfully withstanding interrogation.
3. Do behave with dignity and reserve under interrogation, so that you command the respect of your captors.
4. Do maintain your resolution and morale; and encourage your comrades to do the same.
5. Do empty your pockets before going on operations.
6. Do destroy your aircraft, maps, and documents whenever possible. Remember that incriminating articles and papers can often be disposed of before the enemy has a chance to search you.
7. Do keep your eyes and ears open after capture – you may learn much that may be of value both to your country and yourself if you succeed in escaping.

--5--

1. Don't be truculent or aggressive under interrogation. You may regret it.
2. Don't try to fool your interrogators. They will be experts at their job, and in any battle of wits you are bound to lose in the end. Once you begin to talk, they have got you where they want you. Say *nothing and go on saying it*.

3. Don't imagine that you can find every microphone. You can't.
4. Don't talk shop. A careless word may cost old comrades their lives. If you have plans to discuss, do it in the open air, but remember even trees have ears.
5. Don't accept old prisoners on trust.
6. Don't believe enemy propaganda, and don't let your comrades do so either.
7. Don't broadcast, no matter what inducement is offered.
8. Don't fraternize. The enemy is not in the habit of wasting his time, whisky, and cigars on those who have nothing to give him in return.
9. Don't give your parole, except under special circumstances.
10. Don't betray those who help you to escape. A careless word after you have reached safety may cost them their lives.
11. Don't write direct to any service address in the UK, and don't reveal in your letter that the addressee is in any way connected with the services. Remember that the German censor will closely examine all your correspondence, and will note what you write and to whom you write.
12. Don't carry these instructions on you or in your aircraft. They are to help you and not the enemy.

A prisoner is always surrounded by his Enemies. Trust no one.

Rights of a prisoner

1. The rights of a prisoner of war are fully safeguarded by the Geneva Convention of 1929, and this should be displayed in every camp. Insist on this being done.
2. There is a neutral protecting power to whom all serious complaints can be addressed through the camp commandant.
3. If you escape to a neutral country, claim your freedom and report to the nearest British representative.

Timeline of Prison Camp Evacuations

13 July 1944: evacuation of Stalag Luft VI at Heydekrug to Stalag Luft IV at Gross Tychow. A forced march and transit by ship to Swinemunde. Other route by forced march and cattle train to Stalag XX-A at Thorn in Poland.

24 December 1944: PoW work camps near Koningsberg evacuated.

27 December 1944 to April 1945: Stalag VIII-B at Teschen began their forced march through Czechoslovakia, towards Dresden, then towards Stalag XIII-D at Nuremberg, and finally on to Stalag VII-A at Moosburg in Bavaria.

19 January 1945: evacuation from Stalag Luft VII Bankau, Poland begins. Prisoners force marched then loaded onto cattle trucks and taken to Stalag III, south of Berlin.

20 January 1945: Stalag XX-A at Thorn, Poland started evacuation.

22 January 1945: Stalag 344 at Lamsdorf, Silesia was evacuated.

23 January 1945: evacuation began at Stalag XX-B, Danzig.

27 January 1945: Allied forces liberate Auschwitz.

27 January 1945: evacuation of Stalag Luft III, Sagan to either Stalag III-A at Luckenwalde near Berlin, or to Marlag und Milag Nord, near Bremen, or to Stalag XIII-D, near Nuremberg, then onto Stalag VII-A Moosburg. Balaria compound was evacuated 29 January 1945.

6 February 1945 to March 1945: evacuation from Stalag Luft IV at Gross Tychow, begining an eighty-six day march to Stalag XI-B and Stalag 357. Many prisoners were later marched onwards toward Lubek and liberated on the march.

8 February 1945: Stalag VIII-C at Sagan was evacuated and marched across Germany to Stalag IX-B near Bad Orb, arriving 16 March.

10 February 1945: Stalag VIII-A at Gorlitz was evacuated.

3 April 1945: Stalag XIII-D at Nuremberg was evacuated.

6 April 1945: Stalag XI-B and Stalag 357 were evacuated.

10 April 1945: Marlag und Milag Nord evacuated. Prisoners liberated on the march.

16 April 1945: Oflag IV-C, Colditz was liberated.

16 April 1945: PoWs left behind at Stalag 357 were liberated.

17 April 1945: Bergen-Belsen concentration camp liberated.

19 April 1945: PoW column was attacked by Allied aircraft at Gresse.

22 April 1945: Stalag III-A liberated by Soviet forces.

27 April 1945: US and Soviet forces met at the River Elbe.

29 April 1945: Stalag VIIA, Moosburg was liberated.

30 April 1945: Berlin falls to the Red Army and Hitler commits suicide.

2 May 1945: Stalag Luft I liberated by Soviet forces.

4 May 1945: German forces surrendered.

8 May 1945: The last PoWs evacuated from Stalag XIB are liberated.

12 May 1945: The Red Army releases Commonwealth and USAAF prisoners at Stalag III-A, Luckenwalde.

13 May 1945: Stalag Luft I prisoners released by Soviets and departed from adjacent airfield.

Main Allied Pow Evacuation Routes West

There were three main Allied PoW evacuation routes to the west, which included:

The northern route

Starting from Stalag Luft VI Heydekrug, East Prussia, via Stalag Luft IV at Gross Tychow in Pomerania, via Stettin to Stalag XI-B, and Stalag 357 at Fallingbostel. Some prisoners were marched from this camp towards Lubeck during the final stages of the war.

The central route

Started from Stalag Luft VII at Bankau, near Kreuzburg in Silesia (now Poland), via Stalag 344 at Lamsdorf, to Stalag VIII-A Gorlitz, then ending at Stalag III-A at Luckenwalde, 30 km south of Berlin.

The southern route

Started at Stalag VIII-B (formerly Stalag VIII-D) at Teschen (not far from Auschwitz), which led through Czechoslovakia towards Stalag XIII-D at Nuremberg, and then onto Stalag VII-A at Moosburg in Bavaria.

Main Allied Pow Evacuation Routes East

Allied PoW camps situated in western Germany were subjected to similar movement orders, but these were movements that engaged far shorter distances. There were two primary routes:

The north-east route

Starting from Dulag Luft Wetzlar, via Oflag IXA, Duberstadt, Brunswick and Stalag 357 at Fallingbostel.

The south-east route

Starting at Stalag XIIIC via Nuremburg to Stalag VII-A Mooseburg.

The Allied prisoner of war evacuations all progressed towards the central core of Germany. It has to be presumed that the last bastions of the German Reich intended to contain the entire prisoner population within the central confines of Germany. This was a most unlikely prospect due to the overwhelming numbers of men. Several theories have been explored in order to establish the thoughts behind the orders to move these extraordinary large numbers of prisoners of war, but in all probability the irrational orders will remain with no clarity of explanation. The entire German command infrastructure collapsed, resulting in the unspecific orders to the commanders of the numerous columns of prisoners remaining; in many instances, the final surrender to Allied forces took place simply as a result of their slow progression towards the Allied lines.

House of Lords PoW Pay Deductions

House of Lords Question 31 October 1980.
PRISONERS OF WAR: PAY DEDUCTION.

My Lords, I beg leave to ask the question which stands in my name on the order paper. The question was as follows:

To ask Her Majesty's government whether the protests by members of the forces who were prisoners of war between 1940 and 1945 about deduction of pay have been considered, and what decision has been reached.

The MINISTER of STATE, MINISTRY of DEFENCE
(Lord Strathcona and Mount Royal)

My Lords, our inquiries into this question have now been completed. A detailed investigation has been carried out by a study group under the leadership of my honourable friend the parliamentary under-Secretary of State for the Royal Air Force. A copy of its full report has been placed in the library. With the leave of the House, I will circulate in the official report a detailed statement of the work of the group and a summary of its conclusions.

In brief, the conclusions are that satisfactory arrangements were made for officers' accounts to be adjusted after the war to take account of money deducted from pay that was not received. It is not possible to prove that every returning prisoner of war had his account adjusted as planned, but all the indications are that the vast majority did receive some money. There remains the complaint that officers should not have had any money deducted from their pay, or alternatively, that it should have been repaid in full after repatriation, as some Commonwealth governments decided to do. The Government decided in September 1945 to refund in full all deductions from the accounts of Japanese PoWs in view of the exceptional hardships endured by these prisoners. It was open to them to apply the same policy to former prisoners of the Germans and the Italians. In the light of their knowledge of the situation at the time they decided not to do so, and there would seem no case for a British government thirty-five years later without the advantage of detailed records or contemporary knowledge to seek to go back on this decision.

This is not to say, however, that the Government are in any way unsympathetic to the problems of former PoWs. The Government feel, therefore, that rather than continue to rake over the remaining evidence from 1945, a more constructive approach would be to consider whether additional assistance could be made available. These possibilities are now being studied.

Following is the statement referred to:

OFFICER PRISONER OF WAR PAY.

Following representations received from Flight Lieutenant Roth regarding the deductions from pay of officers held prisoner in the Second World War, which were made public in an article in *The Daily Telegraph* at the end of August 1980, a study was launched under the chairmanship of the Parliamentary under-Secretary of State for the Royal Air Force Mr. Geoffrey Pattie. Extensive searches were made into the records of all three services, the Public Record Office and the Treasury. Unfortunately, documentary evidence is far from complete. The Navy

Department still hold some officer pay records from the Second World War in ledger form, but no comparable individual pay records exist for the Army or the RAF. Pay records are normally destroyed after six years. The evidence relating to the Army and the RAF is consequently more circumstantial, but it is clear that the policy of all three services with regard to PoWs throughout the war was coordinated by a tri-service committee, and that a common policy on pay matters was followed. My honourable friend has discussed the matter at some length with a number of ex-PoWs and representatives of ex-officer associations.

The study has examined initially the basis of the then Government's policy in relation to PoW pay, and looked for evidence of promulgation of this policy throughout the services. It has then sought evidence of arrangements for handling returning PoWs with particular emphasis on their pay. A key question has been to discover the existence of evidence to indicate that any payments were made thereby giving prima facie proof that machinery was not only established but functioned. Evidence was also sought on the disposal of the camp communal funds.

Some former PoWs have maintained that they were unaware that any deductions from their pay were being made. Although there is no reason to doubt the genuineness of this contention, we have established that the policy of making convention related deductions was promulgated in 1940 in the usual manner, and that further efforts were made later in the war to remind camp leaders that deductions were taking place.

The central complaint is that money was deducted in the United Kingdom on account of pay they were supposed to have received from the detaining authorities when, for prolonged periods, they either received nothing or were paid in worthless camp currency. They contend that they were not given an opportunity to reclaim these monies on repatriation.

The study group is satisfied on the evidence that, from quite early in the war, the authorities here were aware of the somewhat variable standards in relation to camp pay and arrangements were made for adjustments to be made to officers' accounts after the war. We can never know for certain how effective this procedure was, but we do know that over half a million pounds was paid out to ex-RAF PoWs, which does indicate a system that was working tolerably well. For army officers, there is evidence of the payment of claims for adjustment. The Navy Department ledgers provide irrefutable evidence that credits were paid by the Navy to returning officer PoWs. It would be impossible to prove that every returning PoW had his account adjusted as planned, but all the indications are that the vast majority did receive some money.

No evidence has been found to support or refute Flight Lieutenant Roth's allegations that he was threatened with prosecution under the Official Secrets Act if he pursued his claim. The allegation must be regarded as unproven. However, the group was greatly impressed by the meticulous care shown by the reception procedures and the desire to bend over backwards to help returning prisoners. On the question of communal funds, although in general, individuals were not reimbursed for contributions, clear evidence exists that substantial sums were redeemed at the end of the war by the British Government and donated to charity.

There remains the complaint that prisoners should not have had any money deducted from their pay, or alternatively that it should have been repaid in full after repatriation in accordance with the practice of some Commonwealth governments. Her Majesty's Government decided in September 1945 to refund in full all deductions from the accounts of Japanese PoWs. This decision was taken in the light of the appalling experiences that these men had endured. It was open to the Government at the same time to reverse their policy in relation to former prisoners of the Germans and Italians. Her Majesty's Government, with their contemporary knowledge of the situation and with all the records available, decided not to do so, and there would seem to be no reason why a British government thirty-five years later, without the advantage of contemporary insight, should seek to vary this policy. The study group is satisfied that, despite the fact that many important records are missing, the above conclusions are soundly based. The full report has been placed in the libraries of both Houses.

On the basis of the evidence before it, the study group had little alternative but to reach the conclusions it did. That is not to say, however, that the Government are in any way unsympathetic to the problems of former PoWs. The Government feel therefore, that rather than continue to rake over the remaining evidence from 1945, a more constructive response would be to consider whether additional assistance could be made available. These possibilities are now being studied.

Endnotes

1. The approaches to Jade Bay and the infamous docks at Willhelmshaven are known in English terms as the Schillig Roads.
2. *Footprints in the Sands of Time*, Oliver Clutton-Brock (Grubb Street publication)
3. As part of the celebrations for her 100th birthday in Falmouth, a fly-past was arranged from which trailed a banner with the message: 'Happy 100th Birthday Spitfire Annie'. *The Daily Telegraph* 25 October 2011.
4. Rt Hon. Duncan Sandys. MP Royal Artillery 1939-1941, Financial Secretary to the War Office 1941-43, Chairman of Intergovernmental Council for Empire Prisoners of War 1942-43, Parliamentary Secretary Minister of Supplies 1943-44, Chairman War Cabinet Committee for Defence against V-Weapons 1943-45, Minister of Works 1944.
5. Viscountess Nancy Astor 1879-1964 Conservative Member of Parliament.
6. Royal Army Service Corp, EFI expeditionary force institution. These men were NAFFI staff issued with uniforms which provided them with protection of the Geneva Convention.
7. Michael McCallen RASC Kings Regiment awarded the BEM for his service while a prisoner of war. McCallen was a member of the escape committee at Stalag 383 and a long-term prisoner from various camps.
8. Lord Swinton, the then Secretary of State for Air. The shadow scheme facilitated production of components in various factories in particular the motor car industry. The scheme created complete aircraft production by uninterrupted supply of technical staff and consulting engineers. It was supported by a special department called the 'Outside Production Office'.
9. British War production 1939-45 compiled by *The Times*, 1945.
10. Clarence Prouty Shedd and others, *History of the World's Alliance of Young Men's Christian Associations* (London: Published for the World's Committee of Young Men's Christian Associations).
11. The United States of America acted as protecting power for British Commonwealth prisoners of war until they entered the war in December 1941. Switzerland subsequently acted independently for the majority of engaged coun-

tries during the Second World War.

12. IS9 Estimate September 1944. The figure is likely to be higher than this estimate.

13. *Red Cross & St. John: The Official Record of the Humanitarian Services of the War Organization of the British Red Cross Society and Order of St. John of Jerusalem 1939-1947,* compiled by P. G. Cambray and G. G. B. Briggs

14. RCAF Dept National Archives AIK pow intelligence.

15. Military Intelligence Service War Department.

16. Donald Edgar, *The Stalag Men,* John Clare Books, 1982.

17. *They Shall Not Grow Old,* Commonwealth Air training Plan Museum Publication.

18. The state political and criminal investigation security agencies

19. The SD was tasked with the detection of actual or potential enemies of the Nazi leadership and the neutralization of that opposition.

20. Source: Nazi Conspiracy and Aggression, Vol. II. USGPO, Washington, 1946, pp. 248-302.

21. Re: Beards of prisoners of war. Prisoners of war wearing beards for religious reasons, e.g. Indians & orthodox clergymen, may continue to do so. Individuals enjoying a non-prisoner status, such as medical officers, army chaplains, and medical corps personnel may also keep their beards, if any. (Taken from Allied regulations imposed upon German PoWs).

22. Air Ministry Order A253/38 provided the conditions of service for direct entrant air observers.

23. Airmen endorsed replacement logbooks with the hours and operations flow as 'carried over' from the lost flying logbook. This is frequently seen from air crew that participated in the fall of France period.

24. Also used was the term 'Man of confidence' both indicating the elected post of representing the men within the camp concerned.

25. TRE was combined with the Radar Research and Development Establishment in 1953 to form the Radar Research Establishment.

26. Shot down in a Halifax during a raid upon Gelsenkirchen on 25 June 1943.

27. History of the International Red Cross.

28. Stalag Luft III Arthur Durand 1989.

29. Each fort was numbered and linked with additional constructions in Posen.

30. Gifts of War Presentation Spitfires by Boot & Sturtivant 2005.

31. Four copies of the German radio message exist as sent to Fighter Command and then forwarded to Bentley Priory by dispatch rider.

32. The occupied French Island marking the most north-westernmost point of France (Brittany).

33. Treble One Squadron Records Reg Wyness and letter to Colin Pateman from Brian Spranger 111 Sqd.

34. Wing Commander F. W. Hilton service number 32195 PoW number 1591 Stalag luft I.

35. *578 Squadron Based at Burn* by Hugh Cawdron, 1995.

36. Heinrich Haslob : Henry was an intelligence officer known to the PoWs as 'Henry the butcher' because he had once lived in New York where he owned a butcher shop.

37. Cecil Thomas Weir, known as 'Ginger', served in the Royal Air Force after the war and rose to the rank of Air Vice Marshal.

38. Barrack block 6 resident in room 7.

39. Eagles Victorious by H. J. Martin, p. 283.

40. War crime commission file 1628. Case number 11.

41. The Germans issued food tins punctured to avoid cans being stored for escape purposes.

42. F/Lt B DeLarge Polish Air Force had been shot down in Wellington LN393 by a flak ship off Brest on 12 November 1943. His crew had been engaged in dropping sea mines. He was awarded the Polish Virtuti Militari Cross No. 11561.

43. Judeth Cameron daughter of Captain Nichols RAMC.

44. Behind Barb wire.com US MIS statistics.

45. Within Bomber Command some Squadrons were given a Commonwealth identity and efforts were made to staff them with a high percentage of men from that particular country.

46. Robert Gordon Douglas R106758 aged twenty-eight was buried at Gresse later exhumed and reburied in the Berlin War Cemetery.

47. Rules and Regulations for the operation of German PoW camps [Item 279].

48. Appelplatz, German phrase for Parade Square adopted by all camps.

49. Brandenburg-Neuendorf opened as an aerodrome for the Ardo aircraft factory in 1930.

50. Sagan Kupper is now Zagan-Kopernia Poland.

51. *Flak and Ferrets* by Walter Morison.

52. Military air base.

53. As a rule, all non-flying units (support and flak not otherwise assigned) were assigned to Air District commands known as Luftgaue.

54. Public Record Office WO 208/3338 has his MI.9 interrogation report. Later Member, Order of the British Empire 411 RCAF Squadron Award as per 4 May 1946 *London Gazette* dated 17 May 1946 for services whilst a prisoner of war.

55. The Sergeant escapers by John Dominy.

56. W. J. Charlesworth RCAF PoW who also provided the photograph of Capt Pollock RAMC.

57. Fallingbostel museum statistics.

58. At noon on 20 June 1944.

59. A Gallant company by Jonathan Vance.

60. George Harsh was an American who volunteered to serve in the RCAF after his release from jail. Having received a life sentence for committing murder it was pardoned following his actions in saving an inmate's life. Harsh was shot down in October 1942 whilst operating with 102 Squadron RAF.

61. 44177 Flight Lieutenant Edgar S. Humphreys, 107 Squadron shot down 19 December 1940, recaptured near Sagan, last seen alive 31 March 1944, murdered by Lux and Scharpwinkel, cremated at Liegnitz.

62. Driver Walter Breithaupt.

63. French Pilot Lt Bernard W. M. Scheidhauer, 131 Squadron, captured 18 November 1942.

64. This trial started at No. 1 War Crimes Court at Hamburg on 1 July 1947. The documents concerning the trial are contained in the Judge Advocate General's Office 1939-45 War Crimes Papers group WO 235 DJAG No. 703-721. Case Number 288.

65. An executioner was required following the Nuremberg war trials. Pierrepoint, the British executioner was flown secretly into Germany to hang 200 convicted Nazi war criminals, including Josef Kramer, the commandant of Bergen-Belsen concentration camp, and Irma Grese, the sadistic SS guard at Belsen and Auschwitz.

66. This trial started at No.1 War Crimes Court at Hamburg on 11 October 1948. The documents concerning the trial are contained in the Judge Advocate General's Office 1939-45 War Crimes Papers group WO 235 DJAG No. 969-971. Case Number 354

67. Sir Arthur Street died 24 February 1951. A memorial service was held in St Martins in the Field the same location where his son had his life commemorated seven years previously.

68. TNA: PRO AIR 2/6723; CGHDM, draft report, 'Battle of Britain' clasp to the 1939-43 Star, 24 July 1944, TNA: PRO AIR 2/ 6723; CGHDM, Campaign Stars and the Defence Medal, cmd. 6633, May 1945.

69. *Honour the Air Force* by Michael Matron

70. *London Gazette* p5727 Bankruptcy Act Case number 2001.

71. Flight Lieutenant Charles Green claimed a Bf109 on 23 May 1940. He then took command of 91 Squadron but was shot down and wounded. He later claimed a Do 17 destroyed and two Bf 109s probably destroyed (one shared). After a spell off operations in 1941, he joined 600 Squadron flying Beaufighters in the nightfighter role and went to the Middle East. By February 1944 he had claimed a further nine confirmed kills (including four in one night), two 'probables' and one more damaged. He survived the war with the rank of Group Captain, having won a DSO. Source: *Aces High* published by Shores and Williams.

72. 'Jack' Zafouk 311 Squadron Wellington Navigator shot down 17 July 1941 during a raid upon Hamburg.

73. Two Czech parachutists were trained in England for the planned assassination of Heydrich. They attempted to shoot him in his staff car but the gun failed to fire. The backup plan of a hand grenade bomb was successful, wounding him seriously. Reinhard Heydrich died ten days later due to his injuries.

74. On 5 March 1943 a successful tunnel escape took place involving thirty-four men from Oflag XXIB. Lt Cdr Buckley escaped in company with a Danish officer, Jorgen Thalbitzer. Both men attempted to cross from Copenhagen to neutral

Sweden by canoe but they were unsuccessful. The Danish officer's body was washed ashore some time later but Lt Cdr Buckley's body was never found. He was posthumously mentioned in dispatches for his services as a PoW. *London Gazette*, dated 4 June 1946.

75. Pilot Officer B. Scheidhaver served with 131 (County of Kent) Squadron. He was forced to land on the island of Jersey after his Spitfire EN830 sustained flak damage on 18 November 1942. His Spitfire was recovered to Germany and used as a test bed airframe which later flew with the Luftwaffe with several modifications.

76. After the war, Alex Cassie served in the Air Ministry where he developed psychometric tests for potential aircrew. *Telegraph* media obituary.

77. National archives of Australia: A705, 166/5/603.

78. MI9 ex-PoW questionnaire 1945.

79. Foreign Office despatch (T526/526/373) of 10 January 1948: 'Flight Lieutenant Libert joined the Belgian Section of the Royal Air Force Volunteer Reserve in 1942 after having escaped from enemy occupied territory. He has endured many vicissitudes. In 1940 as a fighter pilot he was severely wounded and burned and while serving with No. 349 Squadron his aircraft was shot down over France and he was captured. He again sustained severe burns but with great courage and fortitude he refused treatment because he would not divulge information which might be useful to the enemy. As a prisoner of war Flight Lieutenant Libert has set an excellent example to all his fellow prisoners.'

80. Boots or shoes were frequently torn from the feet of airmen as they escaped by parachute; it was not unusual to see recently captured air crews hobbling along with just one piece of footwear.

81. *Guardian* news and media, United Kingdom; published article 2 September 2007.

82. *Flight Magazine*, published March 1945

83. *They Shall Grow Not Old: A Book of Remembrance* by Les Allison and Harry Hayward.

84. *Footprints on the Sands of Time* by Oliver Clutton-Brock.

85. Uwe Mai: Kriegsgefangenen in Brandenburg, Stalag III A in Luckenwalde 1939-1945, Metropol Verlag, Berlin 1999.

86. Untermenschen – The Nazi term for inferior races.

87. In the Nuremberg Trials after the Second World War, Reinecke was convicted of war crimes and crimes against humanity and sentenced to life imprisonment.

88. Archives of Canada RG24 Vol 25139 J88362 PB Crosswell.

89. *Bomber Command War Diaries* by Middlebrook and Everitt.

90. 2 Group History, Michael Bowyer.

91. 18 Squadron Operational Record Book Entries, National Archives.

92. Letter from Jack Brown, June 1993.

93. Squadron operational record book entries confirmed that actually four aircraft were lost during the operation on the Bizerte-Sidi aerodrome.

94. In later life Norman Eckersley served within the banking industry. He was rewarded with the CBE in 1978 for services to British Commercial interests in San Francisco.

95. In 1940 the RCAF opened a base on Prince Edward Island to support the British Commonwealth Air Training Plan. The base was named RCAF Station Summerside in 1941 and became home to No. 9 Service Flying Training School for pilots, No. 53 Air Cadet Squadron and No. 1 General Reconnaissance School for pilots and navigators. Planes used for training during the Second World War included the Harvard and the Anson.

96. 211 Squadron was under control of 224 Group. The Beaufighter wing had been formed in late 1942.

97. The Victoria Cross is publicly displayed at the Australian War Memorial, Canberra, Australia.

98. Trim controls are used to relieve the pilot of the need to maintain constant pressure on the flight controls. Trim systems usually consist of cockpit controls and small hinged devices attached to the trailing edge of one or more of the primary flight control surfaces. They are designed to help minimize a pilot's workload by aerodynamically assisting movement and position of the flight control surface to which they are attached.

99. The Imperial War Museum Reference ID JFU 243 holds film footage taken of the 17 divisions meeting with the column of prisoners on 29 April 1945

100. A force composed mainly of former Indian prisoners of war captured by the Japanese in Malaya, which sought to overthrow British rule in India.

101. HMSO CMND 6832.

102. Information via David Satchell, cousin by marriage to Kenneth Holland.

103. *Tee Emm* was written by the staff of the magazine *Punch* (and particularly Anthony Armstrong), who had been seconded to the Air Ministry for the duration of the war to make technical manuals readable. They were very successful in that respect, the character Pilot Officer Prune features significantly within these documents.

104. Steve Brew, 41 Squadron Archives.

105. RAF photo reconnaissance sorties to the coast of France were coded as 'Popular' operations in Squadron record books. Tactical reconnaissance sorties were flown with the ability to attack ground targets should they present themselves as targets of opportunity.

106. 38 Squadron Wellington N2953 RAF Marham to the Black Forrest. Bomber Command Losses by Chorley.

107. The Red Cross transported the individual cardboard food parcels inside large wooden crates. The crates were a good supply of materials that were transformed into numerous items with the camps. The theatre no doubt looked awash with large Red Cross symbols which featured within the seating arrangements.

108. *Arsenic and Old Lace* was produced by Tony Hudson.

109. Kenneth Mackintosh died in 2006.

110. AIR 40/269, National Archives.

111. Lancaster LL716 had been on strength with 115 Squadron before joining 514 Squadron, the aircraft had recorded 256 hours prior to its loss over France in August 1944.

112. MI9 Liberation report Baxter.

113. The notorious Gestapo Headquarters in Avenue Foch, central Paris.

114. *Newcastle News Chronicle* report and MI9 report, 9 October 1945.

115. Philip Lamason was born in Napier, New Zealand 15 September 1918. He worked in the livestock industry and later joined the RNZAF. In 1941 he sailed for England where he joined 218 Squadron, Bomber Command. He later served in 15 Squadron and was awarded the DFC and Bar. After the war he returned to New Zealand where he died in May 2012.

116. *No time for Fear* by Victor Gammon, p. 198.

117. National Archives AIR 40/269, report on occupancy of Marlag-Milag Camp.

118. Beaufighter Mk I, T5164 'O' of 248 Squadron took off from Ta' Qali, Malta, at 16.15 hrs to escort nine Beauforts of 86 Squadron on a shipping strike on a convoy that had left Messina bound for Benghazi. The convoy was located 19 km off Paxos Island, but during the attack the Beaufighter was hit by AA fire and was forced to ditch 19 km west of Corfu.

119. A court of enquiry was held in relation to this incident. Wing Commander Scragg described the incident as showing utter callousness and disregard for human life.

120. John Topham served in the Coldstream Guards 1933-37, Newcastle City Police 1937-40, RAFVR 1940-46, Newcastle City Police 1946-1951, RAF 1951-66.

121. Source: WO 208/3242,65.

122. *The Bomber Command War Diaries*, p. 636.

123. www.pegasusarchive.org

124. *The Prisoners of War*, published by the Department of the British Red Cross in May 1942.

125. Air Publication 1548 – 1936 Third Edition, April 1944.

Bibliography

Chorley, W. R. *Bomber Command Losses* (Midland Counties Publications, 1992)

Churchill College Archives

Clutton-Brock, Oliver *Footprints on The Sands of Time* (Grubb Street Publications, 2003)

Commonwealth Air Training Plan Museum *They Shall not Grow Old* (1996)

Durand, A. *Stalag Luft III* (Patrick Stephens Publishing, 1989)

Gammon, V. *No Time for Fear* (Arms & Armour Publishing, 1998)

Holmes, Harry *Avro Lancaster the Definitive Record* (Airlife, 1997)

Hutton, C. *Official Secret* (Max Parrish Publishing 1960)

International Red Cross Archives

Lagrandeur, P. *We Flew We Fell We Lived* (Grubb Street Publications, 2007)

Maton, M. *Honour the Air Forces* (Token Publishing, 2004)

Maton, M. *Honour those mentioned MID despatches* (Token, Publishing 2010)

Middlebrook, M. and C. Everitt *Bomber Command War Diaries* (Viking Penguin Books, 1985)

Morison, W. *Flak & Ferrets* (Sentinel Publishing, 1995)

National Archives under the terms of the Open Government Licence

Nickless, P., B. Nutt, F. Wells, S. Hamblin and J. Brace *YMCA Wartime Logbooks*

Prisoners of War Naval & Air Forces of Great Britain & The Empire 1939-1945 (Hayward and Son)

Royal Air Force 1939-1945, Vols I II & III (HMSO, 1953)

Vance, J. *Gallant Company: The Men of The Great Escape* (Pacifica Military History, 2000)